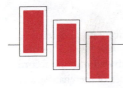

Exploring Chemistry with Electronic Structure Methods

Second Edition

D0139165

James B. Foresman

Æleen Frisch

Gaussian, Inc.
Pittsburgh, PA

Gaussian, Gaussian 90, Gaussian 92, Gaussian 94 and *Gaussian 94W* are registered trademarks of Gaussian, Inc. All other trademarks and registered trademarks are the properties of their respective holders.

For more information about the Gaussian program, contact:
> Gaussian, Inc.
> Carnegie Office Park, Building 6
> Pittsburgh, PA 15106 U.S.A.
> *voice:* 412-279-6700
> *fax:* 412-279-2118
> *email:* info@gaussian.com

Colophon: This book was created on a Gateway 2000 486-based computer using FrameMaker, FreeHand, ChemDraw, Photoshop and FreezeFrame. Body text is set in 9/11 Minion; headings and captions are set in Futura.

ISBN 0-9636769-3-8

Printing History:

		Corresponds to:
April 1993	First Edition.	*Gaussian 92* Revision D.1 and higher.
March 1994	Second Printing.	
August 1996	Second Edition.	*Gaussian 94* Revision D.2 and higher.

Printed in the U.S.A.

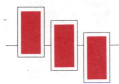

Quick Topic Finder

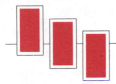

Table of Contents

Part 1: Essential Concepts & Techniques

Part 2: Model Chemistries

Part 3: Applications

Appendices

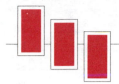

List of Examples and Exercises

Table of Input Files

The following table lists the input files corresponding to the various examples and exercises in this work. These files are located in the subdirectories quick, examples and exercise of the explore subdirectory of the *Gaussian* directory tree. Files have the extension .com on UNIX and VMS systems, and .GJF on Windows systems.

The final column of the table lists the CPU time required for running the job on our reference computer system, a DEC AlphaServer 2100$^{5/250}$; all jobs were run using a single processor. For multi-step jobs, the timing figure indicates the total CPU time for all job steps. Filenames and CPU times for long jobs (> 30 minutes) are in **boldface** type, and filenames and CPU times for very long jobs (> 2 hours) are in **boldface red** type.

	Input File	Corresponding Example/Exercise	Description of Job	CPU Time (hrs:mins:secs:)
Quick Start	qs	Exercise QS.1	Water single point energy	0:00:08.2
	water.pdb	Exercise QS.2	Converting a PDB file	0:00:08.2
Chapter 2	e2_01	Example 2.1	Formaldehyde energy	0:00:09.1
	e2_02	Example 2.2	Methane NMR properties	0:00:20.8
	2_01	Exercise 2.1	Propene energy	0:00:15.1
	2_02a	Exercise 2.2	Dichloro-difluoro-ethane (RR form)	0:01:06.4
	2_02b	Exercise 2.2	Dichloro-difluoro-ethane (SS form)	0:01:06.8
	2_02c	Exercise 2.2	Dichloro-difluoro-ethane (meso form)	0:01:04.9
	2_03	Exercise 2.3	Acetone energy	0:00:26.8
	2_04	Exercise 2.4	Ethylene energy	0:00:09.7
	2_05a	Exercise 2.5	Butane NMR properties	0:03:01.8
	2_05b	Exercise 2.5	Trans 2-butene NMR properties	0:02:45.2
	2_05c	Exercise 2.5	2-Butyne NMR properties	0:02:45.6
	2_06	Exercise 2.6	C_{60} energy	**0:44:31.9**
	2_07	Exercise 2.7	Conventional vs.direct CPU usage study	**1:26:46.8**
	2_08a	Exercise 2.8	Stability of oxygen	0:00:36.8
	2_08b	Exercise 2.8	Stability of ozone	0:05:03.5
Chapter 3	e3_01	Example 3.1	Ethylene geometry optimization	0:00:44.2
	e3_02	Example 3.2	Fluoroethylene optimization	0:01:56.4
	e3_03	Example 3.3	$H_3CO \rightarrow H_2COH$ TS opt. (QST2)	0:02:07.2
	3_01a	Exercise 3.1	Propene optimization (180°)	0:02:01.8
	3_01b	Exercise 3.1	Propene optimization (0°)	0:01:57.7

	Input File	Corresponding Example/Exercise	Description of Job	CPU Time (hrs:mins:secs:)
Chapter 3	3_02a	Exercise 3.2	Vinyl alcohol optimization (0°)	0:02:12.4
	3_02b	Exercise 3.2	Vinyl alcohol optimization (180°)	0:01:48.2
	3_02c	Exercise 3.2	Acetaldehyde optimization	0:01:40.2
	3_03	Exercise 3.3	Planar vinyl amine optimization	0:01:56.1
	3_04	Exercise 3.4	Chromium hexacarbonyl optimization	0:17:54.5
	3_05a	Exercise 3.5	Benzene optimization & NMR props.	**1:00:06.4**
	3_05b	Exercise 3.5	TMS optimization & NMP properties	**1:45:01.8**
	3_06a	Exercise 3.6	$C_{60}O$ optimizations (PM3)	0:16:32.0
	3_06b	Exercise 3.6	$C_{60}O$ optimizations (HF)	11:14:52.2
	3_07	Exercise 3.7	$SiH_2 + H_2 \rightarrow SiH_4$ TS optimization	0:02:23.2
	3_08	Exercise 3.8	Bicyclo[2.2.2]octane optimizations with different coordinate systems	**1:53:28.5**
Chapter 4	e4_01	Example 4.1	Formaldehyde frequencies	0:00:43.4
	e4_02a	Example 4.2	Trans 1-fluoropropene (0°) freqs.	0:09:03.9
	e4_02b	Example 4.2	Trans 1-fluoropropene (180°) freqs.	0:09:29.1
	e4_02c	Example 4.2	Cis 1-fluoropropene (0°) freqs.	0:11:19.7
	e4_02d	Example 4.2	Cis-Trans TS for 1-fluoropropene	**0:20:28.9**
	4_01a	Exercise 4.1	Vinyl alcohol (180°) frequencies	0:02:37.8
	4_01b	Exercise 4.1	Vinyl alcohol (0°) frequencies	0:02:39.0
	4_02a	Exercise 4.2	Vinyl amine (planar) frequencies	0:02:44.7
	4_02b	Exercise 4.2	Vinyl amine TS opt. + frequencies	0:03:21.3
	4_03a	Exercise 4.3	Ethylene frequencies	0:00:41.1
	4_03b	Exercise 4.3	Fluoroethylene frequencies	0:01:54.1
	4_03c	Exercise 4.3	Propene frequencies	0:02:53.7
	4_04a	Exercise 4.4	Acetaldehydefrequencies	0:02:12.8
	4_04b	Exercise 4.4	Acrolein frequencies	0:05:18.6
	4_04c	Exercise 4.4	Formamide frequencies	0:01:54.8
	4_04d	Exercise 4.4	Acetone frequencies	0:07:16.9
	4_04e	Exercise 4.4	Acetyl chloride frequencies	0:06:03.3
	4_04f	Exercise 4.4	Methyl acetate frequencies	0:17:38.1
	4_05a	Exercise 4.5	Strained hydrocarbons frequencies	**0:55:19.1**
	4_05b	Exercise 4.5	Larger strained hydrocarbons freqs.	2:01:23.1
	4_06a	Exercise 4.6	3-Fluoropropene optimization	0:14:53.9

	Input File	Corresponding Example/Exercise	Description of Job	CPU Time (hrs:mins:secs:)
Chapter 4	4_06b	Exercise 4.6	$CH_2F–CH=CH_2 \leftrightarrow CHF=CH–CH_3$ TS	0:20:25.7
Chapter 5	e5_01	Example 5.1	Methanol vs. methoxide anion	0:01:12.2
	e5_02	Example 5.2	Optimization of PO	**0:42:36.0**
	5_01	Exercise 5.1	Basis set effects on H–F bond length	0:15:02.0
	5_02	Exercise 5.2	$M(CO)_6$ optimizations (LANL2DZ)	**1:09:30.5**
	5_03a	Exercise 5.3	Benzene NMR properties by basis set	**0:44:37.7**
	5_03b	Exercise 5.3	TMS NMR properties by basis set	**1:11:06.8**
	5_04	Exercise 5.4	N,N-Dimethyl-formamide opt. + freq.	3:24:00.7
	5_05	Exercise 5.5	Basis set structure (via methanol)	0:00:15.0
	5_06	Exercise 5.6	6-31G** vs. 6-31G†† basis sets	0:04:25.3
Chapter 6	e6_01	Example 6.1	TPP AM1 molecular orbitals	0:11:40.3
	e6_02	Example 6.2	HF Dimer semi-empirical study	0:05:12.8
	e6_03	Example 6.3	HF bond energy	0:05:07.5
	e6_04	Example 6.4	Ozone optimizations	3:30:31.6
	e6_05a	Example 6.5	CO_2 atomization energy: HF	0:02:00.7
	e6_05b	Example 6.5	CO_2 atomization energy: SVWN	0:03:44.4
	e6_05c	Example 6.5	CO_2 atomization energy: SVWN5	0:03:47.8
	e6_05d	Example 6.5	CO_2 atomization energy: BLYP	0:09:01.9
	e6_05e	Example 6.5	CO_2 atomization energy: B3LYP	0:09:34.2
	e6_05f	Example 6.5	CO_2 atomization energy: B3PW91	0:09:35.6
	e6_05g	Example 6.5	CO_2 atomization energy: MP2	0:05:25.7
	e6_06	Example 6.6	F_3^- frequencies	**0:30:16.1**
	6_01a	Exercise 6.1	Isobutane and n-butane AM1 opts.	0:00:08.0
	6_01b	Exercise 6.1	Isobutane and n-butane PM3 opts.	0:00:08.1
	6_01c	Exercise 6.1	Isobutane and n-butane HF opts.	0:06:39.8
	6_02a	Exercise 6.2	N-butane (anticlinal) AM1 opt.	0:00:20.1
	6_02b	Exercise 6.2	N-butane (anticlinal) HF opt.	0:08:25.6
	6_03	Exercise 6.3	Malonaldehyde optimizations	5:46:30.4
	6_03x	Exercise 6.3	Malonaldehyde optimization (B3LYP)	**0:54:13.9**
	6_04	Exercise 6.4	FOOF optimizations	**0:34:49.7**
	6_05a	Exercise 6.5	Acetaldehyde QCISD(T) energy	0:11:22.6
	6_05b	Exercise 6.5	Ethylene oxide QCISD(T) energy	0:13:04.9
	6_06a	Exercise 6.6	Cyano radical spin polarization	**1:35:34.7**

	Input File	Corresponding Example/Exercise	Description of Job	CPU Time (hrs:mins:secs:)
Chapter 6	6_06b	Exercise 6.6	Allyl radical spin polarization	0:06:47.9
	6_06c	Exercise 6.6	Be-sub. allyl radical spin polarization	0:20:24.0
	6_06d	Exercise 6.6	Mg-sub. allyl radical spin polarization	**0:32:06.5**
	6_06e	Exercise 6.6	S-sub. allyl radical spinpolarization	0:17:41.5
	6_07a	Exercise 6.7	$K^+F_3^-$ frequencies	**1:09:02.4**
	6_07b	Exercise 6.7	$Na^+F_3^-$ frequencies	2:02:50.1
	6_07c	Exercise 6.7	$Cs^+F_3^-$ frequencies	**1:14:51.4**
	6_08	Exercise 6.8	HNCN radical hyperfine coupling	**0:36:36.5**
	6_09	Exercise 6.9	Destruction of ozone by atomic chlorine	15:16:41.3
Chapter 7	e7_01	Example 7.1	Atomization energy of PH_2	0:05:57.1
	e7_02	Example 7.2	Electron affinity of PH_2	0:03:55.6
	e7_03	Example 7.3	Ionization potential of PH_2	0:03:48.9
	e7_04	Example 7.4	Proton affinity of PH_3	0:16:55.9
	e7_05	Example 7.5	G2 proton affinity of PH_3	0:13:49.1
	e7_06	Example 7.6	CBS-4 proton affinity of PH_3	0:17:45.4
	7_01a	Exercise 7.1	Atomization energy of water	0:03:23.9
	7_01b	Exercise 7.1	Ionization potential of water	0:01:39.3
	7_01c	Exercise 7.1	Electron affinity of OH	0:02:54.9
	7_01d	Exercise 7.1	Proton affinity of water	0:01:21.8
	7_02a	Exercise 7.2	Chlorine destruction of ozone (G2)	**1:42:52.6**
	7_02b	Exercise 7.2	Chlorine destruction of ozone (CBS-4)	0:18:29.4
	7_02c	Exercise 7.2	Chlorine destruction of ozone (CBS-Q)	**0:56:24.4**
Chapter 8	e8_01a	Example 8.1	Electron density of nit. chlorobenzene	0:18:44.6
	e8_01b	Example 8.1	Electron density of nit. nitrobenzene	0:22:45.6
	e8_02	Example 8.2	H_3O^+ hydration reaction	0:08:07.8
	e8_03	Example 8.3	$H_2 + CO \leftrightarrow H_2CO$ PES	0:08:24.3
	e8_04	Example 8.4	$H_2CO \leftrightarrow$ trans HCOH PES	0:10:58.5
	e8_05	Example 8.5	Isodesmic reaction	**0:37:53.7**
	e8_06	Example 8.6	CO_2 atom. energy via isodesmic rx.	0:06:07.2
	e8_07	Example 8.7	Ethane and SiH_4 heats of formation	3:25:03.0
	8_01a	Exercise 8.1	Li hydration reaction	0:09:51.5
	8_01b	Exercise 8.1	Water calcs. for hydration reactions	0:03:28.4
	8_01c	Exercise 8.1	Water dimer hydration reaction	**0:41:45.9**

	Input File	Corresponding Example/Exercise	Description of Job	CPU Time (hrs:mins:secs:)
Chapter 8	8_02a	Exercise 8.2	CH PES scan	0:08:44.9
	8_02b	Exercise 8.2	CH_4 PES scan	2:14:42.9
	8_03	Exercise 8.3	HOCH cis-trans TS	0:19:54.8
	8_04	Exercises 8.4 & 8.5	Allyl cation population analyses	0:01:12.4
	8_06	Exercise 8.6	Allyl cation Atoms-in-Molecules analysis	**0:55:44.7**
	8_07	Exercise 8.7	$Si^+ + SiH_4$ PES IRC	**1:09:21.0**
	8_08	Exercise 8.8	Isodesmic reactions	**0:53:45.5**
	8_09a	Exercise 8.9	Trifluoromethane (isodesmic reaction)	**0:38:16.9**
	8_09b	Exercise 8.9	Benzene (isodesmic reaction)	2:53:47.4
	8_10	Exercise 8.10	S_N2 reactions	**0:39:26.4**
Chapter 9	e9_01	Example 9.1	Ethylene excited states	0:00:21.1
	e9_02	Example 9.2	Formaldehyde excited states	0:03:54.4
	9_01	Exercise 9.1	Methylenecyclopropene excited states	0:03:47.4
	9_02	Exercise 9.2	Formaldehyde excited state optimization	0:03:47.8
	9_03	Exercise 9.3	Acrolein excited state optimization	0:22:53.5
	9_04a	Exercise 9.4	Benzene excited states (6-31G*)	0:01:24.2
	9_04b	Exercise 9.4	Benzene excited states (6-31+G*)	0:03:24.2
	9_05a	Exercise 9.5	Acrolein orbitals for CAS	0:00:14.4
	9_05b	Exercise 9.5	CASSCF acrolein excitation energy	0:11:39.6
	9_06a	Exercise 9.6	Butadiene orbitals for CAS	0:00:10.8
	9_06b	Exercise 9.6	CASSCF(4,4) butadiene ground state	**0:35:49.3**
	9_06c	Exercise 9.6	CASSCF(4,6) butadiene ground state	0:26:13.6
	9_06d	Exercise 9.6	Butadiene conical intersection	**0:38:55.2**
Chapter 10	**e10_01a**	Example 10.1	Dichloroethane rotational barrier in solution (IPCM model)	**1:02:12.6**
	e10_01b	Example 10.1	Dichloroethane rotational barrier in solution (Onsager model)	0:21:43.3
	e10_02a	Example 10.2	Formaldehyde opt. & volume calc.	0:01:21.7
	e10_02b	Example 10.2	Formaldehyde in acetonitrile (SCIPCM)	**0:56:32.5**
	e10_02c	Example 10.2	Formaldehyde in acetonitrile (Onsager)	0:01:49.6
	10_01a	Exercise 10.1	Dichloroethane in solution (IPCM)	2:52:17.1
	10_01b	Exercise 10.1	Dichloroethane in solution (HF Onsager)	0:01:13.5
	10_01c	Exercise 10.1	Dichloroethane in solution (MP2 Onsager)	**0:42:53.6**

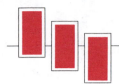

List of "To the Teacher" Boxes

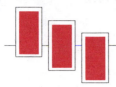

Acknowledgments

Many people helped with this work. We are grateful to the many readers who read all or part of the manuscript of the second edition: K. B. Wiberg (Yale University), George Petersson (Wesleyan University), Mike Robb (King's College, London), Berny Schlegel and his research group (Wayne State University and Gaussian, Inc.), Doug Fox and David Moses (Gaussian, Inc.), John Montgomery, Jim Cheeseman, Mike Frisch and Gary Trucks (Lorentzian, Inc.), Andrew Livelsberger (York College of PA; Rice University), Joe Ochterski and Carlos Sosa (Cray Research), and Krishnan Raghavachari (AT&T Bell Laboratories/Lucent Technologies). We also continue to thank the readers of the first edition of this book: Ken Fountain (Northeast Missouri State University), Robert Higgins (Fayetteville State University), James Lobue (Ursinus College), John Ranck (Elizabethtown College), Arlen Viste (Augustana College), Martin Head-Gordon (University of California, Berkeley), Bill Ellis (Lorentzian, Inc.), and David Turner (Scientific Computing Associates). Arlen Viste, Michael Tsai (Univiversity of Alabama, Birmingham), Errol Lewars (Trent University), and Ross Nobes (Molecular Simulations) provided helpful bug reports on the first edition. The errors that remain are our own.

John Montgomery, Mike Robb, K. B. Wiberg, Gustavo Scuseria (Rice University), Ian Carmichael (University of Notre Dame), Sason Shaik (University of Rochester), M. W. (Richard) Wong (University of Queensland), Krishnan Raghavachari, Charlie Bauschlicher (NASA), Carlos Sosa (Cray Research) and David Tozer (Cambridge University), and Jim Cheeseman, Mike Frisch and Gary Trucks were also extremely helpful in developing some of the examples and exercises in this book. We thank them for their inspirational scientific work, their patience, and their quick email responses.

John Carpenter and Carlos Sosa of Cray Research generously provided the computer time and technical assistance for the resource use study in Chapter 6.

The figures of the $C_{60}O$ isomers in Chapter 3 are reprinted by permission from *Chem. Phys. Letters.*

This book also benefits from the excellent copy editing of Carolyn Ball and Laura Lasala. Laura Lasala, Gina Onushco, Judy Loukides and Christine Ashline also provided invaluable assistance in the production process.

Finally, the authors thank all of the important people in their lives who allowed this project to be a central focus for such a long time.

About This Work

Exploring Chemistry with Electronic Structure Methods serves as an introduction to the capabilities of and procedures for this variety of computational chemistry. It is designed to teach you how to use electronic structure modeling to investigate the chemical phenomena of interest to you. This work was developed using the *Gaussian* series of computational chemistry programs for all of its specific examples and exercises (specifically *Gaussian 94*). Other program(s) could be substituted, provided that the necessary features and capabilities were available.

Gaussian is capable of predicting many properties of molecules and reactions, including the following:

- ✦ Molecular energies and structures
- ✦ Energies and structures of transition states
- ✦ Bond and reaction energies
- ✦ Molecular orbitals
- ✦ Multipole moments
- ✦ Atomic charges and electrostatic potentials
- ✦ Vibrational frequencies
- ✦ IR and Raman spectra
- ✦ NMR properties
- ✦ Polarizabilities and hyperpolarizabilities
- ✦ Thermochemical properties
- ✦ Reaction pathways

Computations can be carried out on systems in the gas phase or in solution, and in their ground state or in an excited state. *Gaussian* can serve as a powerful tool for exploring areas of chemical interest like substituent effects, reaction mechanisms, potential energy surfaces, and excitation energies.

Who Should Read This Book?

Several different types of chemists will benefit from reading this work:

- ✦ Experimental research chemists with little or no experience with computational chemistry may use this work as an introduction to electronic structure calculations. They will discover how electronic structure theory can be used as an adjunct to their experimental research to provide new insights into chemical problems.

◆ Students of physical chemistry, at the advanced undergraduate or beginning graduate level, will find this work a useful complement to standard texts, enabling them to experiment with the theoretical constructs discussed there.

◆ Experienced *Gaussian* users may use this book to acquaint themselves with the program's newest features.

Overview and Goals

This work is structured as a study guide, and it employs a hands-on approach to teaching you how to use electronic structure theory to investigate chemical systems. It is suitable for either individual, self-paced study or classroom use. Naturally, not every section will be relevant to all readers. Accordingly, chapters are designed to be as self-contained as possible; you should focus on those parts which address your research needs and interests.

Examples and Exercises

Each chapter focuses on a single topic, and includes explanations of the chemical properties or phenomena under consideration and the relevant computational procedures, one or two detailed examples of setting up such calculations and interpreting their results, and several exercises designed to both provide practice in the area and to introduce its more advanced aspects. Full solutions are provided for all exercises.

Many exercises include new material that expands on themes first introduced in the text. Accordingly, you may find it beneficial to read through each problem and solution even if you do not choose to complete every exercise. For this second edition, we have added new exercises covering advanced aspects of the current topic to most chapters. This material constitutes an advanced track through the work. Experienced researchers may wish to examine the advanced track even in the earlier, more elementary chapters where the basic concepts are very familiar.

The molecules considered in both the worked examples in the text and the exercises have been chosen to minimize the amount of CPU time necessary to complete a non-trivial calculation of each type. We've deliberately chosen systems that, for the most part, can be modeled with minimal cost because our goal here is to focus on the chemistry, rather than on *Gaussian*'s features and research capabilities. Note, however, that although the molecules we will consider are relatively small, the methods you will learn are applicable to any size system. However, we have used methods and basis sets which are appropriate to research-level calculations. Nevertheless, virtually all of the exercises can be run under any post-1994 version of *Gaussian*, including Windows versions such as *Gaussian 94W* (although some jobs may have elapsed times of hours or even days on slower PC's). Readers with limited computing resources may want to reduce the level of theory and/or basis set size for some or all jobs.

A long study
(>30 mins. on
the reference
computer)

**A very long
study** (>2 hrs.)

Examples and exercises involving particularly computationally-intensive studies have been marked with one of the icons in the margin. We provide a complete list of all examples and exercises, together with their associated job files and CPU times on a reference computer system, beginning on page xiv. We haven't even attempted to cover all of *Gaussian*'s features. Instead, we've tried to focus on those of most general applicability. Once you understand these, you'll be in a position to explore the rest of *Gaussian*'s capabilities on your own.

Input Files for the Examples and Exercises

Input files for all examples and exercises are included with *Gaussian* (although you will probably want to try setting up your own first for the exercises). In *Gaussian 94*, they are stored in the following default directory locations:

System Type	Directory Location	File Extension
UNIX systems	`$g94root/g94/explore`	`.com`
VMS systems	*Disk*:`[G94.Explore]`	`.COM`
Windows systems	*X*:`\G94W\Explore`	`.GJF`

Example 0:
Sample Example
file: sample

For VMS and Windows systems, the appropriate disk name must be prepended to the directory location. There are subdirectories under the `explore` directory named `examples` and `exercise`, which hold the input files for the examples in the text and for the exercises at the end of each chapter, respectively (the corresponding filename is given in the margin at the start of each example and exercise); the input files for the *Quick Start* section are located in the subdirectory `quick` in the same location. If you do not find these files in the designated location on your system, contact your system administrator for assistance in determining where *Gaussian* is installed.

Organizational Structure

This book begins with a *Gaussian Quick Start* tutorial designed to help new *Gaussian* users begin using the program right away. The remainder of the work is divided into three main parts:

◆ Part 1, *Essential Concepts & Techniques*, introduces computational chemistry and the principal sorts of predictions which can be made using electronic structure theory. It presents both the underlying theoretical and philosophical approach to electronic structure calculations taken by this book and the fundamental procedures and techniques for performing them.

◆ Part 2, *Model Chemistries*, provides an in-depth examination of the accuracy, scope of applicability and other characteristics and trade-offs of all of the major well-defined electronic structure models. It also gives some general recommendations for selecting the best model for investigating a particular problem.

◆ Part 3, *Applications*, discusses electronic structure calculations in the context of real-life research situations, focusing on how it can be used to illuminate a variety of chemical problems.

Contents of this Work

Each of the chapters in this work is described briefly below:

◆ Chapter 1, "Computational Models and Model Chemistries," provides an overview of the computational chemistry field and where electronic structure theory fits within it. It also discusses the general theoretical methods and procedures employed in electronic structure calculations (a more detailed treatment of the underlying quantum mechanical theory is given in Appendix A).

◆ Chapter 2, "Single Point Energy Calculations," discusses computing energies at specific molecular structures, as well as the related molecular properties that may be predicted at the same time.

Note that much of the discussion of *Gaussian* input has been moved to Appendix B in this second edition.

◆ Chapter 3, "Geometry Optimizations," describes how to locate equilibrium structures of molecules, or, more technically, stationary points on the potential energy surface. It includes an overview of the various commonly used optimization techniques and a consideration of optimizing transition structures as well as minimizations.

◆ Chapter 4, "Frequency Calculations," discusses computing the second derivatives of the energy and using it to predict IR and Raman frequencies and intensities and vibrational normal modes. It also considers other uses of second derivatives, including characterizing stationary points found during optimizations as minima or transition states.

◆ Part 2, "Model Chemistries," begins with Chapter 5, "Basis Set Effects." This chapter discusses the most important standard basis sets and presents principles for basis set selection. It also describes the distinction between open shell and closed shell calculations.

◆ Chapter 6, "Selecting an Appropriate Theoretical Method," discusses the model chemistry concept introduced in Chapter 1 in detail. It covers the strengths, computational cost and limitations of a variety of popular methods, beginning with semi-empirical models and continuing through Hartree-Fock, Density Functional Theory, and electron correlation methods.

◆ Chapter 7, "High Accuracy Energy Models," describes several research procedures for predicting very accurate thermodynamic and energetic properties of systems, including G1, G2, G2(MP2) and several Complete Basis Set (CBS) models.

◆ Part 3, "Applications," begins with Chapter 8, "Studying Chemical Reactions and Reactivity," which discusses using electronic structure theory to investigate chemical problems. It includes consideration of reaction path features to investigate the routes between transition structures and the equilibrium structures they connect on the reaction's potential energy surface.

◆ Chapter 9, "Modeling Excited States," discusses predicting the properties of excited states of molecules, including structures and vibrational frequencies. An exercise in the advanced track considers CASSCF methods.

◆ Chapter 10, "Modeling Systems in Solution," discusses how to model systems in solution. It describes available solvation models and the sorts of systems and properties which may be studied with them.

◆ Appendix A, "The Theoretical Background," contains an overview of the quantum mechanical theory underlying *Gaussian*. It also includes references to the several detailed treatments available.

◆ Appendix B, "Overview of *Gaussian* Input," provides a summary of the *Gaussian* input file format. It also discusses techniques for creating Z-matrix representations of molecular systems.

Where to Get Additional Information

We hope that the discussions here will stimulate your interest in computational chemistry in general and *Gaussian* in particular. Each chapter provides references to the original studies from which the examples and exercises are drawn as well as to other works of related interest.

More detailed information about the *Gaussian 94* program can be found in the *Gaussian 94 User's Reference* and *Gaussian 94 Programmer's Reference*.

Typographic and Graphical Conventions

In this book, we have used the following typographical and graphical conventions.

Full or partial *Gaussian* input sets are set in fixed-width type and are set off from normal text like this:

```
# RHF/STO-3G Opt SCF=Direct Test
```

Similarly, general syntax statements for *Gaussian* input are set off from the text, set in fixed-width type. Within syntax statements, literal keywords appear in fixed-width type while replaceable parameters—items for which you must substitute the appropriate value—are set in normal italic type:

```
# method/basis_set [Test]
```

Optional items appear in square brackets (which are not themselves typed when the item is included).

When *Gaussian* input keywords, like **RHF**, appear within normal text, they are set in boldface sans-serif type. Basis set names when referred to as keywords are also set in boldface sans-serif type. Basis set names used in a generic way are set in normal type.

Gaussian output is also set off from normal text, set in fixed-width type, and enclosed in a shadowed box. Comments about the output are set in red sans-serif type and appear to the left of the output:

Comment on the *Gaussian* output

```
SCF DONE:  E(RHF) =  -74.9607165382    A.U. AFTER    8 CYCLES
              CONVG  =    0.2843D-09           -V/T =   2.0050
              S**2  =    0.0000
```

A few UNIX and VMS command examples appear in the text, mostly in the *Gaussian Quick Start* section, which precedes the text proper. These commands are set off from normal text and set in fixed-width type (but have no box surrounding them). Commands that the user must type appear in boldface fixed-width type, and computer prompts and messages appear in normal fixed-width type:

```
% grep "SCF DONE" tut000.log
SCF DONE:  E(RHF) =  -74.9607165382 ...
```

When UNIX and VMS commands and file or pathnames appear within normal text, they are set in bold and normal sans-serif type (respectively).

Gaussian 94W menu options and display labels are set in boldface sans-serif type, following the usual Windows convention.

Italic type is used to indicate special terms, like *basis set*, the first time they appear in the text. Italicized terms will be defined immediately following their introduction.

Finally, we have included advice to teachers at appropriate points throughout this work. They are enclosed in a red shaded box. The first one of these "To The Teacher" boxes appears at the end of this section.

To The Teacher: About This Guide

It is our intention that this book might be used as an instructional unit in a variety of undergraduate and graduate chemistry courses (in addition to serving as an overview of electronic structure theory for research chemists). Accordingly, we have provided *To The Teacher* boxes such as this one at appropriate points throughout the text. They will contain hints for introducing and discussing material in the classroom, suggestions for further exercises, clarification of answers given in the text, and pointers to additional reference material.

Note that the exercises in this work are not ordered and can be used in other sequences. Omitting earlier exercises will not generally affect later ones. The exercises are suitable as either homework or laboratory exercises, and they have been designed so that the work may be easily divided among a group of students.

We'd love to hear about your experiences using this book for educational purposes. Please also feel free to let us know how this book could better meet the needs of your students and courses. You can contact us at *explore@gaussian.com*.

Running Gaussian

This chapter breaks into two branches: one for the Windows version (here *Gaussian 94W*), and one for all of the workstation and supercomputer versions. Although their capabilities are identical, their user interfaces are different enough to warrant separate sections. The output produced by both of them is identical, and so we have recombined the two threads as we take our first look at *Gaussian* output in "A Quick Tour of *Gaussian* Output" on page xlix. At that point, and throughout the remainder of this book, the text will apply to all versions of *Gaussian*. The few interface differences between versions will be noted as appropriate.

The first subsection discusses running *Gaussian* on UNIX and VMS systems and uses *Gaussian 94* as an example. The *Gaussian 94W* tutorial begins on page xxxviii.

Tutorial for UNIX and VMS Systems

This tutorial assumes that *Gaussian 94* is already installed on your computer. Instructions for doing so are included with your program package.

Executing a *Gaussian* job involves the following steps:

+ Setting up the *Gaussian* environment (usually handled by your login initialization file).
+ Preparing the input file.
+ Running the program, either interactively or via a batch queue.
+ Examining and interpreting the output.

We'll discuss each of these steps in turn.

1. Execute the appropriate commands to set up the *Gaussian* environment on your system.

You must execute the *Gaussian 94* initialization file included with the program in order to run it. This file sets the values of some environment variables (UNIX) or logical names (VMS) needed by the program. Usually, this file is executed from within your user initialization file (i.e., .login, .profile, or LOGIN.COM, as appropriate), although you can also run the commands by hand.

These are the commands needed to prepare to run *Gaussian 94*:

UNIX: C Shell
```
% setenv g94root directory
% source $g94root/g94/bsd/g94.login
```

UNIX: Bourne Shell
```
$ g94root=directory; export g94root
$ . $g94root/g94/bsd/g94.profile
```

VMS
```
$ @disk:[G94.VMS.EDT]G94Login.Com
```

UNIX users will need to specify the location of the *Gaussian 94* tree on their system. VMS users will need to specify the disk location of the [G94] directory.

You may want to add these commands to your user initialization file now if you haven't already done so. VMS users will also want to include a line like the following in their LOGIN.COM file, setting their working set to its maximum value:

```
$ Set Work/NoAdjust/Quota=65536/Limit=65536
```

Next, we'll prepare a *Gaussian* input file for an energy calculation on water.

2. Start any text editor and enter the following into a new file:

UNIX
```
#T RHF/6-31G(d) Test
```

VMS
```
$ RunGauss
#T RHF/6-31G(d) Test
```

VMS users begin their input file by executing the command to run *Gaussian*; input to the program follows. UNIX users will redirect their input file to standard input of the *Gaussian 94* command.

The line beginning with **#** is the *route section* for this job. The first line of the route section always begins with a pound sign in the first column (UNIX folks: this is *not* a comment marker). **#T** requests terse output from the program (only the essential results), **#** alone requests normal (traditional) *Gaussian* output, and **#P** requests more detail in the output file.

The route section specifies the procedure and basis set we want to use for this calculation:

Keyword	Meaning
RHF	Restricted Hartree-Fock (*restricted* means that there are no unpaired electrons in our molecule).
6-31G(d)	Use the 6-31G(d) basis set (which is a useful and often-recommended basis set).

We've chosen a restricted (**R**) Hartree-Fock (**HF**) calculation using the 6-31G(d) basis set (**6-31G(d)**).

All route sections must include a procedure keyword and a basis set keyword. Additional keywords further specify the type of calculation desired and additional options.

We've included only one additional keyword, **Test**, which says this is a test calculation whose results should not be entered into the *Gaussian* archive (if used at your site).

3.   Next, enter a blank line into the file, followed by a one-line description of the calculation.

Your file will now look something like this:

```
#T RHF/6-31G(d) Test

My first Gaussian job: water single point energy
```

This new line forms the *title section* for the job, which provides a description of the calculation for the job output and archive entry. It is not otherwise used by the program.

4.   Enter another blank line after the title section, followed by these four lines:

```
0  1
O -0.464  0.177  0.0
H -0.464  1.137  0.0
H  0.441 -0.143  0.0
```

This information makes up the *molecule specification section*, in this case for water. The first line of the molecule specification gives the charge and spin multiplicity for the molecule as two free-format integers. In this case, our molecule is neutral (charge 0), and has spin multiplicity 1 (a singlet). Spin multiplicity is discussed in Chapter 2, and molecule specifications in general are discussed in Appendix B.

The remaining three lines specify the element type and Cartesian coordinates (in angstroms) for each of the atoms in the molecule.

5.   **End the file with another blank line.**

The completed input file looks like this:

Exercise QS.1: Water Single Point Energy
file: qs.com

```
#T RHF/6-31G(d) Test

My first Gaussian job: water single point energy

0 1
O -0.464  0.177  0.0
H -0.464  1.137  0.0
H  0.441 -0.143  0.0
```

VMS users will have the **RunGauss** command preceding this input in their version of the file.

6.   **Save the file under the name h2o.com, and exit from the editor.**

Notice that we never stated what kind of computation to perform. By default, *Gaussian* performs an energy calculation, which is what we want.

We're now ready to run this calculation.

7.   **Execute this *Gaussian* job, using the appropriate command:**

UNIX
```
% g94 <h2o.com >& h2o.log          C shell
$ g94 <h2o.com 2>&1 >h2o.log       Bourne shell
```

VMS
```
$ @H2O.Com/Output=H2O.Log
```

This job should complete very quickly. You may run the job in the background if desired with commands like these:

UNIX
```
% g94 <h2o.com >& h2o.log &        C shell
$ g94 <h2o.com 2>&1 >h2o.log &     Bourne shell
```

VMS
```
$ Spawn/NoWait/Notify/In=H2O.Com/Out=H2O.Log
```

The job's output goes to the file h2o.log. We'll look at the output in more detail later. For now, we'll examine it only briefly.

8. Display the contents of the log file on the terminal screen.

Once all of it has been displayed, verify that the job completed normally. A line like the following will appear at or near the end of the file:

```
Normal termination of Gaussian 94.
```

Resource usage statistics are also included.

Next, we'll look for the results of our computation: the energy of the system.

9. Search the output file for the string "SCF Done".

Using the appropriate search utility for your system, you'll find the following line:

```
SCF Done: E(RHF) = -76.0098706218 A.U. after  6 cycles
```

This indicates that the energy of the system, computed at the Hartree-Fock level, is about -76.00987 hartrees.

Converting a Structure from a Graphics Program

Molecule specifications can be entered by hand or be converted from the output of a graphics program. We'll perform a simple conversion here, converting the water molecule structure saved in Brookhaven Protein Data Bank (PDB) format. The file water.pdb in the quick subdirectory contains a PDB format structure for water.

Exercise QS.2: Converting a PDB File
file: water.pdb

The NewZMat utility is provided with *Gaussian* to perform conversions between different data file formats. We'll use it to convert this PDB file to *Gaussian* input.

10. Execute the following NewZMat command:

UNIX
```
% newzmat -ipdb $g94root/g94/tutor/quick/water.pdb water.com
```

VMS
```
$ NewZMat -IPDB disk:[G94.Tutor.Quick]Water.PDB []Water.Com
```

This command will create a new *Gaussian* input file. **NewZMat** may prompt you for the charge and multiplicity to use; accept the default values offered.

11. Edit the new input file.

Notice that NewZMat has set up a Hartree-Fock calculation by default, using the 6-31G(d) basis set. The molecule specification in the generated file is also in Z-matrix format rather than Cartesian coordinates. You can now edit this file to modify the procedure, basis set, and type of run desired. We won't bother running this file, since it is the same job as the one we just completed.

Batch Processing

Although we ran the water calculation interactively, we recommend batch processing for *Gaussian* jobs on multiuser systems where a batch facility is available. On some systems, such as those at supercomputer centers, only batch processing is allowed. VMS users may execute water.com as a batch job using the Submit command. On UNIX systems supporting the NQS batch facility, the **subg94** command provided with *Gaussian 94* may be used. Here is an example:

```
% subg94 queue-name h2o.com
```

where *queue-name* is the name of the desired batch queue. The output from the job will automatically go to the file water.log. Alternatively, on UNIX systems, *Gaussian* jobs may be run in the background at lowered priority by initiating them with the **nice** command:

```
% nice g94 <h2o.com >h2o.log &
```

This concludes the UNIX and VMS-specific portion of the tutorial. Turn to page xlix to continue learning about *Gaussian*, where we examine *Gaussian* output.

Tutorial for Windows Systems

This tutorial assumes that you have already installed *Gaussian* on your PC and that you know how to navigate within Windows and run programs from the Program Manager. These instructions assume that you are using Windows 3.1; Windows 95 users will need to adjust them for the changes introduced in that operating system.

The following steps are necessary to run a *Gaussian* calculation:

+ Start the program.
+ Load or enter *Gaussian* input.

✦ Start execution of the job.
✦ Examine and interpret the output.

1. Start the program by double clicking on the *Gaussian 94W* icon.

Gaussian 94W

This icon is usually located in the **G94W** program group. If you moved this icon to a different program group, select it from the appropriate location.

The main program window is now open.

2. Locate each of the labeled items in the illustration below in the window on your screen.

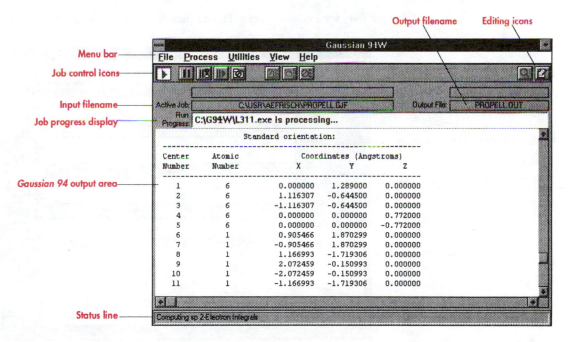

We'll examine each of these items in turn.

Before you can run a *Gaussian* job, you must provide the program with the input it needs. The **File** menu is used to create a new input file or to modify an existing one.

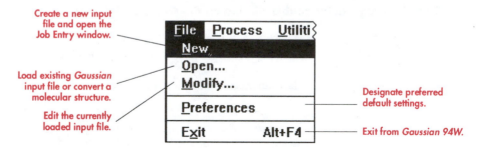

Create a new input file and open the Job Entry window.

Load existing *Gaussian* input file or convert a molecular structure.

Edit the currently loaded input file.

Designate preferred default settings.

Exit from *Gaussian 94W*.

3. Select New from the File menu to create a new Gaussian input file.

The **Job Entry** window now appears. This diagram indicates the major input sections:

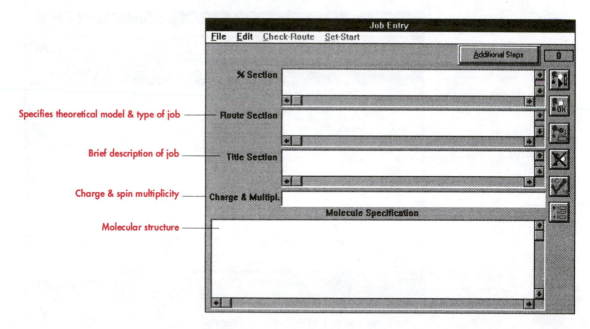

Specifies theoretical model & type of job

Brief description of job

Charge & spin multiplicity

Molecular structure

We'll fill in this window with the input for an energy calculation on water.

This window is divided into several separate individually scrollable sections, each of which will hold a different part of the Gaussian input. The cursor is initially placed in the **% Section** section. You move the cursor to the next section by pressing the Tab key;

Shift Tab moves the cursor to the previous section. Or, you can move directly to any section by clicking in it with the mouse.

4. Move the cursor to the second section of the window, which is labeled Route Section.

This section is used to enter the *route section* of the job, which contains instructions for running the calculation.

5. Type the following line into the window:

```
#T RHF/6-31G(d) Test
```

The route section specifies the procedure and basis set we want to use for this calculation:

Keyword	Meaning
RHF	Restricted Hartree-Fock (*restricted* means that there are no unpaired electrons in our molecule)
6-31G(d)	Use the 6-31G(d) basis set (which is a useful and often-recommended basis set).

We've chosen a restricted (**R**) Hartree-Fock (**HF**) calculation using the 6-31G(d) basis set (**6-31G(d)**).

Lines in the route section begin with a **#** sign. **#T** requests terse output from the program (only the essential results), **#** alone requests normal (traditional) *Gaussian* output, and **#P** requests the maximum amount of detail in the output file.

All route sections must include a procedure keyword and a basis set keyword. Additional keywords further specify the type of calculation desired and additional options.

We've also included only one additional keyword, **Test**, which says this is a test calculation whose results should not be archived in the *Gaussian* archive (although archiving is not available for *Gaussian 94W*).

6. Move the cursor to the third section of the window, labelled Title section.

The *title section* of a *Gaussian* input file contains a brief (usually one-line) description of the job. Enter something like the following into this section:

```
My first Gaussian job: water single point energy
```

The title section appears in the output and is stored in the *Gaussian* archive entry but is not otherwise used by the program.

7.   Move the cursor to the next section of the window, labelled Charge & Multipl.

This section and the one following it (**Molecule Specification**) specify the structure of the molecule system to be investigated. This section holds the charge on the molecule and its spin multiplicity. Each of them is entered as an integer on this line, with one or more spaces separating them.

Since water is a neutral molecule, its charge is 0. *Spin multiplicity* refers to the arrangement of the electrons within the molecule. Water has no unpaired electrons, so it is a singlet and its spin multiplicity is 1 (Spin multiplicity is discussed in Chapter 2, and molecule specifications in general are discussed in Appendix B).

8.   Enter the following values into the Charge and Multiplicity section:

Charge & Multipl. | 0 1

The **Molecule Specification** section holds the type and positions of each of the atoms in the molecule. For this job, we'll enter our water molecule's structure in Cartesian coordinates.

9.   Enter the following data into the Molecule Specification section:

```
O -0.464    0.177    0.0
H -0.464    1.137    0.0
H  0.441   -0.143    0.0
```

This completes the input needed for this job. The completed screen should look similar to the one illustrated on the next page. We will save this input to a file for future reference and then run the job.

10.   Select Save File from the File menu.

This directs the program to save the input you typed in to a file. Select the desired directory location in the standard Windows save dialog box, and give the input file the name H2O.GJF. GJF is the extension used for *Gaussian* input files on Windows systems (standing for *Gaussian Job File*).

Exercise QS.1: Water Single Point Energy
file: qs.gjf

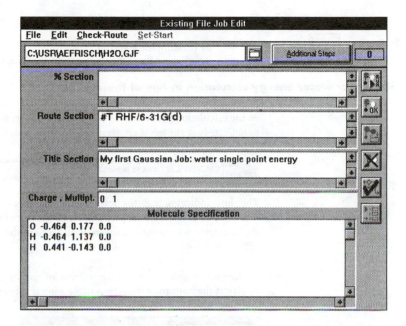

The top three icons on the right side of this window can be used to return to the main menu in various ways:

Icon	Action	Corresponding File Menu Option
	Return to the main menu.	**Exit**
	Return to the main menu and begin executing the job.	**Exit & Run**
	Discard input and return to the main menu.	**Abandon Data**

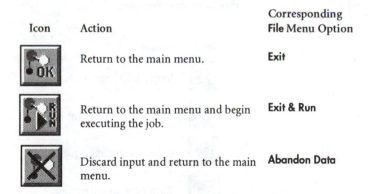

11. Select Exit from the File menu or click on the exit icon with the mouse.

This will return you to the main program window. Notice that the **Output File** display now contains the name of the file where output from this job will go, Water.Out. Output will also appear in the large window below the **Run Progress** display.

Gaussian 94W jobs may be started in two ways:

The Run icon

✦ By pressing the **Run** icon
✦ By selecting **Begin Processing** from the **Process** menu.

12. Start your water energy calculation in one of these ways.

As the calculation proceeds, the **Run Progress** display line will be periodically updated to indicate how the job is progressing. Here is a typical display:

Run
Progress: C:\G94W\L301.exe is processing...

This line indicates that the job is currently executing Link 301. All versions of *Gaussian* are divided into approximately 75 modules known as *links*, having names of the form L*nnn* where *nnn* is a one to four digit number. As you gain experience, many of these links will become familiar to you.

To aid you in this process, a description of the current link appears in the status display at the bottom of the screen while a job is running:

Performing Berny Optimization

You may pause or terminate a running job by using items from the **Process** menu or their corresponding icons:

Icon	Action	Corresponding **Process** Menu Item
⏸	Immediately pause job.	**Pause**
⏸	Pause after the current link.	**Pause @ Next Link**
⏯	Resume executing a paused job.	**Resume**
⏹	Terminate the current job.	**Kill Job**

Output is added to the output display area as it is produced by the program. This area is horizontally and vertically scrollable and may be examined at any point throughout job execution.

When the job finishes, the **Run Progress** area displays this message:

> Run
> Progress | Processing Complete.

The output window still contains the output from the job. We'll look at it briefly now and in more detail a bit later.

13. Examine the job output, and locate the following lines near the end of the output window:

```
Job cpu time:  0 days  0 hours  0 minutes 12.6 seconds.
File lengths (MBytes):  RWF= 5 Int= 1 D2E= 0 Chk= 1 Scr= 0
Normal termination of Gaussian 94.
```

This display indicates that the job was successful. It also shows some statistics about resource usage by the job.

14. Move back through the output until you find the line containing "SCF Done."

It is located approximately three screens back from the end of the output:

```
SCF Done: E(RHF) = -76.0098706218 A.U. after  6 cycles
```

This is the one of the quantities predicted by this calculation. It indicates that the energy of the system, computed at the Hartree-Fock level, is about -76.00987 hartrees.

Converting a Structure from a Graphics Program

Exercise QS.2: Converting a PDB File
file: water.pdb

Input for *Gaussian 94W* can be created in many different ways:

✦ Via the **Job Entry** window.

✦ As a text file created with any editor, using the same format used by other *Gaussian* versions (discussed in the previous section).

✦ By converting output from a drawing program and then editing the generated input.

We'll look at a simple example of the latter method here, converting the water molecule structure saved in Brookhaven Protein Data Bank (PDB) format.

15. Select the Open... option from the File menu.

This option is used to open existing input files and to convert files in other formats to *Gaussian* input. We're going to convert a file saved in Brookhaven Protein Data Bank (PDB) format.

Once you have selected this option, a file selection dialog box will appear:

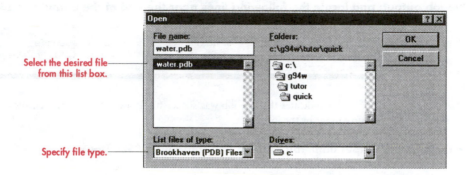

Select the desired file from this list box.

Specify file type.

The menu in the lower right part of the dialog box allows you to specify the type of file that you want to open. This setting defaults to *Gaussian 94W* input files.

16. Select Brookhaven (PDB) Files from the List files of type menu, and then open the file water.pdb, located in the quick subdirectory.

The **NewZMat File Conversion** window will appear:

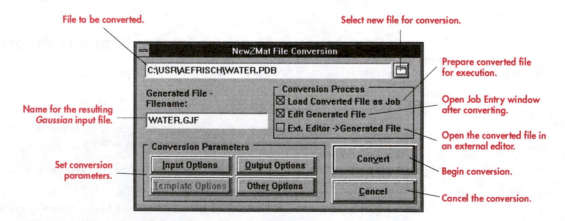

File to be converted.

Select new file for conversion.

Prepare converted file for execution.

Name for the resulting *Gaussian* input file.

Open Job Entry window after converting.

Open the converted file in an external editor.

Set conversion parameters.

Begin conversion.

Cancel the conversion.

This window controls how the generated file is made. The default filename is the same as that of the input file, with the extension .GJF.

17. Make sure that both the Load Generated File and Edit Generated File options are checked, and then click the Convert button.

The first of these options loads the created input into memory in preparation for execution by *Gaussian 94W*. The second one automatically opens the **Job Entry** window with the generated input.

The **NewZMat** utility will convert the file, and then open the Job Entry window. Notice that **NewZMat** has set up a Hartree-Fock calculation using the 6-31G(d) basis set by default. The molecule specification in the generated file is also in Z-matrix format rather than Cartesian coordinates. See Appendix B for details on the Z-matrix molecule specification format.

18. Create a title, specify terse output with #T, and then save the file by selecting Save from the File menu.

We could now begin executing this job by selecting **Exit & Run** option from the **File** menu. However, don't do that now. Instead, we'll run this job using a different technique in the next subsection.

19. Select Exit from the File menu to return to the main program window.

Drag-and-Drop Execution

Gaussian 94W provides another quick way of running a job. If an input file has already been prepared, then you can use the *drag-and-drop* method of running it. It involves these steps (in Windows 3.1):

✦ Open the Windows **File Manager** and locate the desired input file by selecting its directory in the left side of the window and locating it in the list box on the right side.

✦ Start *Gaussian 94W* if it is not already running. The main program window may be open, or the application may be iconified, but no job should be currently running.

✦ Select and drag the desired input file from the **File Manager** into the *Gaussian 94W* main program window or on top of its minimized icon. The file will turn into a small page icon with a plus sign at its center:

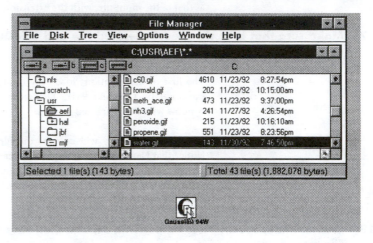

✦ Release the mouse button and the job will be loaded.

If the **Run Dropped Files** preference is set, the job will also begin executing as soon as it is dropped. If not, as is the default, you must explicitly initiate execution in one of the available ways.

20. Try this technique with the Water.GJF input file you saved earlier.

Allow the job to complete executing, and leave the program open as we'll use this setup when we look at *Gaussian* output in the next major section of this chapter.

Gaussian 94W also includes a batch processing facility; see the *Gaussian 94W Reference* pamphlet for details.

This concludes the Windows-specific portion of the tutorial. Go on to the next subsection to continue learning *Gaussian*, where we examine *Gaussian* output in some detail.

A Quick Tour of *Gaussian* Output

Edit Output File icon

In this section, we'll use an editor to examine the output from our water single point energy calculation in more detail. UNIX and VMS users should open the file h2o.log using an editor. *Gaussian 94W* users may also use any editor to examine the file directly; alternatively, an editing session may be started from the main program window by clicking on the **Edit Output File** icon in the upper right corner.[†] Note that this icon is active only after a *Gaussian 94W* job has completed.

Exercise QS.3: Sample *Gaussian* Output

We'll look at the main features of this output now. Locate the corresponding section in your file with your editor as you read each comment. Note that the output from your system may vary slightly. Not every numerical value will necessarily agree to the last decimal place, although differences should appear only beyond the fifth decimal place. This subsection concludes the *Gaussian* tutorial.Once you have completed it, you will be ready to learn about the various types of *Gaussian* jobs as well as the model chemistries the program offers.

This is the copyright notice for *Gaussian 94*. Its appearance indicates that the program has begun executing.

```
Entering Gaussian System, Link 0=g94
Input=h2o.com
Output=h2o.log
Initial command:
/mf/g94/l1.exe /scratch/g94-17042.inp -scrdir=/scratch/
Entering Link 1 = /mf/g94/l1.exe PID=      18580.

     Copyright (c) 1988,1990,1992,1993,1995 Gaussian, Inc.
               All Rights Reserved.

This is part of the Gaussian 94(TM) system of programs. It is
based on the Gaussian 92(TM) system (copyright 1992
Gaussian, Inc.), the Gaussian 90(TM) system (copyright 1990
Gaussian, Inc.), the Gaussian 88(TM) system (copyright 1988
Gaussian, Inc.), the Gaussian 86(TM) system (copyright 1986
Carnegie Mellon University), and the Gaussian 82(TM) system
(copyright 1983 Carnegie Mellon University). Gaussian is a
federally registered trademark of Gaussian, Inc.

This software is provided under written license and may be
used, copied, transmitted, or stored only in accord with that
written license.

...
```

[†] The editor invoked when pressing this icon defaults to **Notepad**, but any available editor may be specified using the **ASCII Editor** field in the **Preferences** window; you can access the **Gaussian 94W Preferences** window by selecting the **Preferences** item from the **File** menu in the main program window. Note that some editors, including **Notepad**, have length limitations which may be exceeded by some *Gaussian* output files.

This is the official citation for the *Gaussian 94* **program, which should be included in its entirety in all papers presenting results obtained by running** *Gaussian 94* **and** *Gaussian 94W.*

This is the version of *Gaussian 94* **that is running, in this case, Revision C.3. Include this information in any questions or problem reports you send to Gaussian, Inc.**

The route section, title section, and molecule specification from the input file are displayed next.

The standard orientation is the coordinate system used internally by the program as it performs the calculation, chosen to optimize performance. The origin is placed at the molecule's center of nuclear charge. Here, the oxygen atom sits on the Y-axis above the origin, and the two hydrogen atoms are placed below it in the XY plane.

```
Gaussian, Inc.
Carnegie Office Park, Building 6, Pittsburgh, PA 15106 USA

Cite this work as:
Gaussian 94, Revision C.3,
M. J. Frisch, G. W. Trucks, H. B. Schlegel, P. M. W. Gill,
B. G. Johnson, M. A. Robb, J. R. Cheeseman, T. Keith,
G. A. Petersson, J. A. Montgomery, K. Raghavachari,
M. A. Al-Laham, V. G. Zakrzewski, J. V. Ortiz, J. B. Foresman,
J. Cioslowski, B. B. Stefanov, A. Nanayakkara, M. Challacombe,
C. Y. Peng, P. Y. Ayala, W. Chen, M. W. Wong, J. L. Andres,
E. S. Replogle, R. Gomperts, R. L. Martin, D. J. Fox,
J. S. Binkley, D. J. Defrees, J. Baker, J. P. Stewart,
M. Head-Gordon, C. Gonzalez, and J. A. Pople,
Gaussian, Inc., Pittsburgh PA, 1995.

**************************************************
Gaussian 94:  IBM-RS6000-G94RevC.3 26-Sep-1995
              25-Nov-1995
**************************************************
------------------
#T RHF/6-31G(d) Test
------------------

---------------
Water HF Energy
---------------
Symbolic Z-matrix:
   Charge = 0 Multiplicity = 1
O      -0.464    0.177     0.
H      -0.464    1.137     0.
H       0.441   -0.143     0.
------------------------------------------------------------
                    Z-MATRIX (ANGSTROMS AND DEGREES)
CD Cent Atom  N1   Length/X   N2    Alpha/Y   N3    Beta/Z    J
------------------------------------------------------------
   1   1  O   0    -.464000         .177000         .000000
   2   2  H   0    -.464000        1.137000         .000000
   3   3  H   0     .441000        -.143000         .000000
------------------------------------------------------------
Framework group   CS[SG(H2O)]
Deg. of freedom   3
                    Standard orientation:
------------------------------------------------------------
Center      Atomic            Coordinates (Angstroms)
Number      Number          X            Y            Z
------------------------------------------------------------
   1          8          .000000      .110843      .000000
   2          1          .783809     -.443452      .000000
   3          1         -.783809     -.443294      .000000
------------------------------------------------------------
```

```
Rotational constants (GHZ):   919.1537631   408.1143172   282.6255042
Isotopes: O-16,H-1,H-1
    19 basis functions        36 primitive gaussians
     5 alpha electrons         5 beta electrons
         nuclear repulsion energy        9.1576073710 Hartrees.
Projected INDO Guess.
Initial guess orbital symmetries:
       Occupied  (A')  (A')  (A')  (A')  (A")
       Virtual   (A')  (A')  (A')  (A')  (A')  (A")  (A')  (A')  (A')  (A')
                 (A')  (A')  (A")  (A")
Warning!  Cutoffs for single-point calculations used.
SCF Done:  E(RHF) =  -76.0098706218     A.U. after     6 cycles
               Convg  =      .3332D-04            -V/T =   2.0027
               S**2   =      .0000


*********************************************************************
               Population analysis using the SCF density.
*********************************************************************
Orbital Symmetries:
       Occupied  (A')  (A')  (A')  (A')  (A")
       Virtual   (A')  (A')  (A')  (A')  (A')  (A")  (A')  (A')  (A")  (A')
                 (A")  (A')  (A')  (A')
 The electronic state is 1-A'.
Alpha occ. eigenvals-- -20.55796 -1.33618 -.71426 -.56023  -.49562
Alpha virt. eigenvals--    .21061    .30388 1.04585 1.11667  1.15963
Alpha virt. eigenvals-- 1.16927 1.38460 1.41675 2.03064 2.03551
Alpha virt. eigenvals -- 2.07410 2.62759 2.94215 3.97815
           Condensed to atoms (all electrons):
Total atomic charges:
                  1
    1  O    -.876186
    2  H     .438090
    3  H     .438096
Sum of Mulliken charges=       .00000
...
Electronic spatial extent (au):  <R**2>=     18.9606
Charge=        .0000 electrons
Dipole moment (Debye):
    X=   -.0001    Y=  2.1383    Z=   .0000  Tot=  2.1383


Test job not archived.
1\1\GINC-MJF\SP\RHF\6-31G(d)\H2O1\AEFRISCH\25-Nov-1995\0\\#T RHF/6-31G(
d) TEST\\Water HF Energy\\0,1\O,0,-0.464,0.177,0.\H,0,-0.464,1.137,0.\H
,0,0.441,-0.143,0.\\Version=IBM-RS6000-G94RevC.3\State=1-A'\HF=-76.0098
706\RMSD=3.332e-05\Dipole=0.6868725,0.4857109,0.\PG=CS [SG(H2O1)]\\@

Children are likely to live up to what you believe of them.
   -- Lady Bird Johnson
Job cpu time:  0 days  0 hours  0 minutes  5.8 seconds.
File lengths (MBytes): RWF=  5 Int=   0 D2E=   0 Chk=   1 Scr=   1
Normal termination of Gaussian 94
```

This line indicates the predicted energy computed by our single point calculation. It also indicates the values of the convergence criteria in the SCF computation. Appendix A discusses the iterative nature of SCF methods in more detail.

A Mulliken population analysis follows the SCF energy results. This analysis partitions the charge on the molecule by atom.

The section labelled `Total atomic charges` indicates the estimated total charge on each atom in the molecule. Here, the oxygen atom has a negative charge balancing the slight positive charge on each of the hydrogen atoms.

This section gives the dipole moment for this molecule, in the standard orientation. This dipole moment has only a negative Y component, and its magnitude is 1.69 debye. By convention, the dipole moment "points" in the direction of positive charge. Referring back to the standard orientation for this molecule, we note that the oxygen atom is situated on the positive Y-axis. This indicates that the dipole points away from the oxygen atom, toward the positively-charged portion of the molecule.

This is the archive entry corresponding to this job, which summarizes its results.

Successful *Gaussian* jobs end with a quotation chosen at random from a collection stored internally.

CPU time and other resource usage information is presented at the conclusion of the job.

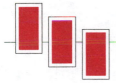

Part 1: Essential Concepts & Techniques

Computational Models & Model Chemistries

All chemists use models.[†] Beginning chemistry students use plastic models to help them understand and visualize the structures of molecules. Recently, both students and experienced researchers have begun to use chemical drawing programs for the same purpose.

Not all models are physical or pictorial objects. For example, the S_N2 mechanism is a simple model for a particular class of reactions that successfully explains a lot of chemistry. What all of these things have in common is that they use a set of pre-defined objects and rules to approximate real chemical entities and processes.

In a similar way, *computational chemistry* simulates chemical structures and reactions numerically, based in full or in part on the fundamental laws of physics. It allows chemists to study chemical phenomena by running calculations on computers rather than by examining reactions and compounds experimentally. Some methods can be used to model not only stable molecules, but also short-lived, unstable intermediates and even transition states. In this way, they can provide information about molecules and reactions which is impossible to obtain through observation. Computational chemistry is therefore both an independent research area and a vital adjunct to experimental studies.

An Overview of Computational Chemistry

There are two broad areas within computational chemistry devoted to the structure of molecules and their reactivity: *molecular mechanics* and *electronic structure theory*. They both perform the same basic types of calculations:

♦ Computing the energy of a particular molecular structure (spatial arrangement of atoms or nuclei and electrons). Properties related to the energy may also be predicted by some methods.

[†] In fact, certain philosophers of science argue that chemistry itself—indeed all science—functions as a model of certain aspects of the physical universe.

✦ Performing geometry optimizations, which locate the lowest energy molecular structure in close proximity to the specified starting structure.[†] Geometry optimizations depend primarily on the gradient of the energy—the first derivative of the energy with respect to atomic positions.

✦ Computing the vibrational frequencies of molecules resulting from interatomic motion within the molecule. Frequencies depend on the second derivative of the energy with respect to atomic structure, and frequency calculations may also predict other properties which depend on second derivatives. Frequency calculations are not possible or practical for all computational chemistry methods.

Molecular Mechanics

Molecular mechanics simulations use the laws of classical physics to predict the structures and properties of molecules. Molecular mechanics methods are available in many computer programs, including MM3, HyperChem, Quanta, Sybyl, and Alchemy. There are many different molecular mechanics methods. Each one is characterized by its particular *force field*. A force field has these components:

✦ A set of equations defining how the potential energy of a molecule varies with the locations of its component atoms.

✦ A series of *atom types*, defining the characteristics of an element within a specific chemical context. Atom types prescribe different characteristics and behavior for an element depending upon its environment. For example, a carbon atom in a carbonyl is treated differently than one bonded to three hydrogens. The atom type depends on hybridization, charge and the types of the other atoms to which it is bonded.

✦ One or more *parameter sets* that fit the equations and atom types to experimental data. Parameter sets define *force constants*, which are values used in the equations to relate atomic characteristics to energy components, and structural data such as bond lengths and angles.

Molecular mechanics calculations don't explicitly treat the electrons in a molecular system. Instead, they perform computations based upon the interactions among the nuclei. Electronic effects are implicitly included in force fields through parametrization.

This approximation makes molecular mechanics computations quite inexpensive computationally, and allows them to be used for very large systems containing many

---

[†] Strictly speaking, optimizations do not always find minimum energy structures. This point will be discussed at length in Chapter 4.

thousands of atoms. However, it also carries several limitations as well. Among the most important are these:

✦ Each force field achieves good results only for a limited class of molecules, related to those for which it was parametrized. No force field can be generally used for all molecular systems of interest.

✦ Neglect of electrons means that molecular mechanics methods cannot treat chemical problems where electronic effects predominate. For example, they cannot describe processes which involve bond formation or bond breaking. Molecular properties which depend on subtle electronic details are also not reproducible by molecular mechanics methods.

Electronic Structure Methods

Electronic structure methods use the laws of quantum mechanics rather than classical physics as the basis for their computations. Quantum mechanics states that the energy and other related properties of a molecule may be obtained by solving the Schrödinger equation:

$$\mathbf{H}\Psi = E\Psi$$

For any but the smallest systems, however, exact solutions to the Schrödinger equation are not computationally practical. Electronic structure methods are characterized by their various mathematical approximations to its solution. There are two major classes of electronic structure methods:

✦ *Semi-empirical methods*, such as AM1, MINDO/3 and PM3, implemented in programs like MOPAC, AMPAC, HyperChem, and *Gaussian*, use parameters derived from experimental data to simplify the computation. They solve an approximate form of the Schrödinger equation that depends on having appropriate parameters available for the type of chemical system under investigation. Different semi-emipirical methods are largely characterized by their differing parameter sets.

✦ *Ab initio methods*, unlike either molecular mechanics or semi-empirical methods, use no experimental parameters in their computations. Instead, their computations are based solely on the laws of quantum mechanics—the first principles referred to in the name *ab initio*—and on the values of a small number of physical constants:

❖ The speed of light
❖ The masses and charges of electrons and nuclei
❖ Planck's constant

Gaussian offers the entire range of electronic structure methods. This work provides guidance and examples in using all of the most important of them.

Ab initio methods compute solutions to the Schrödinger equation using a series of rigorous mathematical approximations. These procedures are discussed in detail in Appendix A, *The Theoretical Background*.

Semi-empirical and ab initio methods differ in the trade-off made between computational cost and accuracy of result. Semi-empirical calculations are relatively inexpensive and provide reasonable qualitative descriptions of molecular systems and fairly accurate quantitative predictions of energies and structures for systems where good parameter sets exist.

In contrast, ab initio computations provide high quality quantitative predictions for a broad range of systems. They are not limited to any specific class of system. Early ab initio programs were quite limited in the size of system they could handle. However, this is not true for modern ab initio programs. On a typical workstation, *Gaussian 94* can compute the energies and related properties for systems containing a dozen heavy atoms in just a few minutes. It can handle jobs of up to a few hundred atoms, and it can predict the structures of molecules having as many as one hundred atoms on the same size computer system.[†] Corresponding larger systems can be handled on supercomputer systems, based upon their specific CPU performance characteristics.

The ab initio methods in *Gaussian* are also capable of handling any type of atom, including metals. *Gaussian* computes a variety of molecular properties in addition to the energies and structures. *Gaussian* can investigate molecules in their excited states and in solution.

Density Functional Methods

Recently, a third class of electronic structure methods have come into wide use: *density functional methods*.[‡] These DFT methods are similar to ab initio methods in many ways. DFT calculations require about the same amount of computation resources as Hartree-Fock theory, the least expensive ab initio method.

DFT methods are attractive because they include the effects of *electron correlation*—the fact that electrons in a molecular system react to one another's motion and attempt to keep out of one another's way—in their model. Hartree-Fock calculations consider this effect only in an average sense—each electron sees and

---

[†] Such large calculations will take on the order of one to a few days, depending on the exact molecular system and computer system. However, even larger calculations are possible, provided you are willing to allocate the necessary CPU resources to them. What constitutes a "practical" calculation is ultimately a matter of individual judgement. We'll look at how resource requirements vary with molecule size and calculation type at appropriate points in the course of this work.

[‡] Whether density functional methods are ab initio methods or not is a controversial question which we will not attempt to address.

reacts to an averaged electron density—while methods including electron correlation account for the instantaneous interactions of pairs of electrons with opposite spin.[†] This approximation causes Hartree-Fock results to be less accurate for some types of systems. Thus, DFT methods can provide the benefits of some more expensive ab initio methods at essentially Hartree-Fock cost. See Appendix A for more details about these methods.

Model Chemistries

The theoretical philosophy underlying *Gaussian* is characterized by the following principle:

> A theoretical model should be *uniformly applicable* to molecular systems of any size and type, up to a maximum size determined only by the practical availability of computer resources.

This is in contrast to an alternate view which holds that the highest—most accurate—level of theory which is practical ought to be used for any given molecular system. The Schrödinger equation can be approximated much more closely for small systems than for large ones (and can even be solved exactly for the smallest possible system: the hydrogen atom). However, using different levels of theory for different size molecules makes comparing results among systems unreliable.

This principle has a number of implications:

✦ A theoretical model should be *uniquely defined* for any given configuration of nuclei and electrons. This means that specifying a molecular structure is all that is required to produce an approximate solution to the Schrödinger equation; no other parameters are needed to specify the problem or its solution.

✦ A theoretical model ought to be *unbiased*. It should rely on no presuppositions about molecular structure or chemical processes which would make it inapplicable to classes of systems or phenomena where these assumptions did not apply. It should not in general invoke special procedures for specific types of molecules.

The implementation of such a theoretical model is termed a theoretical-model chemistry, or simply a *model chemistry*.

[†] This is a bit of an oversimplification (see Appendix A).

Once a theoretical model has been defined and implemented, it should be systematically tested on a variety of chemical systems, and its results should be compared to known experimental values. Once a model demonstrates that it can reproduce experimental results, it can be used to predict properties of systems for which no data exist.

Other desirable features of a model chemistry include:

+ *Size consistency*: the results given for a system of molecules infinitely separated from one another ought to equal the sum of the results obtained for each individual molecule calculated separately. Another way of describing this requirement is that the error in the predictions of any method should scale roughly in proportion to the size of the molecule. When size consistency does not hold, comparing the properties of molecules of different sizes will not result in quantitatively meaningful differences.

+ Reproducing the *exact solution for the relevant n-electron problem*: a method ought to yield the same results as the exact solution to the Schrödinger equation to the greatest extent possible. What this means specifically depends on the theory underlying the method. Thus, Hartree-Fock theory should be (and is) able to reproduce the exact solution to the one electron problem, meaning it should be able to treat cases like H_2^+ and HeH^+ essentially exactly.

 Higher order methods similarly ought to reproduce the exact solution to their corresponding problem. Methods including double excitations (see Appendix A) ought to reproduce the exact solution to the 2-electron problem, methods including triple excitations, like QCISD(T), ought to reproduce the exact solution to the three-electron problem, and so on.

+ *Variational*: the energies predicted by a method ought to be an upper bound to the real energy resulting from the exact solution of the Schrödinger equation.

+ *Efficient*: calculations with a method ought to be practical with existing computer technology.

+ *Accurate*: ideally, a method ought to produce highly accurate quantitative results. Minimally, a method should predict qualitative trends in molecular properties for groups of molecular systems.

Not every model can completely achieve all of these ideals. We'll look at the characteristics of the various methods in *Gaussian* in Appendix A.

Defining Model Chemistries

Gaussian includes many different model chemistries. The theoretical model chemistries in *Gaussian* have been subjected to the testing procedure described previously and so may be recommended for general use with any system for which they are computationally feasible.

Model chemistries are characterized by the combination of theoretical procedure and basis set. Every calculation performed with *Gaussian* must specify the desired theoretical model chemistry in addition to specifying the molecular system to consider and which results to compute for it.

Method

The *Gaussian* program contains a hierarchy of procedures corresponding to different approximation methods (commonly referred to as different *levels of theory*). Theoretical descriptions for each of them may be found in Appendix A. The ones we'll be concerned with most often in this work are listed in the following table:

Keyword	Method	Availability
HF	Hartree-Fock Self-Consistent Field	Through 2nd derivatives
B3LYP	Becke-style 3-Parameter Density Functional Theory (using the Lee-Yang-Parr correlation functional)	Through 2nd derivatives
MP2	2nd Order Møller-Plesset Perturbation Theory	Through 2nd derivatives
MP4	4th Order Møller-Plesset Perturbation Theory (including Singles, Doubles, Triples and Quadruples by default)	Energies only
QCISD(T)	Quadratic CI (Single, Doubles & Triples)	Energies only

More accurate methods become correspondingly more expensive computationally. Recommended uses of each level of theory will be discussed throughout the work, and a consideration of the entire range of electronic structure methods is the subject of Chapter 6.

Basis Set

A *basis set* is a mathematical representation of the molecular orbitals within a molecule. The basis set can be interpreted as restricting each electron to a particular region of space. Larger basis sets impose fewer constraints on electrons and more accurately approximate exact molecular orbitals. They require correspondingly more computational resources. Available basis sets and their characteristics are discussed in Chapter 5.

Open vs. Closed Shell

Although not strictly part of a model chemistry, there is a third component to every *Gaussian* calculation involving how electron spin is handled: whether it is performed using an *open shell* model or a *closed shell* model; the two options are also referred to as *unrestricted* and *restricted* calculations, respectively. For closed shell molecules, having an even number of electrons divided into pairs of opposite spin, a spin restricted model is the default. In other words, closed shell calculations use doubly occupied orbitals, each containing two electrons of opposite spin.

Open shell systems—for example, those with unequal numbers of spin up and spin down electrons—are usually modeled by a spin unrestricted model (which is the default for these systems in *Gaussian*).[†] Restricted, closed shell calculations force each electron pair into a single spatial orbital, while open shell calculations use separate spatial orbitals for the spin up and spin down electrons (α and β respectively):

Unrestricted calculations are needed for systems with unpaired electrons, including:

◆ Molecules with odd numbers of electrons (e.g. some ions).
◆ Excited states.
◆ Other systems with unusual electronic structure (for example, 2 or more unpaired outer electrons).
◆ Processes such as bond dissociation which require the separation of an electron pair and for which restricted calculations thus lead to incorrect products (even though there is an even number of electrons).

In *Gaussian*, open shell calculations are requested by prepending the method keyword with a **U** (for unrestricted); similarly, closed shell calculations use an initial **R** (for example, **RHF** versus **UHF**, **RMP2** versus **UMP2** and so on).[‡]

Compound Models

Traditional electronic structure energy calculations consist of a single job. However, a calculation at a very accurate level of theory can take a very long time to complete. In an effort to achieve high accuracy results at less computational cost, several new model chemistries have been defined as a series of calculations to be run and a

---

[†] It is also possible to define spin restricted open shell models (keyword prefix **RO**). See the *Gaussian User's Reference* for more information.

[‡] For some cases, additional measures must be taken to force an unrestricted wavefunction to be used (for example, **Guess=Mix** or **Guess=Alter**).

procedure for combining their results to predict an energy value for the molecule under investigation. Even though multiple calculations are run, their total computational cost is still significantly less than that of the single, high-accuracy model which they are designed to approximate.

We will consider several of these multi-job models in Chapter 7, including Gaussian-1 and Gaussian-2 theory and their variants and several Complete Basis Set (CBS) methods.

References

J. B. Foresman, "Ab Initio Techniques in Chemistry: Interpretation and Visualization," Chapter 14 in *What Every Chemist Should Know About Computing*, Ed. M. L Swift and T. J. Zielinski (ACS Books, Washington, D.C., 1996).

A. Szabo and N. S. Ostlund, *Modern Quantum Chemistry* (McGraw-Hill, New York, 1982).

W. J. Hehre, L. Radom, P. v. R. Schleyer, and J. A. Pople, *Ab Initio Molecular Orbital Theory* (Wiley, New York, 1986).

M. J. Frisch, Æ. Frisch and J. B. Foresman, *Gaussian 94 User's Reference* (Gaussian, Inc., Pittsburgh, 1995).

Chapter 2

Single Point Energy Calculations

In this chapter, we'll elaborate further on the type of calculation we performed in the *Quick Start*. A single point energy calculation is a prediction of the energy[†] and related properties for a molecule with a specified geometric structure. The phrase *single point* is key, since this calculation is performed at a single, fixed point on the potential energy surface[‡] for the molecule. The validity of results of these calculations depends on having reasonable structures for the molecules as input.

Single point energy calculations are performed for many purposes, including the following:

✦   To obtain basic information about a molecule.

✦   As a consistency check on a molecular geometry to be used as the starting point for an optimization.

✦   To compute very accurate values for the energy and other properties for a geometry optimized at a lower level of theory.

✦   When it is the only affordable calculation for a system of interest.

Single point energy calculations can be performed at any level of theory and with small or large basis sets. The ones we'll do in this chapter will be at the Hartree-Fock level with medium-sized basis sets, but keep in mind that high accuracy energy computations are set up and interpreted in very much the same way.

Setting Up Energy Calculations

Setting up an input file for a *Gaussian* single point energy calculation follows the steps we used in the *Quick Start*. To request this type of calculation, you must supply the following information:

✦   The type of job and level of theory for the calculation.
✦   A title for the job.

[†] That is, the sum of the electronic energy and nuclear repulsion energy of the molecule at the specified nuclear configuration. This quantity is commonly referred to as the *total energy*. However, more complete and accurate energy predictions require a thermal or zero-point energy correction (see Chapter 4, p. 68).
[‡] This term is defined in detail in Chapter 3.

✦ The structure of the molecule: its charge and spin multiplicity and the locations of the nuclei in space.

These items form the route section, the title section, and the molecule specification section of the input file, respectively. We'll look at each of them again briefly as we set up an input file for an energy calculation on formaldehyde.

The Route Section

The route section of a *Gaussian* input file specifies the kind of job you want to run as well as the specific theoretical method and basis set which should be used. All of these items are specified via keywords. Recall that the first line of the route section begins with a **#** sign (or **#T** to request terse output).

A single point energy is the default calculation type in *Gaussian*, so no special keyword is needed in the route section to request one (although you can include the **SP** keyword if you want to); simply specifying a procedure and basis set in the route section requests a single point energy calculation. We'll be running our formaldehyde calculation at the Hartree-Fock level, using the 6-31G(d) basis set.

Here are some other useful keywords for single point energy calculations (and other types of jobs as well):

Keyword	Effect
Test	Prevents *Gaussian* from entering this job's results into the site archive.
Pop=Reg	Displays highest five occupied and lowest five virtual molecular orbitals and other information not included in the output by default. Use **Pop=Full** to display all orbitals.
Units	Specifies that alternate units have been used in the molecule specification (discussed later in this section).
SCF=Tight	Requests that the wavefunction convergence criteria be made more rigorous. The default criteria for single point energy calculations are chosen as the best tradeoff between accuracy and computation speed, and they are generally accurate enough for comparing the energies of similar molecules and for predicting properties such as molecular orbitals and the dipole moment. **SCF=Tight** can be used to compute the energy using even tighter SCF convergence criteria. See Exercise 2.6 for more details about this topic.

We'll be including **Pop=Full** in our job in order to include information about all of the molecular orbitals in the output.

The Title Section

This section of the input file consists of one or more lines describing the calculation in any way that the user desires. It often consists of just one line, and the section ends with a blank line.

The Molecule Specification Section

All molecule specifications require that the *charge* and *spin multiplicity* be specified (as two integers) on the first line of this section. The structure of the molecule follows, in either Cartesian coordinates, internal coordinates (a Z-matrix), or a combination of the two.

Charge on the Molecule

The charge is a positive or negative integer specifying the total charge on the molecule. Thus, 1 or +1 would be used for a singly-charged cation, -1 designates a singly-charged anion, and 0 represents a neutral molecule.

Spin Multiplicity

The *spin multiplicity* for a molecule is given by the equation $2S + 1$, where S is the total spin for the molecule. Paired electrons contribute nothing to this quantity. They have a net spin of zero since an alpha electron has a spin of $+\frac{1}{2}$ and a beta electron has a spin of $-\frac{1}{2}$. Each unpaired electron contributes $+\frac{1}{2}$ to S. Thus, a singlet—a system with no unpaired electrons—has a spin multiplicity of 1, a doublet (one unpaired electron) has a spin multiplicity of 2, a triplet (two unpaired electrons of like spin) has a spin multiplicity of 3, and so on.

Molecular Structure

The structure of the molecular system to be investigated follows the initial charge and spin multiplicity line in the molecule specification section. The structure may be obtained in a variety of ways: from the coordinates generated by or converted from a drawing program (as demonstrated in the *Quick Start*), by constructing a Z-matrix by hand (see Appendix B), from the experimental literature, from the results of a previous calculation, and so on.

Multi-Step Jobs

Multiple *Gaussian* calculations can be performed from a single input file. See Appendix B (page 294) for details on multi-step jobs.

Locating Results in *Gaussian* Output

Example 2.1: Formaldehyde Single Point Energy

file: **e2_01**

In this section, we'll identify the major results predicted by a single point energy calculation by looking at the output of a calculation on formaldehyde. Here is the complete input file:

```
#T RHF/6-31G(d) Pop=Full Test

Formaldehyde Single Point

0 1
C  0.0   0.0  0.0
O  0.0   1.22 0.0
H  0.94 -0.54 0.0
H -0.94 -0.54 0.0
```

Here we give the molecule specification in Cartesian coordinates. The route section specifies a single point energy calculation at the Hartree-Fock level, using the 6-31G(d) basis set. We've specified a restricted Hartree-Fock calculation (via the **R** prepended to the **HF** procedure keyword) because this is a closed shell system. We've also requested that information about the molecular orbitals be included in the output with **Pop=Reg**.

We'll look at each of the major items separately, in the order in which they appear in the output.

Standard Orientation Geometry

This section displays positioning of the atoms in the molecule used by the program internally, in Cartesian coordinates. This orientation is chosen for maximum calculation efficiency, and corresponds to placing the center of nuclear charge for the molecule at the origin. Most molecular properties are reported with respect to the standard orientation. Note that this orientation usually does not correspond to the one used in the input molecule specification; the latter is printed earlier in the output as the "Z-matrix orientation."

Here is the standard orientation generated for formaldehyde:

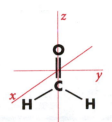

```
                 Standard orientation:

Center Atomic        Coordinates (Angstroms)
Number Number      X          Y          Z

  1        6     0.000000   0.000000  -0.542500
  2        8     0.000000   0.000000   0.677500
  3        1     0.000000   0.940000  -1.082500
  4        1     0.000000  -0.940000  -1.082500
```

The molecule is positioned in the YZ-plane, with the C=O bond coinciding with the Z-axis.

Energy

The total energy of the system, computed at the Hartree-Fock level, is given by this line of the output:

```
SCF Done: E(RHF) = -113.863697598     A.U. after 6 cycles
```

One hartree is 627.51 kcal-mol⁻¹

The value is in hartrees. The number of cycles it took the SCF calculation to converge is also given on this line (refer to Appendix A for a discussion of the iterative nature of the SCF method). When we discuss energies in this work, we will generally use hartrees (atomic units); when we discuss energy differences, kcal-mol⁻¹ will often be a more convenient unit (especially when comparing calculation predictions to experimental results).

In a higher level energy calculation, values for the energy computed using the more accurate procedure appear shortly after the Hartree-Fock energy. Here is the output from a formaldehyde calculation done at the MP2 level (**RMP2** replaces **RHF** in the route section:

```
E2 =   -0.3029540001D+00     EUMP2 =   -0.11416665769315D+03
```

The number following EUMP2 is the predicted energy at the MP2 level, approximately -114.16666 hartrees.

Here is part of the energy output from an MP4 calculation:

```
SCF DONE:  E(RHF) = -113.863697598 A.U. AFTER 6 CYCLES
...
E2 =    -0.3029540001D+00    EUMP2 =  -0.11416665769315D+03
...
E3= -0.25563412D-02 EUMP3= -0.1141669850323D+03
E4(DQ)= -0.13383605D-02 UMP4(DQ)= -0.1141669872345D+03
E4(SDQ)= -0.31707330D-02 UMP4(SDQ)= -0.1141678953224D+03
E4(SDTQ)= -0.10020409D-01 UMP4(SDTQ)= -0.114168745328D+03
```

Notice that the energies for all of the lower-level methods—HF, MP2, MP3, MP4(DQ) and MP4(SDQ)—are also given in a full MP4(SDTQ) calculation.

Molecular Orbitals and Orbital Energies

The **Pop=Reg** keyword in the route section requested data about the molecular orbitals be included in the output. They appear at the beginning of the population analysis section (output is shortened):

```
Molecular Orbital Coefficients
                      1         2         3         4         5
                   (A1)--O   (A1)--O   (A1)--O   (A1)--O   (B2)--O
      EIGENVALUES — -20.58275 -11.33951 -1.39270 -0.87260 -0.69717
   1  1 C   1S      0.00000   0.99566 -0.11059 -0.16263  0.00000
   2        2S     -0.00047   0.02675  0.20980  0.33995  0.00000
   3        2PX     0.00000   0.00000  0.00000  0.00000  0.00000
   4        2PY     0.00000   0.00000  0.00000  0.00000  0.42014
   5        2PZ    -0.00007   0.00066  0.17258 -0.18448  0.00000
  16  2 O   1S      0.99472   0.00038 -0.19672  0.08890  0.00000
  17        2S      0.02094  -0.00025  0.44186 -0.20352  0.00000
  18        2PX     0.00000   0.00000  0.00000  0.00000  0.00000
  19        2PY     0.00000   0.00000  0.00000  0.00000  0.32128
  20        2PZ    -0.00153   0.00029 -0.13538 -0.14221  0.00000
  31  3 H   1S      0.00002  -0.00210  0.03017  0.17902  0.19080
  33  4 H   1S      0.00002  -0.00210  0.03017  0.17902 -0.19080
```

The atomic orbital contributions for each atom in the molecule are given for each molecular orbital, numbered in order of increasing energy (the MO's energy is given in the row labeled EIGENVALUES preceding the orbital coefficients). The symmetry of the orbital and whether it is an occupied orbital or a virtual (unoccupied) orbital appears immediately under the orbital number.

When looking at the orbital coefficients, what is most important is their relative magnitudes with respect to one another within that orbital (regardless of sign). For example, for the first—lowest energy—molecular orbital, the carbon 2s and $2p_z$, the oxygen 1s, 2s, and $2p_z$ and the 1s orbitals on both hydrogens all have non-zero coefficients. However, the magnitude of the 1s coefficient on the oxygen is much, much larger than all the others, and so this molecular orbital essentially corresponds to the oxygen 1s orbital. Similarly, the important component for the second molecular orbital is the 1s orbital from the carbon atom.

The highest occupied molecular orbital (HOMO) and lowest unoccupied molecular orbital (LUMO) may be identified by finding the point where the occupied/virtual code letter in the symmetry designation changes from O to V.

Here are the energies and symmetry designations for the next set of molecular orbitals for formaldehyde:

	6 (A1)--O	7 (B1)--O	8 (B2)--O	9 (B1)--V	10 (A1)--V
EIGENVALUES —	-0.63955	-0.52296	-0.44079	0.13572	0.24842

For formaldehyde, molecular orbital number 8 is the HOMO, and molecular orbital number 9 is the LUMO. In this case, the energy also changes sign at the point separating the occupied from the unoccupied orbitals.

Molecule lies in a plane perpendicular to the page

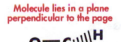

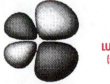

LUMO
(π^*)

E ↑

HOMO
(n)

To The Teacher: Molecular Orbitals

When discussing molecular orbitals, three-dimensional models or visualization software may be very instructive.

However, it is also important to emphasize that orbitals are actually mathematical conveniences and not physical quantities (despite how real models may make them seem). While the energy, electron density, and optimized geometry are physical observables, the orbitals are not. In fact, several different sets of orbitals can lead to the same energy. Nevertheless, orbitals are very useful in qualitative descriptions of bonding and reactivity.

Charge Distribution

By default, *Gaussian* jobs perform a Mulliken population analysis, which partitions the total charge among the atoms in the molecule. Here is the key part of output for formaldehyde:

```
Total atomic charges:
1 C   0.128551
2 O  -0.439946
3 H   0.155697
4 H   0.155697
Sum of Mulliken charges= 0.00000
```

This analysis places a slight negative charge on the oxygen atom and divides the balancing positive charge between the remaining three atoms.

Mulliken population analysis is an arbitrary scheme for assigning charges. Indeed, all such schemes are ultimately arbitrary. Atomic charges—unlike the electron density—are not a quantum mechanical observable, and are not unambiguously predictable from first principles. Other methods for assigning charges to atoms are explored in Exercises 8.4 and 8.5 (beginning on page 194).

Dipole and Higher Multipole Moments

Gaussian also predicts dipole moments and higher multipole moments (through hexadecapole). The dipole moment is the first derivative of the energy with respect to an applied electric field. It is a measure of the asymmetry in the molecular charge distribution, and is given as a vector in three dimensions. For Hartree-Fock calculations, this is equivalent to the expectation value of X, Y, and Z, which are the quantities reported in the output.

Here are the predicted dipole and quadrupole moments for formaldehyde:

```
Dipole moment (Debye):
X=     0.0000    Y=    0.0000    Z=  -2.8427   Tot= 2.8427
Quadrupole moment (Debye-Ang):
XX= -11.5395   YY= -11.3085   ZZ= -11.8963
XY=   0.0000   XZ=   0.0000   YZ=   0.0000
```

The dipole moment is broken down into X, Y, and Z components. In this case, the dipole moment is entirely along the Z-axis. By referring to the standard orientation for the molecule, we realize that this is pointing away from the oxygen atom, which is

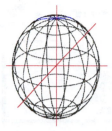

the negatively charged part of the molecule. Dipole moments are always given in units of debye.[†]

Quadrupole moments[‡] provide a second-order approximation of the total electron distribution, providing at least a crude idea of its shape. For example, equal XX, YY, and ZZ components indicate a spherical distribution. This is approximately the case for formaldehyde. One of these components being significantly larger than the others would represent an elongation of the sphere along that axis. If present, the off-axis components represent trans-axial distortion (stretching or compressing) of the ellipsoid. Quadrupole (and higher) moments are generally of significance only when the dipole moment is 0.

Another way of obtaining information about the distribution of electrons is by computing the polarizability. This property depends on the second derivative of the energy with respect to an electric field. We'll examine the polarizability of formaldehyde in Chapter 4.

CPU Time and Other Resource Usage

Gaussian jobs report the CPU time used and the sizes of their scratch files upon completion. Here is the data for our formaldehyde job:

```
Job cpu time: 0 days 0 hours 0 minutes 9.1 seconds.
File lengths (MBytes): RWF= 5 Int= 0 D2E= 0 Chk= 1 Scr= 1
```

Predicting NMR Properties

Example 2.2: Methane NMR Shielding Constants
file: e2_02

NMR shielding tensors are another property that can be computed in the context of a single point energy calculation. Such a calculation is requested by including the **NMR** keyword in the route section for the job. For example:

```
#T RHF/6-31G(d) NMR Test
```

We will run this job on methane at the Hartree-Fock level using the 6-31G(d) basis; our molecule specification is the result of a geometry optimization using the B3LYP Density Functional Theory method with the same basis set. This combination is cited

---

[†] Dipole moments are strictly determined for neutral molecules. For charged systems, its value depends on the choice of origin and molecular orientation.

[‡] You must use **#** rather than **#T** in order for quadrupole and higher moments to be included in the output.

by Cheeseman and coworkers as the minimum recommended model chemistry for predicting NMR properties.

Here is the predicted shielding value for the carbon atom in methane:

```
GIAO Magnetic shielding tensor (ppm):
  1  C     Isotropic =   199.0522   Anisotropy =      0.0000
   XX=    199.0522   YX=    .0.0000   ZX=      0.0000
   XY=      0.0000   YY=   199.0522   ZY=      0.0000
   XZ=      0.0000   YZ=     0.0000   ZZ=    199.0522
   Eigenvalues:    199.0522    199.0522    199.0522
```

The output gives the predicted value for each atom in the molecule in turn. Here we see that the predicted value for the carbon atom is about 199.1 parts-per-million.

Shielding constants reported in experimental studies are usually shifts relative to a standard compound, often tetramethylsilane (TMS). In order to compare predicted values to experimental results, we also need to compute the absolute shielding value for TMS, using exactly the same model chemistry. Here is the relevant output for TMS:

```
GIAO Magnetic shielding tensor (ppm):
  1  C     Isotropic =   195.1196   Anisotropy =     17.5214
```

To obtain the predicted shift for the carbon atom in methane, we subtract its absolute value from that of the reference molecule, resulting in a predicted shift of -3.9 ppm, which is in reasonable agreement with the experimental value of -7.0. Note the sign convention for shifts: a negative number indicates that there is more shielding in the specified molecule than in the reference molecule, and a positive number indicates that there is less shielding than in the reference molecule.

Exercises

Exercise 2.1: Propene Single Point Energy

file: **2_01**

Run a single point energy calculation on propene and determine the following information from the output:

◆ What is the standard orientation of the molecule? In what plane do most of the atoms lie?
◆ What is the predicted Hartree-Fock energy?
◆ What is the magnitude and direction of the dipole moment for propene?

◆ Describe the general nature of the predicted charge distribution.

Use the 6-31G(d) basis set for your calculation. Obtain the structure for propene from one of the sources we have discussed, or see Appendix B for detailed information on setting up a Z-matrix for propene.

Solution

Here is the route section for this job:

```
#T RHF/6-31G(d) Test
```

Here is the standard orientation from the output:

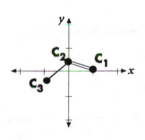

```
                    Standard orientation:
     ──────────────────────────────────────────────────────
     Center   Atomic        Coordinates (Angstroms)
     Number   Number       X           Y           Z
     ──────────────────────────────────────────────────────
        1        6      1.273694    0.103415    0.000000
        2        6      0.000000    0.519712    0.000000
        3        6     -1.131346   -0.495403    0.000000
        4        1      1.496403   -0.953373    0.000000
        5        1      2.077545    0.824680    0.000000
        6        1     -0.222709    1.576500    0.000000
        7        1     -2.088089    0.026845    0.000000
        8        1     -1.058621   -1.120498    0.889981
        9        1     -1.058621   -1.120498   -0.889981
     ──────────────────────────────────────────────────────
```

The plane of the molecule corresponds to the XY-plane (since most of the Z values are 0), with the two other hydrogens slightly in front of and behind it. The three carbons are oriented as in the diagram.

The Hartree-Fock/6-31G(d) energy is -117.06570 hartrees:

```
SCF Done: E(RHF) = -117.065698056     A.U. after 6 cycles
```

Here is the output giving the dipole moment and atomic charges:

```
Total atomic charges:
              1
   1  C   -0.388420
   2  C   -0.156442
   3  C   -0.507090
   4  H    0.170180
   5  H    0.173519
   6  H    0.183866
   7  H    0.165399
   8  H    0.179494
   9  H    0.179495
Sum of Mulliken charges= 0.00000
...
Dipole moment (Debye):
X= -0.2982   Y= -0.0310   Z= 0.0000   Tot= 0.2998
```

The dipole moment has a magnitude of about 0.3 debye, mostly in the negative X direction. This is a weak dipole moment, indicating that the centers of positive and negative charge are relatively close together in this molecule.

The negative charges are confined to the carbons, with the one on the middle carbon being appreciably smaller than that on the other two carbons. Each hydrogen has a small positive charge. ∎

Exercise 2.2: 1,2-Dichloro-1,2-Difluoroethane Conformer Energies

files: **2_02a (RR)**
       2_02b (SS)
       2_02c (meso)

Make a table of the energies and dipole moments for the three stereoisomers of 1,2-dichloro-1,2-difluoroethane (stoichiometry: CHFCl–CHFCl). You'll need to set up and run a HF/6-31G(d) single point energy calculation for each form.

Here are the three forms:

All three molecules are positioned so that the carbons and chlorines all lie in the plane of the paper, with other atoms above or below it as indicated. (Appendix B contains detailed instructions for setting up Z-matrices for these molecules.)

Solution

Running all three jobs yields the following results:

Form	Energy	μ
RR	-1194.7153	$-2.8\hat{z}$
SS	-1194.7153	$-2.8\hat{z}$
meso	-1194.7178	0.0

1 hartree = 627.51 kcal mol⁻¹

The RR and SS forms have exactly the same values for the energy and the dipole moment. The energy difference between them and the meso form is about 2.5 millihartrees, which corresponds to about 1.5 kcal mol⁻¹. This is a small but significant difference in energy.

The RR and SS forms both have a dipole moment of 2.8 debye along the negative Z-axis. To locate this within the molecule, we need to examine the standard orientation. Here is the output for the RR form:

```
              Standard orientation:

 Center     Atomic        Coordinates (Angstroms)
 Number     Number      X          Y          Z

    1          6      0.000000   0.765000  -0.278044
    2          6      0.000000  -0.765000  -0.278044
    3         17     -1.660072   1.349604  -0.278044
    4         17      1.660072  -1.349604  -0.278044
    5          9      0.645709   1.222315   0.840358
    6          1      0.511868   1.130642  -1.168210
    7          9     -0.645709  -1.222315   0.840358
    8          1     -0.511868  -1.130642  -1.168210
```

Here is a graph showing the positions of the carbon and chlorine atoms in the XY-plane, ignoring their common Z-coordinate:

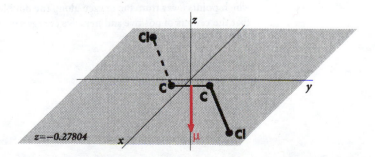

If we define the positive Z direction as up, the hydrogen atoms lie below this plane, and the fluorine atoms lie above it. The dipole moment points down, toward the hydrogen atoms, which is where we expect the positive charge to be. The same is true for the SS form.

The meso form has no dipole moment. If we look again at the structure, this makes sense, since the molecule has a center of inversion. ■

Exercise 2.3: Acetone Compared to Formaldehyde
file: 2_03

Acetone has a structure similar to formaldehyde, with methyl groups replacing the hydrogens on the carbon atom. What is the effect of making this substitution? What properties change, and which ones do not? (Use the same model chemistry as for the previous exercise.)

Solution

Here is a table of the major results for the two jobs:

Molecule	Energy	Dipole Moment
Formaldehyde	-113.86370	-2.84 $\hat{z}$
Acetone	-191.95961	-3.26 $\hat{z}$

Although the energies are very different, comparing them directly is of little value. Energies for two systems can be compared only when the number and type of nuclei are the same. Thus, we could compare the energies of the alternate forms of 1,2-dichloro-1,2-difluoroethane, and we can compare the energies for the reactants and products of reactions when the total number of nuclei of each type are the same. But we cannot make any meaningful statement about formaldehyde versus acetone based upon comparing their energies.

We can compare their dipole moments, however. In this case, we note that the methyl groups in acetone have the effect of increasing the magnitude of the dipole moment, which points away from the oxygen along the double bond in both cases. This means that the centers of positive and negative charge are farther apart in acetone than they are in formaldehyde. ■

Exercise 2.4: Ethylene and Formaldehyde Molecular Orbitals

file: **2_04**

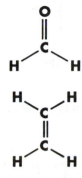

Ethylene is another molecule that is similar to formaldehyde. The two compounds are isoelectronic. In the case of ethylene, the oxygen in formaldehyde is replaced by a carbon with two additional hydrogens attached to it.

Compare the dipole moment of ethylene and formaldehyde. Then compare the HOMO and LUMO in both molecules. Use the data from the formaldehyde example earlier in this chapter.

Here is the output for the relevant orbitals for formaldehyde for reference:

				6 (A1)--O	7 (B1)--O	8 (B2)--O	9 (B1)--V	10 (A1)--V
EIGENVALUES		--		-0.63955	-0.52296	-0.44079	0.13572	0.24842
1 1	C	1S		0.01941	0.00000	0.00000	0.00000	-0.12212
2		2S		-0.06072	0.00000	0.00000	0.00000	0.14897
3		2PX		0.00000	0.32522	0.00000	0.40259	0.00000
4		2PY		0.00000	0.00000	-0.19817	0.00000	0.00000
5		2PZ		-0.37596	0.00000	0.00000	0.00000	-0.21086
6		3S		0.03976	0.00000	0.00000	0.00000	1.98096
7		3PX		0.00000	0.21235	0.00000	0.71120	0.00000
8		3PY		0.00000	0.00000	-0.04485	0.00000	0.00000
9		3PZ		-0.08854	0.00000	0.00000	0.00000	-0.74976
10		4XX		0.00549	0.00000	0.00000	0.00000	-0.00273
11		4YY		0.02734	0.00000	0.00000	0.00000	-0.01266
12		4ZZ		-0.01933	0.00000	0.00000	0.00000	-0.00459
13		4XY		0.00000	0.00000	0.00000	0.00000	0.00000
14		4XZ		0.00000	0.03558	0.00000	-0.03289	0.00000
15		4YZ		0.00000	0.00000	0.06034	0.00000	0.00000
16 2	O	1S		-0.06967	0.00000	0.00000	0.00000	-0.00099
17		2S		0.15358	0.00000	0.00000	0.00000	-0.01034
18		2PX		0.00000	0.49029	0.00000	-0.38148	0.00000
19		2PY		0.00000	0.00000	0.56588	0.00000	0.00000
20		2PZ		0.50940	0.00000	0.00000	0.00000	0.05334
21		3S		0.32365	0.00000	0.00000	0.00000	0.10031
22		3PX		0.00000	0.35352	0.00000	-0.52798	0.00000
23		3PY		0.00000	0.00000	0.44338	0.00000	0.00000
24		3PZ		0.28718	0.00000	0.00000	0.00000	0.05069
25		4XX		0.00485	0.00000	0.00000	0.00000	0.00130
26		4YY		0.00745	0.00000	0.00000	0.00000	-0.01009
27		4ZZ		-0.03495	0.00000	0.00000	0.00000	-0.00048
28		4XY		0.00000	0.00000	0.00000	0.00000	0.00000
29		4XZ		0.00000	-0.04166	0.00000	0.00355	0.00000
30		4YZ		0.00000	0.00000	-0.01928	0.00000	0.00000
31 3	H	1S		0.09100	0.00000	-0.18068	0.00000	-0.04749
32		2S		0.07400	0.00000	-0.22489	0.00000	-1.47348
33 4	H	1S		0.09100	0.00000	0.18068	0.00000	-0.04749
34		2S		0.07400	0.00000	0.22489	0.00000	-1.47348

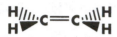

Chapter 2 | *Single Point Energy Calculations*

Solution

Molecules lie in a plane perpendicular to the page

Lowest unoccupied molecular orbital for formaldehyde (top) and ethylene

Highest occupied molecular orbital for formaldehyde (top) and ethylene

Here are the dipole moments for the two molecules:

Formaldehyde	-2.84$\hat{z}$ *(away from the oxygen atom)*
Ethylene	0.0

While the oxygen atom induces a dipole moment in formaldehyde, the center of inversion in ethylene results in no dipole moment.

Here are the HOMO and LUMO for ethylene (some non-significant lines have been removed from the output):

				8 (B3U)--O	9 (B3U)--V
	EIGENVALUES --			-0.37467	0.18399
1 1	C	1S		0.00000	0.00000
3		2PX		0.37552	0.33994
7		3PX		0.30346	0.74838
14		4XZ		-0.02553	0.02420
16 2	C	1S		0.00000	0.00000
18		2PX		0.37552	-0.33994
22		3PX		0.30346	-0.74838
29		4XZ		0.02553	0.02420
31 3	H	1S		0.00000	0.00000
33 4	H	1S		0.00000	0.00000
35 5	H	1S		0.00000	0.00000
37 6	H	1S		0.00000	0.00000

LUMO

HOMO

Since both molecules have the same number of electrons, the orbital numbered 8 is the HOMO, and the one numbered 9 is the LUMO in both cases. However, they are not the same type orbitals. Let's consider ethylene first.

In ethylene, both the HOMO and LUMO are formed primarily from p_x orbitals from the two carbons. The carbons lie in the YZ-plane, and so the p_x orbitals lie above and below the C-C bond. In the HOMO, the orbitals have like signs, and so they combine to form a bonding π molecular orbital. In contrast, in the LUMO, they have opposite signs, indicating that they combine to form an antibonding π^* molecular orbital.

Orbitals 7 and 9 (the latter is the LUMO) of formaldehyde exhibit this same character. Orbital 7 is a bonding π orbital, and orbital 9 is a π^*. However, the π orbital formed of the p_x orbitals from the carbon and the oxygen (which also lie in the YZ plane) is not the HOMO. Instead, an orbital formed from p_y orbitals from the carbon and the oxygen and from the s orbitals on the hydrogens is the highest occupied orbital. The contributions from the carbon and oxygen are situated along the double bond while the HOMO in ethylene was perpendicular to this bond.

This difference is due to the two lone pairs on the oxygen. Of the six valence electrons on the oxygen atom, two are involved in the double bond with the carbon, and the other four exist as two lone pairs. In Chapter 4, we'll examine the IR spectra for these two molecules. The orbitals suggest that we'll find very different frequencies for the two systems. In Chapter 9, we'll look at the transition to the first excited state in formaldehyde. ■

Exercise 2.5: NMR Properties of Alkanes, Alkenes and Alkynes

files: **2_05a**
2_05b
2_05c

The NMR magnetic shielding for atoms like carbon is affected greatly by what it is bonded to and the type of bond to its neighbor. Use the inner carbon atoms of normal butane as the reference atom and calculate the shift in ^{13}C isotropic shielding for 2-butene and 2-butyne. Can you explain these shifts as a function of the changing molecular environments?

Run your NMR calculations at the HF/6-31G(d) level; here are the structures of the three molecules calculated at the B3LYP/6-31G(d) level:

	butane		
C	0.000000	0.767105	0.000000
C	0.000000	-0.767105	0.000000
C	1.407571	1.372311	0.000000
C	-1.407571	-1.372311	0.000000
H	1.372874	2.467846	0.000000
H	-1.372874	-2.467846	0.000000
H	1.974414	1.056859	0.884767
H	1.974414	1.056859	-0.884767
H	-1.974414	-1.056859	0.884767
H	-1.974414	-1.056859	-0.884767
H	-0.554359	1.127932	-0.878287
H	-0.554359	1.127932	0.878287
H	0.554359	-1.127932	-0.878287
H	0.554359	-1.127932	0.878287

	trans 2-butene		
C	0.000000	0.667614	0.000000
C	0.000000	-0.667614	0.000000
C	1.226946	-1.535762	0.000000
C	-1.226946	1.535762	0.000000
H	-0.957948	-1.192291	0.000000
H	0.957948	1.192291	0.000000
H	2.143559	-0.935724	0.000000
H	-2.143559	0.935724	0.000000
H	1.251318	-2.192033	0.880777
H	1.251318	-2.192033	-0.880777
H	-1.251318	2.192033	0.880777
H	-1.251318	2.192033	-0.880777

	2-butyne		
C	0.000052	0.000000	-0.604592
C	-0.000052	0.000000	0.604592
C	0.000016	0.000000	-2.066136
C	-0.000016	0.000000	2.066136
H	-1.021490	0.000000	-2.466263
H	0.510752	-0.884627	-2.466360
H	0.510752	0.884627	-2.466360
H	1.021490	0.000000	2.466263
H	-0.510752	-0.884627	2.466360
H	-0.510752	0.884627	2.466360

Note that the inner carbon atoms are the first two atoms listed for each compound. The predicted NMR shielding values will appear in the output in the same order as the atoms are listed in the molecule specification section.

Solution   The predicted absolute shielding value for the central carbons in butane is 176.3 ppm, which is what we will use as the reference value, subtracting the computed shielding values for the outer carbons in butane and for each type of carbon in the other two compounds from it.

Here are the predicted shifts with respect to the C2 carbon in butane (all values are given in ppm):

Compound	C1 (outer)		C2 (inner)	
	calc.	exp.	calc.	exp.
butane	-7.8	-11.8	0.0	0.0
2-butene	-5.3	-7.6	101.0	100.8
2-butyne	-19.1		48.5	48.4

The agreement with experiment is very good for these cases even with this inexpensive model.

For the C2 carbons, the shielding decreases greatly as we move from the alkane to the alkene. This is due to that fact that the sp3 orbitals have a greater ability to oppose the applied magnetic field. The shift is much smaller when moving to the alkyne, which has been explained by the fact that the π bonding present in an sp environment creates a cylinder of electric charge acting to oppose the applied magnetic field. ∎

To The Teacher: Magnetic Properties

For another dramatic illustration of chemical shifts, have students calculate the magnetic shielding of nitrogen in pyridine and compare it to its saturated cyclohexane analogue.

Advanced Exercise 2.6: C$_{60}$ Single Point Energy

file: 2_06

Fullerene compounds have receieved a lot of attention in recent years. In this exercise we predict the energy of C$_{60}$ and look at its highest occupied molecular orbital, predicted at the Hartree-Fock level with the 3-21G basis set[†]. Include **SCF=Tight** in the route section of the job.

Solution

Here is the route section for the job:

```
#T HF/3-21G SCF=Tight Pop=Reg Test
```

The predicted energy is -2259.04767 hartrees. The HOMO is plotted at the left.

If you forget to include **SCF=Tight** in your job, it will probably have failed, giving error messages something like the following:

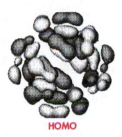

HOMO

```
>>>>>>>>>> Convergence criterion not met.
SCF Done:  E(RHF) = ...
...
Convergence failure -- run terminated.
```

These messages indicate that the SCF calculation, which is an iterative process, failed to converge. The predicted energy should accordingly be ignored. ∎

Advanced Exercise 2.7: CPU Resource Usage by Calculation Size

file: 2_07

This exercise is concerned with resource usage as a function of system size and introduces the use of the direct SCF method in *Gaussian* jobs (it is the default). Compare the total CPU time required to compute the Hartree-Fock energies of the series of hydrocarbons described below, using the 6-31G(d) basis set for the conventional SCF algorithm (**SCF=Conven**) and the direct SCF method (the default algorithm). Use **SCF=Tight** to request stricter convergence criteria for the SCF wavefunction for the direct jobs (tight convergence is the default for the conventional SCF algorithm). Also, include the keyword **IOP(5/19=1)** in the direct SCF calculations, which prevents them from being run entirely in memory (*in-core*).[‡]

[†] We select a smaller basis set than usual in order to keep the calculation manageable.

[‡] By default, *Gaussian* will substitute the in-core method for direct SCF when there is enough memory because it is faster. When we ran these computations, we explicitly prevented *Gaussian* from using the in-core method. When you run your jobs, however, the in-core method will undoubtedly be used for some jobs, and so your values may differ. An in-core job is identified by the following line in the output: `Two-electron integrals will be kept in memory`.

Plot the CPU time used for each method as a function of the number of carbon atoms (N). Theoretically, CPU time required should scale as the fourth power of the number of carbon atoms (N^4). How do the actual times depend on N?

The systems we'll use in this exercise are hydrocarbons of the form C_nH_{2n+2}, where n runs from 1 to some upper limit ≤ 10. The place to stop depends on the CPU capacity of your system. Users of *Gaussian 94W* will probably want to go no higher than 7 or 8. We used the 6-31G(d) basis set, but you could substitute a smaller one to save time (3-21G or STO-3G).

Basis Function Data in *Gaussian* Output

Gaussian output indicates the number of basis functions for a molecule in its output, just below the standard orientation:

```
Isotopes: H-1,C-12,H-1,H-1,H-1
   23 basis functions      44 primitive gaussians
    5 alpha electrons       5 beta electrons
      nuclear repulsion energy       13.4353902217 Hartrees.
```

This output is for CH_4, which uses 23 basis functions with the 6-31G(d) basis set.

Solution

The basic strategy behind the direct SCF method is recomputing certain intermediate quantities within the calculation—specifically the two-electron integrals—as needed, rather than storing them on disk. This has the advantage of making it possible to study systems which would require more disk space than is available on the system.

Direct SCF also has a significant performance advantage over the conventional algorithm for large systems. There is always a crossover point in terms of molecule size beyond which direct SCF will be faster than the conventional algorithm. The exact location of this crossover varies according to the characteristics of the computer system running the program.

Here are the results we obtained by running these hydrocarbon single point energy calculations on a DEC AlphaStation $600^{5/266}$ computer (in CPU seconds). In the table, *N* is the number of carbons in the system:

SCF CPU and Disk Requirements by Problem Size for Linear C_NH_{2N+2}

N	# Basis Functions	Conventional SCF		Direct SCF
		MB for INT file	*CPU seconds*	*CPU seconds*
1	23	2	8.6	12.8
2	42	4	11.9	19.8
3	61	16	23.2	38.8

SCF CPU and Disk Requirements by Problem Size for Linear C_NH_{2N+2}

| N | # Basis Functions | Conventional SCF | | Direct SCF |
		MB for INT file	CPU seconds	CPU seconds
4	80	42	48.7	72.1
5	99	92	95.4	122.5
6	118	174	163.4	186.8
7	137	290	354.5	268.0
8	156	437	526.5	375.0
9	175	620	740.2	488.0
10	194	832	1028.4	622.1

Here is our plot. It is a log-log plot, so we can estimate the exponent for N by computing the slope of each line. The actual scaling for the direct algorithm is more like $N^{2.5}$ than N^4:

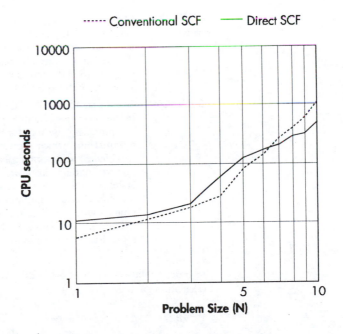

For this computer system, the crossover point where direct SCF beats the conventional algorithm happens at around 120 basis functions ($\sim N=7$). This level may be lower for some vector processors. ∎

Advanced Exercise 2.8: SCF Stability Calculations

files: **2_08a** (O$_2$)
2_08b (O$_3$)

In this exercise, we introduce SCF stability calculations. A stability calculation determines whether the wavefunction computed for the molecular system is stable or not: in other words, whether there is a lower energy wavefunction corresponding to a different solution of the SCF equations. If the wavefunction is unstable, then whatever calculation you are performing is not being done on the expected/desired state of the molecule. For example, if a stability calculation indicates an unstable wavefunction for a system for which you were attempting to model its ground state, then the calculation does *not* in fact correspond to the ground state, and any energy comparisons for or other conclusions about the ground state based on it will be invalid.

When Wavefunction Stability Should Be Tested

The stability of SCF solutions for unknown systems should *always* be tested. Stability considerations apply to and may be tested for in calculations using Density Functional Theory methods as well.

The following *Gaussian* keywords will be of use:

Keyword	Effect
Stable	Tests the stability of the SCF solution computed for the molecule. This involves determining whether any lower energy wavefunction exists for the system, obtained by relaxing constraints placed on it by default (e.g., allowing the wavefunction to become open shell or reducing the symmetry of the orbitals).
Stable=Opt	Test the stability of the SCF solution and reoptimize the wavefunction to the lower energy solution if any instability is found. When we speak of optimizing the wavefunction, we are *not* referring to a geometry optimization, which locates the lowest energy conformation near a specified starting molecular structure. Predicting an SCF energy involves finding the lowest energy solution to the SCF equations. Stability calculations ensure that this optimized electronic wavefunction is a minimum in wavefunction space—and not a saddle point—which is an entirely separate process from locating minima or saddle points on a nuclear potential energy surface. See Appendix A for more details on the internals of SCF calculations.

In order to illustrate how stability calculations work, we'll run the following RHF calculation on molecular oxygen:

```
#T RHF/6-31G(d) Stable Test

Oxygen stability: RHF on singlet (!!)

0 1
O
O 1 1.22
```

We can be sure that the RHF wavefunction for molecular oxygen is unstable, since we know the ground state of the molecule is a triplet. The output from the stability calculation confirms this:

```
The wavefunction has an RHF -> UHF instability.
```

This indicates that there is a UHF wavefunction which is lower in energy than the RHF wavefunction, which is what we expect in this case. Note that instabilities can be of many different types. The most common kinds are:

✦ The lowest energy wavefunction is a singlet, but not a closed shell singlet (e.g., biradicals). This is an RHF-to-UHF instability.

✦ There is a lower-lying triplet state than the singlet (the current case). This is an RHF-to-UHF instability.

✦ There is more than one solution to the SCF equations for the system, and the calculation procedure converges to a solution which is not the minimum (often a saddle point in wavefunction space). This indicates an RHF-to-RHF or UHF-to-UHF instability, depending on the wavefunction type.

Run a stability calculation on the true (triplet) ground state of molecular oxygen. What is the energy difference between the ground state and the singlet state?

Once you have completed this first calculation, devise and run calculations which will determine the lowest energy electronic state for ozone. Use the experimental geometry: O–O bond lengths=1.272 Å, O–O–O bond angle=116.8°.

Solution   Running a **Stable** calculation indicates that the computed UHF wavefunction for triplet molecular oxygen is stable:

```
The wavefunction is stable under the perturbations considered.
```

The predicted energy, which appears in the SCF summary section preceding the stability analysis output, is -149.61266 hartrees, which is about 53.5 kcal/mol lower than that corresponding to the RHF wavefunction (-149.52735).

Since we knew molecular oxygen is a triplet, we should have performed this calculation as an open shell calculation.

Ozone is a singlet, but it has an unusual electronic structure and is thus often difficult to model. An **RHF Stable=Opt** calculation finds an RHF→UHF instability, and the reoptimization of the wavefunction leads to a UHF solution with an energy of -224.34143 hartrees.

At this point, we might expect that a UHF calculation would be sufficient. However, when we perform a **UHF Stable=Opt** calculation, the predicted wavefunction is again found to be unstable:

```
The wavefunction has an internal instability.
```

Reoptimization of the wavefunction again leads to the same lower-energy electronic state as was found by the RHF calculation. Even for a UHF calculation, it is necessary to modify the default electronic configuration in order to specify the proper ground state of ozone. This is not surprising given the known significantly biradical character of ozone resulting from the coupling of the singly-occupied π orbitals on the terminal oxygen atoms.

In order to specify the proper electronic state, ozone calculations should be performed as unrestricted calculations, and the keyword **Guess=Mix** should always be included. This keyword tells the program to mix the HOMO and LUMO within the wavefunction in an effort to destroy α-β and spatial symmetries, and it is often useful in producing a UHF wavefunction for a singlet system. Running a **UHF Guess=Mix Stable** calculation confirms that the resulting wavefunction is stable, and it predicts the same energy (-224.34143 hartrees) as the previous **Stable=Opt** calculations.

Specific electronic states may also be specified using the **Guess=Alter** keyword, which allows you to explicitly designate orbital occupancies. See the *Gaussian User's Reference* for details.

As a final note, be aware that Hartree-Fock calculations performed with small basis sets are many times more prone to finding unstable SCF solutions than are larger calculations. Sometimes this is a result of spin contamination; in other cases, the neglect of electron correlation is at the root. The same molecular system may or may not lead to an instability when it is modeled with a larger basis set or a more accurate method such as Density Functional Theory. Nevertheless, wavefunctions should still be checked for stability with the **SCF=Stable** option. ■

References

NMR Calculations

J. R. Cheeseman, G. W. Trucks, T. A. Keith and M. J. Frisch, "A Comparison of Models for Calculating Nuclear Magnetic Resonance Shielding Tensors," *J. Chem. Phys.*, **104**, 5497 (1996).

Experimental NMR Results

Methane: A. K. Jameson and C. J. Jameson, *Chem. Phys. Lett.* **134**, 461 (1987).

Butane, 2-Butene, 2-Butyne: R. M. Silverstein, G. C. Bassler and T. C. Morril, *Spectroscopic Identification of Organic Compounds*, 5th ed. (Wiley, New York, 1991), 236-239.

General: H.-O. Kalinowski, S. Berger and S. Braun, *Carbon-13 NMR Spectroscopy* (Wiley, New York, 1988).

C_{60}

K. Raghavachari and C. M. Rohlfing, *J. Phys. Chem.* **95**, 5768 (1991).

Direct SCF

R. C. Raffenetti, *Chem. Phys. Lett.* **20**, 335 (1973).

J. Almlof, K. Korsell, and K. Faegri, Jr., *J. Comp. Chem.* **3**, 385 (1982).

M. Head-Gordon and J. A. Pople, *J. Chem. Phys.* **89**, 5777 (1988).

Hydrocarbon Series

H. B. Schlegel and M. J. Frisch, "Computational Bottlenecks in Molecular Orbital Calculations," in *Theoretical and Computational Models for Organic Chemistry*, ed. S. J. Formosinho et. al. (Kluwer Academic Pubs., NATO-ASI Series C 339, The Netherlands, 1991), 5-33.

SCF Stability and Convergence

H. B. Schlegel and J. J. W. McDouall, "Do You Have SCF Stability and Convergence Problems?" in C. Ögretir and I. G. Csizmadia, eds., *Computational Advances in Organic Chemistry* (Kluwer Academic Pubs., NATO-ASI Series C 330, The Netherlands, 1991), 167-85.

Geometry Optimizations

So far, we've considered calculations which investigate a molecular system having a specified geometric structure. As we've seen, structural changes within a molecule usually produce differences in its energy and other properties.

The way the energy of a molecular system varies with small changes in its structure is specified by its *potential energy surface*. A potential energy surface is a mathematical relationship linking molecular structure and the resultant energy. For a diatomic molecule, it is a two-dimensional plot with the internuclear separation on the X-axis (the only way that the structure of such a molecule can vary), and the energy at that bond distance on the Y-axis, producing a curve. For larger systems, the surface has as many dimensions as there are degrees of freedom within the molecule.

Potential Energy Surfaces

A potential energy surface (PES) is often represented by illustrations like the one below. This sort of drawing considers only two of the degrees of freedom within the molecule, and plots the energy above the plane defined by them, creating a literal surface. Each point corresponds to the specific values of the two structural variables—and thus represents a particular molecular structure—with the height of the surface at that point corresponding to the energy of that structure.

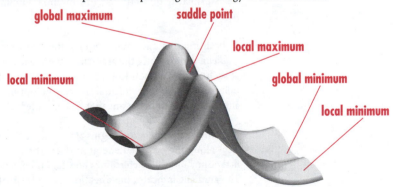

There are three *minima* on this potential surface. A minimum is the bottom of a valley on the potential surface. From such a point, motion in any direction—a physical metaphor corresponding to changing the structure slightly—leads to a higher energy. A minimum can be a *local minimum*, meaning that it is the lowest point in some limited region of the potential surface, or it can be the *global minimum*, the lowest energy point anywhere on the potential surface. Minima occur at equilibrium structures for the system, with different minima corresponding to different conformations or structural isomers in the case of single molecules, or reactant and product molecules in the case of multicomponent systems.

Peaks and ridges correspond to maxima on the potential energy surface. A peak is a maximum in all directions (i.e., both along and across the ridge). A low point along a ridge—a mountain pass in our topographical metaphor—is a local minimum in one direction (along the ridge), and a maximum in the other. A point which is a maximum in one direction and a minimum in the other (or in all others in the case of a larger dimensional potential surface) is called a *saddle point* (based on its shape).[†] For example, the saddle point in the diagram is a minimum along its ridge and a maximum along the path connecting minima on either side of the ridge. A saddle point corresponds to a transition structure connecting the two equilibrium structures.

Locating Minima

Geometry optimizations usually attempt to locate minima on the potential energy surface, thereby predicting equilibrium structures of molecular systems. Optimizations can also locate transition structures. However, in this chapter we will focus primarily on optimizing to minima. Optimizations to minima are also called *minimizations*.

At both minima and saddle points, the first derivative of the energy, known as the *gradient*, is zero. Since the gradient is the negative of the forces, the forces are also zero at such a point. A point on the potential energy surface where the forces are zero is called a *stationary point*. All successful optimizations locate a stationary point, although not always the one that was intended.

A geometry optimization begins at the molecular structure specified as its input, and steps along the potential energy surface. It computes the energy and the gradient at that point, and then determines how far and in which direction to make the next step. The gradient indicates the direction along the surface in which the energy decreases most rapidly from the current point as well as the steepness of that slope.

[†] Or, more precisely, a *first-order saddle point*, where the order indicates the number of dimensions in which the saddle point is a maximum. A second-order saddle point would be a maximum in two dimensions and a minimum in all others. Transition structures are first-order saddle points.

Most optimization algorithms also estimate or compute the value of the second derivative of the energy with respect to the molecular coordinates, updating the matrix of force constants (known as the *Hessian*). These force constants specify the curvature of the surface at that point, which provides additional information useful for determining the next step.

Convergence Criteria

An optimization is complete when it has converged: essentially, when the forces are zero, the next step is very small, below some preset value defined by the algorithm, and some other conditions are met. These are the convergence criteria used by *Gaussian*:

✦ The forces must be essentially 0. Specifically the maximum component of the force must be below the cutoff value of 0.00045 (interpreted as 0).

✦ The root-mean-square of the forces must be essentially 0 (below the defined tolerance of 0.0003).

✦ The calculated displacement for the next step must be smaller than the defined cutoff value of 0.0018 (again, meaning essentially 0).

✦ The root-mean-square of the displacement for the next step must also be below its cutoff value of 0.0012.

Note that the change in energy between the current and next points is not an explicit criterion for convergence. It is reflected in the tests of the size of the next step, since small steps near a minimum will usually result in small changes in the energy.

The presence of four distinct convergence criteria prevents a premature identification of the minimum. For example, in a broad, nearly flat valley on the potential energy surface, the forces may be near zero (within the tolerance) while the computed steps remain quite large as the optimization moves toward the very bottom of the valley. Or, in extremely steep regions, the step size may become very small while the forces remain quite large. Checking the root-mean-squares of the items of interest also guards against bad tolerance values for any of the criteria leading to an incorrect prediction of the minimum.

Criteria for Large, Floppy Molecules

There is one exception to the criteria we just looked at, designed to aid in the optimization of large molecules. When the forces are two orders of magnitude smaller than the cutoff value (i.e., 1/100th of the limiting value), then the geometry is considered converged even if the displacement is larger than the cutoff value. This criteria comes into play on very, very flat potential energy surfaces near the minimum, which is common for large, floppy molecules.

Preparing Input for Geometry Optimizations

The **Opt** keyword in the route section requests a geometry optimization, using the basis set and level of theory specified by the other keywords.

In *Gaussian*, the molecule specification for a geometry optimization can be given in any format desired: Cartesian coordinates, Z-matrix, mixed coordinates. The geometry optimization job will produce the optimized structure of the system as its output.

Previously, the requirements for molecule specifications for geometry optimizations were more stringent, and a large part of learning to perform geometry optimizations consisted of learning how to set them up properly. However, recent research into alternative coordinate systems and optimization procedures has made all of this unnecessary. This topic is considered in Exercise 3.8 (page 57); see the references for further information.

Example 3.1: Ethylene Optimization

file: **e3_01**

Ethylene is a highly symmetric molecule. Here is the input file for an optimization of its geometry:

```
#T RHF/6-31G(d) Opt Test

Ethylene Geometry Optimization

0 1
C
C 1 CC
H 1 CH 2 HCC
H 1 CH 2 HCC 3 180.
H 2 CH 1 HCC 3 180.
H 2 CH 1 HCC 4 180.
    Variables:
CC=1.31
CH=1.07
HCC=121.5
```

The values of 180° for all three dihedral angles specify the molecule in a planar orientation.

Examining Optimization Output

We'll now look at the output from the ethylene optimization. After some initial output from the setup portion of the optimization job, *Gaussian* displays a section like the following for each step (the items pointed to by dotted lines do not appear in terse **#T** output):

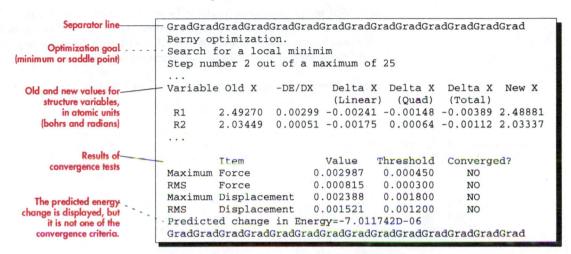

The maximum displacement is the largest change in any coordinate in the molecular structure. The threshold column indicates the cutoff value for each criterion. The new structure generated at this step follows this output.

When all four values in the `Converged?` column are YES, then the optimization is completed and has converged, presumably to a local minimum. For the ethylene optimization, convergence happens after 3 steps:

Step	# YES's
1	0
2	0
3	4

After each step is taken, a single point energy calculation follows at the new point on the potential energy surface, producing the normal output for such a calculation. When the optimization converges, it knows that the current structure is the final one, and accordingly ends the calculation at that point. Therefore, the energy for the optimized structure is found in the single point energy computation for the previous step—in other words, it appears *before* the successful convergence test in the output.

Here is the predicted energy for ethylene:

```
SCF Done: E(RHF) = -78.0317186026    A.U. after 6 cycles
```

Single point energy calculations ought to be run from optimized structures. This energy for ethylene corresponds to a stationary point on the potential energy surface. In this case, it happens to be a minimum. In Chapter 4, we'll discuss distinguishing between stationary points using the second derivatives of the energy.

The final optimized structure appears immediately after the final convergence tests:

Predicted bond lengths (R), bond angles (A) and dihedral angles (D) for the optimized structure.

Initially was 1.31
Initially was 1.07

Initially was 121.5

Optimized structure expressed in the standard orientation.

```
-- Stationary point found.
                    ---------------------------
                    !   Optimized Parameters   !
                    !  (Angstroms and Degrees) !
 ------------------                              ------------------
 ! Name  Definition        Value        Derivative Info.        !
 --------------------------------------------------------------------
 ! R1    R(2,1)            1.317        -DE/DX =    -0.0001      !
 ! R2    R(3,1)            1.076        -DE/DX =     0.          !
 ! R3    R(4,1)            1.076        -DE/DX =     0.          !
 ! R4    R(5,2)            1.076        -DE/DX =     0.          !
 ! R5    R(6,2)            1.076        -DE/DX =     0.          !
 ! A1    A(2,1,3)        121.7952       -DE/DX =     0.          !
 ! A2    A(2,1,4)        121.7952       -DE/DX =     0.          !
 ! A3    A(3,1,4)        116.4096       -DE/DX =    -0.0001      !
 ! A4    A(1,2,5)        121.7952       -DE/DX =     0.          !
 ! A5    A(1,2,6)        121.7952       -DE/DX =     0.          !
 ! A6    A(5,2,6)        116.4096       -DE/DX =    -0.0001      !
 ! D1    D(5,2,1,3)      180.           -DE/DX =     0.          !
 ! D2    D(5,2,1,4)        0.           -DE/DX =     0.          !
 ! D3    D(6,2,1,3)        0.           -DE/DX =     0.          !
 ! D4    D(6,2,1,4)      180.           -DE/DX =     0.          !
 --------------------------------------------------------------------
 ...
                         Standard orientation:
 --------------------------------------------------------------------
 Center     Atomic              Coordinates (Angstroms)
 Number     Number          X           Y            Z
 --------------------------------------------------------------------
    1          6         0.000000    0.000000     0.658510
    2          6         0.000000    0.000000    -0.658510
    3          1         0.000000    0.914545     1.225447
    4          1         0.000000   -0.914545     1.225447
    5          1         0.000000   -0.914545    -1.225447
    6          1         0.000000    0.914545    -1.225447
 --------------------------------------------------------------------
```

The `Optimized Parameters` are the predicted bond lengths (named R*n*), bond angles (A*n*) and dihedral angles (D*n*) for the optimized structure. The applicable atom numbers are in parentheses. Atoms in the molecule are numbered according to their order in the molecule specification section. These *center numbers* also appear in the Cartesian coordinates for the optimized structure expressed in the standard orientation which follows the listing of the optimized parameters.

In this example, the two bond lengths changed only slightly, while the C-C-H bond angle increased by about 0.3 degrees.

The remainder of the optimization output file displays the population analysis, molecular orbitals (if requested with **Pop=Reg**) and atomic charges and dipole moment for the optimized structure.

Example 3.2: Fluoroethylene Optimization
file: **e3_02**

Our second example takes another member of the vinyl series, and considers the effect of replacing one of the hydrogens in ethylene with a fluorine. The fluoroethylene optimization converges at step 5. By looking at the optimized parameters for each job, we can compare the structures of the two molecules:

Coordinate	Ethylene	Fluoroethylene
C-C bond length [R(2,1)]	1.32Å	1.31Å
C-R bond length [R(4,1)]	1.08Å	1.33Å
C-C-R bond angle [A(2,1,4)]	121.8°	122.4°
C-C-H bond angle [A(2,1,3)]	121.8°	125.7°

Substituting the fluorine for a hydrogen results in a longer bond length for that substituent with the carbon. It also produces a slight shortening of the C-C bond, resulting in a stronger bond, and larger bond angles for both atoms with the adjacent carbon. The latter has the effect of bringing the atoms closer together on this end of the molecule.

To The Teacher: Further Substitutions

For a more extended study, perform an optimization on each of these molecules:

1,1-difluoroethylene (C_{2v} symmetry)
cis 1,2-difluoroethylene (C_{2v} symmetry)
trans 1,2-difluoroethylene (C_{2h} symmetry)

Compare the effects of the successive fluorine substitutions on the various structural features of the molecule.

Locating Transition Structures

The optimization facility can be used to locate transition structures as well as ground states structures since both correspond to stationary points on the potential energy surface. However, finding a desired transition structure directly by specifying a reasonable guess for its geometry can be challenging in many cases.

Gaussian includes a facility for automatically generating a starting structure for a transition state optimization based upon the reactants and products that the transition structure connects, known as the STQN[†] method. This feature is requested with the **QST2** option to the **Opt** keyword. Input files using this option will include two title and molecule specification sections. The facility generates a guess for the transition structure which is midway between the reactants and products, in terms of redundant internal coordinates.

Example 3.3: Transition State Optimization
file: e3_03

Here is the input file for an optimization of the transition structure for the reaction $H_3CO \rightarrow H_2COH$ (a simple 1,2 hydrogen shift reaction). We specify a UHF calculation (open shell) since the molecular system is a doublet:

```
#T UHF/6-31G(d) Opt=QST2 Test

H3CO --> H2COH Reactants            First title section

0,2                                 First molecule specification section
structure for H₃CO

H3CO --> H2COH Products             Second title section

0,2                                 Second molecule specification section
structure for H₂COH
```

The STQN facility requires that corresponding atoms appear *in the same order within the two molecule specifications* (although it does not matter whether the reactants or the products appear first). The bonding in the two structures does not need to be the same, however.

[†] It uses a linear or quadratic synchronous transit approach to get closer to the quadratic region of the transition state and then uses a quasi-Newton or eigenvalue-following algorithm to complete the optimization.

In the predicted transition structure, the hydrogen atom is weakly linked to both the carbon and oxygen atoms:

Bond	Length
C-O	1.37
C-H	1.28
O-H	1.19

For more difficult cases, *Gaussian* also provides the **QST3** option to **Opt**, which optimizes a transition state structure based on the reactants, products, and a user-provided guess for the geometry of the transition structure. See the *Gaussian 94 User's Reference* for more details.

Handling Difficult Optimization Cases

There are some systems for which the default optimization procedure may not succeed on its own. A common problem with many difficult cases is that the force constants estimated by the optimization procedure differ substantially from the actual values. By default, a geometry optimization starts with an initial guess for the second derivative matrix derived from a simple valence force field. The approximate matrix is improved at each step of the optimization using the computed first derivatives.

Try computing initial force constants

When this initial guess is poor, you need a more sophisticated—albeit more expensive—means of generating the force constants. This is especially important for transition state optimizations. *Gaussian* provides a variety of alternate ways of generating them. Here are some of the most useful associated keywords; consult the *Gaussian User's Reference* for a full description of their use:

Opt=ReadFC   Read in the initial force constants from the checkpoint file created by a frequency calculation (usually run at a lower level of theory or using a smaller basis set), rather than estimating them. This option can help to start an optimization off in the right direction. This option will also require that a **%Chk=***filename* line precede the route section of the input, specifying the name of the checkpoint file.

Opt=CalcFC   Compute the force constants at the initial point using the same method and basis set as for the optimization itself.

Opt=CalcAll	Calculate the force constants at every point in the optimization. This is a very expensive procedure and is only necessary in drastic situations.

Including **ReadFC** is also useful whenever you already have performed a frequency calculation at a lower level of theory. When you have a difficult case and you have no previous frequency job, then **CalcFC** is a good first choice. **CalcAll** should be reserved for the most drastic circumstances.

Increase the maximum number of optimization steps

Sometimes, an optimization will simply require more steps than the default procedure allots to it. You can increase the maximum number of steps with the **MaxCycle** option to the **Opt** keyword (it takes the number of steps as its argument).

Restart a failed optimization

If you have saved the checkpoint file, then it is also possible to restart a failed optimization, using the **Opt=Restart** keyword. See the *Gaussian User's Reference* for details.

Select a better starting structure

If an optimization runs out of steps, do not blindly assume that increasing the number of steps will fix the problem. Examine the output and determine whether the optimization was making progress or not. For example this command will provide a quick summary of an optimization's progress on a UNIX system (blank lines are added for readability):

```
$ egrep 'out of|SCF Don|Converged| NO | YES |exceeded' opt.log \
  | grep -v '\\\\'
SCF Done:  E(RHF) =  -997.032065122     A.U. after    9 cycles
Step number    1 out of a maximum of  20
          Item              Value     Threshold  Converged?
Maximum Force             0.000925    0.000450     NO
RMS      Force            0.000866    0.000300     NO
Maximum Displacement      0.005381    0.001800     NO
RMS      Displacement     0.002118    0.001200     NO

SCF Done:  E(RHF) =  -997.03225652      A.U. after    6 cycles
Step number    2 out of a maximum of  20
          Item              Value     Threshold  Converged?
Maximum Force             0.000532    0.000450     NO
RMS      Force            0.000295    0.000300     YES
Maximum Displacement      0.002544    0.001800     NO
RMS      Displacement     0.001755    0.001200     NO

SCF Done:  E(RHF) =  -997.03219896      A.U. after    8 cycles
Step number    3 out of a maximum of  20
          Item              Value     Threshold  Converged?
Maximum Force             0.003417    0.000450     NO
RMS      Force            0.000447    0.000300     NO
Maximum Displacement      0.006199    0.001800     NO
RMS      Displacement     0.008898    0.001200     NO
```

```
SCF Done:  E(RHF) =  -997.03207811    A.U. after   13 cycles
Step number   4 out of a maximum of  20
         Item                Value      Threshold  Converged?
Maximum Force               0.043772    0.000450    NO
RMS     Force               0.019250    0.000300    NO
Maximum Displacement        0.050102    0.001800    NO
RMS     Displacement        0.039076    0.001200    NO
 ...
Maximum number of steps exceeded.
```

This optimization was very close to a minimum at step two, but then it moved away from it again in subsequent steps. Merely increasing the number of steps will not fix the problem. A better approach is to start a new optimization, beginning with the structure corresponding to step 2 and including the **CalcFC** option in the route section.

You can retrieve an intermediate structure from the output log file manually. Alternatively, you may use the **Geom=(Check,Step=**n**)** keyword to retrieve the structure corresponding to step n from a checkpoint file.

Exercises

Many of the exercises will consider these other members of the vinyl series $(CH_2=CHR)$:

R	Substance
CH_3	propene
OH	vinyl alcohol
NH_2	vinyl amine

Exercise 3.1: Optimizations of Propene Conformers

files: 3_01a (180°)
3_01b (0°)

Perform geometry optimizations of these two propene conformers, where the C-C-C-H dihedral angle is 180° (left) or 0°. What are the differences between the two optimized geometries?

Solution

Both optimizations converge in 4 steps. Each one leads to a different structure (compare the optimized geometries to verify this), and therefore to a different point on the potential energy surface. This means that the same stoichiometry corresponds to two different stationary points on the potential energy surface. If this were not the case, then both of our input structures would converge to the same optimized geometry, although one would probably take much longer to do so than the other.

Here are the energies and dipole moments of the two optimized structures:

		Dipole Moment		
∠ C-C-C-H	Energy	X	Y	Total
0°	-117.07147	-0.305	-0.003	0.305
180°	-117.06818	-0.300	-0.065	0.307

There is an energy difference of about 3 millihartrees between the two forms. In fact, the 0° form represents the global minimum on the potential energy surface for propene. The partial ring-like arrangement of the three carbons and the planar hydrogen from the methyl group is slightly preferred over the other form.

The dipole moments are very similar in magnitude but differ slightly in direction, depending on the location of the in-plane hydrogen atom (attached to the non-double bonded carbon). ■

Exercise 3.2: Optimizations of Vinyl Alcohol Conformers

files: **3_02a (0°)**
3_02b (180°)
3_02c (acteald.)

Perform geometry optimizations of the two vinyl alcohol conformers illustrated below, which are similar to the propene conformers we considered previously. In addition, optimize the illustrated conformation of acetaldehyde, a structural isomer of vinyl alcohol:

vinyl alcohol conformers

acetaldehyde

Do all three of these forms represent minima on the potential energy surface? What are the energy differences among them?

Solution   All three jobs lead to successful optimizations. The three forms do represent three different minima on the potential energy surface. Their respective energies are given in the following table:

System	Conformer	Energy
Vinyl alcohol	$\angle$ C-C-O-H=0°	-152.88889
	$\angle$ C-C-O-H=180°	-152.88539
Acetaldehyde		-152.91596

The lowest energy form is acetaldehyde, about 27 millihartrees below the 0° form of vinyl alcohol. As was true for propene, the vinyl alcohol conformer where the C-C-O-H dihedral angle is 0° is the lower energy conformer. ■

Exercise 3.3: Planar Vinyl Amine Optimization

file: **3_03**   Run a geometry optimization for planar vinyl amine.

Review the optimizations of vinyl series compounds that we have done, and summarize the effect of substituent on the following characteristics:

✦   The C-C double bond
✦   The bond angle between the carbons and the substituent
✦   The dipole moment

Solution   Here are the predicted bond lengths, bond angles and dipole moments:

System	Conformer	R	C=C (Å)	$\angle$ C-C-R (°)	μ
Ethylene		H	1.317	121.8	0.0
Fluoroethylene		F	1.309	122.4	1.53
Propene	$\angle$ C-C-C-H = 0°	CH_3	1.319	125.3	0.31
	$\angle$ C-C-C-H = 180°	CH_3	1.319	124.9	0.31
Vinyl alcohol	$\angle$ C-C-C-H = 0°	OH	1.318	127.0	1.06
	$\angle$ C-C-C-H = 180°	OH	1.315	122.8	2.09
Vinyl amine		NH_2	1.325	127.1	1.71

Fluorine is the only substituent which shortens the C-C bond significantly. Fluorine is highly electronegative and wishes to obtain additional electron density. It attempts to draw it from the two carbons, which move closer together in order to share the remaining electrons more easily as a result.

Let's compare the Mulliken population analysis for ethylene and fluoroethylene:

Ethylene			
Total atomic charges:			
		1	
1	C	-0.352753	
2	C	-0.352753	
3	H	0.176377	
4	H	0.176377	
5	H	0.176377	
6	H	0.176377	

Fluoroethylene			
Total atomic charges:			
		1	
1	C	0.256639	
2	C	-0.472937	
3	H	0.186698	
4	F	-0.365569	
5	H	0.202811	
6	H	0.192357	

The fluorine atom is a significant site of negative charge, in contrast to the hydrogen in ethylene. This results in an unequal charge distribution among the two carbons, with some positive charge located on the carbon bonded to the fluorine, and a larger negative charge on the other one.

The C-C-R bond angle changes significantly in the 0° conformation of vinyl alcohol and in vinyl amine. In all of these vinyl systems, the substituent shortens the C-H bond (on the carbon to which the substituent is attached), most dramatically in the case of the substituents NH_2 and OH.

Ethylene has no dipole moment, and propene has only a very small one. The other systems have nontrivial dipole moments. Thus, the more electronegative substituents produce nontrivial dipole moments, in contrast to a single hydrogen atom or a methyl group. ■

Exercise 3.4: Chromium Hexacarbonyl Optimization

file: 3_04

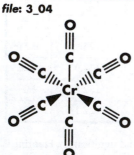

Optimize the structure of chromium hexacarbonyl at the Hartree-Fock level, using the STO-3G or 3-21G basis set. Include **SCF=NoVarAcc** in the route section of your job (this option says to use full convergence criteria throughout the SCF computation, and it aids in convergence for this calculation).

This molecule is most easily input in Cartesian coordinates. Set up an input file for this job, using the following values:

C-Cr distance = 1.94
C-O distance = 1.14

Solution　Here are the results from this job using the two different basis sets. We also include experimental electron diffraction results:

Model	Cr-C	C-O	Energy
RHF/STO-3G	1.79	1.17	-1699.59301
RHF/3-21G	1.93	1.13	-1710.78652
Experiment	1.92	1.16	

Clearly, the 3-21G basis set reproduces the experimental results much better than STO-3G. We'll look at basis set effects in detail in Chapter 5. ■

Advanced Exercise 3.5: NMR Isotropic Chemical Shift for Benzene

files: **3_05a (C₆H₆)**
3_05b (TMS)

Predict the isotropic chemical shift for carbon in benzene with respect to TMS.

In order to do so, you will need to perform Hartree-Fock NMR calculations using the 6-311+G(2d,p) basis set. Compute the NMR properties at geometries optimized with the B3LYP method and the 6-31G(d) basis set. This is a recommended model for reliable NMR predictions by Cheeseman and coworkers. Note that NMR calculations typically benefit from an accurate geometry and a large basis set.

Solution　The basic input file structure is as follows:

```
%Chk=NMR
#T B3LYP/6-31G(d) Opt Test

Opt
```

molecule specification

```
--Link1--
%Chk=NMR
%NoSave
#T RHF/6-311+G(2d,p) NMR Geom=Check Guess=Read Test

NMR
```

charge & spin

You will need to run these jobs for benzene and for TMS (if you want to run the jobs for both molecules simultaneously, you will need to specify different names for the checkpoint file in each input file).

Here are the results of our calculations:

Absolute Shielding Value		Relative Shift	Experiment
TMS	Benzene		
188.7879	57.6198	131.2	130.9

These calculations provide excellent agreement with experiment.

Advanced Exercise 3.6: Optimization of $C_{60}O$ Isomers

files: **3_06a (PM3)**
      3_06b (STO-3G)

Recently, there has been considerable interest in fullerene derivatives. Finding the lowest energy isomer among a variety of choices of attachment is always an interesting and important question. In C_{60}, all carbons are equivalent, but there are two types of C–C bonds:

✦ A bond joining two six member rings: a *6-6 bond*
✦ A bond joining a five member ring to a six member ring: a *5-6 bond*

An oxygen atom can bind to either of these to sites, potentially forming a three member (COC) ring. Thus, there are two possible forms for $C_{60}O$ (see the illustrations on the next page).

Perform an optimization of these two derivatives at the PM3[†] or RHF/STO-3G level in order to discern which is the more favorable isomer (the latter is a very long job). What are the most dramatic structural features that characterize these two isomers? Do the bridging carbons remain bonded in the derivative?

Experimentalists have proposed that oxygen should bind to the 6-6 bond. Does your calculation support or refute this? Can you justify any inconsistencies?

Calculation Hint: You can ensure that the predicted values for the bond lengths and bond angle of interest are included in the optimization output by specifying additional coordinates with the **AddRedundant** option to the **Opt** keyword. It requires an additional input section following the molecule specification. A bond length is specified by listing the atom numbers of the two bonded atoms (numbering follows the atom order in the molecule specification section), and a bond angle is specified by listing the three atom numbers of interest, in the order corresponding to the desired bond angle. See the Technical Note, "Geometry optimizations in *Gaussian 94*," for further details on the use of this keyword (available from Gaussian, Inc.).

[†] Note that no basis set keyword is required for a **PM3** calculation.

Solution   Here are the two isomers:

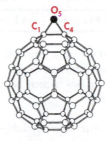 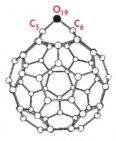

epoxide (6-6 bonded)   open (5-6 bonded)

We have used the **Opt=AddRedundant** keyword in the route section of each job, along with the following additional input sections following the molecule specification (which reflect the atom numbering for our molecule specifications—yours may differ):

AddRedundant Input Section

	epoxide form	*open form*
C-O bond length	1 5	5 19
C-C bond length	1 4	5 6
C-O-C bond angle	1 5 4	5 19 6

Raghavachari has studied this problem in some detail. The following table summarizes his work as well as our own PM3 and HF/STO-3G optimizations:

Result	epoxide isomer (6-6)				open isomer (5-6)			
	MNDO	PM3	HF/STO-3G	HF/3-21G	MNDO	PM3	HF/STO-3G	HF/3-21G
C-C bond length	1.60	1.53	1.53	1.54	2.15	2.16	2.13	2.20
C-O bond length	1.40	1.43	1.43	1.40	1.38	1.40	1.41	1.40
C-O-C bond angle	69.22	64.59	65.06	64.0	102.14	101.0	98.31	103.0

The structures are quite similar for all of the model chemistries we are considering. The second isomer is characterized by a very long bridging carbon distance, indicating that the two carbons are no longer bonded (which is why we refer to it as the "open" form).

Here are the predicted energy differences between the two forms ($\Delta E^{\text{epoxide} - \text{open}}$) at the various levels of theory:

MNDO	PM3	HF/STO-3G	HF/3-21G
5.8 kcal/mol	6.5 kcal/mol	-15.5 kcal/mol	9 kcal/mol

It appears that the open isomer is the ground state structure, given the agreement between the two semi-empirical methods and HF/3-21G. HF/STO-3G predicted the structures of the two isomers reasonably well, but it does a very poor job on the energy difference.

Raghavachari offers several possible explanations for this unexpected result:

✦ Kinetic factors may be important (we have only compared two equilibrium structure energies without investigating the barrier between them).

✦ Experimentalists have not yet found the lowest energy isomer.

✦ A better theoretical model is required to adequately study this problem (although this is fairly unlikely as the HF/3-21G model chemistry generally performs well on systems of this type).

Advanced Exercise 3.7: A 1,1 Elimination Transition State Optimization
file: 3_07

Predict the structure of the transition structure for the following reaction:

$$SiH_4 \rightarrow SiH_2 + H_2$$

What are the predicted Si-H and H-H bond lengths for the departing H atoms?

Solution

Here is our input file (we choose to use traditional Z-matrices for the two molecule specifications):

```
#T RHF/6-31G(d) Opt=(QST2,AddRedundant) Test

SiH2 + H2 --> SiH4 Reactants

0,1
Si
X 1 1.0
H 1 1.48 2 55.0
H 1 1.48 2 55.0 3 180.0
H 1 R 2 A1 3 90.0
H 1 R 5 A2 2 180.0

R=2.0
A1=80.0
```

Note the long bond length.

```
A2=22.0

SiH2 + H2 --> SiH4 Products

0,1
Si
X 1 1.0
H 1 1.48 2 55.0
H 1 1.48 2 55.0 3 180.0
H 1 R 2 A1 3 90.0
H 1 R 5 A2 2 180.0

R=1.48
A1=125.2
A2=109.5

4 5
```

We are interested in the H-H bond length, so we specify the coordinate bonding those two atoms to the **AddRedundant** option so that its value will be included in the printout of the optimized structure (the Si-H bond lengths will be included by default).

The geometry converges in 9 steps, resulting in the structure at the left.

Advanced Exercise 3.8: Comparing Optimization Procedures

file: 3_08

Optimizations in redundant internal coordinates have more to recommend them than merely easy input setup. They also represent the most efficient approach to geometry optimizations developed to date, overcoming the difficulties and deficiencies of both Cartesian coordinates and Z-matrices (internal coordinates).

Optimize the structure of bicyclo[2.2.2]octane using three different optimization procedures:

+ Using redundant internal coordinates, which is the default procedure when you specify the **Opt** keyword.
+ In Cartesian coordinates, requested with the **Opt=Cartesian** keyword. (Note that it does not matter whether the *input* is expressed in Cartesian coordinates or not; the optimization will be carried out in these coordinates when this keyword is specified).
+ In internal coordinates, requested with the **Opt=Z-Matrix** keyword.

Compare the number of optimization steps required by each procedure. Which one was the most efficient and converged the most quickly?

The illustration on the left displays the structure of the carbon ring in this molecule. The illustration on the right includes all of the atoms in the molecule.

Solution   The table below lists the results for the three jobs:

Procedure	# Steps	CPU seconds
Redundant Internal Coordinates	8	1646.0
Cartesian Coordinates	13	2622.9
Internal Coordinates	12	2539.6

Clearly, the optimization in redundant internal coordinates completes significantly more quickly. There is little difference between the optimizations done in Cartesian and internal coordinates for this case. ■

References

Cr(CO)₆ Bond Distance L.O. Brockway, R.V.G. Evans, M.W. Lister, *Trans. Faraday Society*, **34**, 1350 (1938).

Experimental NMR Results R. E. Wasylishen, S. Mooibroek and J. B. Macdonald, *J. Chem. Phys.* **81**, 1057 (1984).

NMR Calculations J. R. Cheeseman, G. W. Trucks, T. A. Keith and M. J. Frisch, "A Comparison of Models for Calculating Nuclear Magnetic Resonance Shielding Tensors," *J. Chem. Phys.*, **104**, 5497 (1996).

C₆₀O Experimental K. M. Creegan, J. L. Robbins, W. K. Robbins, J. M. Millar, R. D. Sherwood, P. J. Tindall, D. M. Cox, A. B. Smith, J. P. McCauley, D. R. Jones, and R. T. Gallagher, *J. Am. Chem. Soc.* **114**, 1103 (1992).

C₆₀O Theoretical K. Raghavachari, "Structure of C₆₀O: unexpected ground state geometry," *Chem. Phys. Lett.* **195**, 221 (1992).

Coordinate Systems and Optimization Procedures C. Peng, P. Y. Ayala, H. B. Schlegel and M. J. Frisch, *J. Comp. Chem.* **17**, 49 (1996).

P. Pulay, G. Fogarasi, F. Pang and J. E. Boggs, *J. Am. Chem. Soc.* **101**, 2550 (1979).

P. Pulay and G. Fogarasi, *J. Chem. Phys.* **96**, 2856 (1992).

G. Fogarasi, X. Zhou, P. Taylor and P. Pulay, *J. Am. Chem. Soc.* **114**, 8191 (1992).

J. Baker, *J. Comp. Chem.* **14**, 1085 (1993).

H. B. Schlegel, "A Comparison of Geometry Optimization with Mixed Cartesian and Internal Coordinates," *Int. J. Quant. Chem.: Quant. Chem. Symp.* **26**, 243 (1992).

J. Baker and W. J. Hehre, "The Death of the Z-Matrix," *J. Comp. Chem.* **12**, 606 (1991).

Berny Optimization Method H. B. Schlegel, *J. Comp. Chem.*, **3**, 214 (1982).

STQN Method C. Peng and H. B. Schlegel, *Israel J. Chem.* **33**, 449 (1993).

Optimizations in *Gaussian 94* Æ. Frisch, M. J. Frisch and D. J. Fox, "Technical Note: Geometry Optimizations in *Gaussian 94*," *Gaussian NEWS*, Summer 1995, 5-8 [also reprinted in the Release Notes for *Gaussian 94* and merged into the second printing of the *Gaussian 94 User's Reference*].

M. J. Frisch, Æ. Frisch and J. B. Foresman, *Gaussian 94 User's Reference* (Gaussian, Inc., Pittsburgh, PA, 1995) [**Opt** keyword discussion in chapter 3].

Approaching Difficult Convergence Cases H. B. Schlegel, "Some Practical Suggestions for Optimizing Geometries and Locating Transition States," in *New Theoretical Concepts for Understanding Organic Reactions*, ed. J. Bertràn (Kluwer Academic Pubs., NATO-ASI Series C 267, The Netherlands, 1989), 33-55.

Review of Optimization and TS Searching Methods H. B. Schlegel, "Geometry Optimization on Potential Energy Surfaces," in *Modern Electronic Structure Theory*, Ed. D. R. Yarkony, 2 vols. (World Scientific Publishing: Singapore, 1994).

Chapter

4

Frequency Calculations

In This Chapter:

Computing Vibrational Frequencies

Interpreting Normal Modes

Characterizing Stationary Points

This chapter discusses running frequency calculations using *Gaussian*. Frequency calculations can serve a number of different purposes:

◆ To predict the IR and Raman spectra of molecules (frequencies and intensities).

◆ To compute force constants for a geometry optimization.

◆ To identify the nature of stationary points on the potential energy surface.

◆ To compute zero-point vibration and thermal energy corrections to total energies as well as other thermodynamic quantities of interest such and the enthalpy and entropy of the system.

Predicting IR and Raman Spectra

Energy calculations and geometry optimizations ignore the vibrations in molecular systems. In this way, these computations use an idealized view of nuclear position.[†] In reality, the nuclei in molecules are constantly in motion. In equilibrium states, these vibrations are regular and predictable, and molecules can be identified by their characteristic spectra.

Gaussian can compute the vibrational spectra of molecules in their ground and excited states. In addition to predicting the frequencies and intensities of spectral lines, the program can also describe the displacements a system undergoes in its normal modes. Put another way, it can predict the direction and magnitude of the nuclear displacement that occurs when a system absorbs a quantum of energy.

Molecular frequencies depend on the second derivative of the energy with respect to the nuclear positions. Analytic second derivatives are available for the Hartree-Fock (**HF** keyword), Density Functional Theory (primarily the **B3LYP** keyword in this book), second-order Møller-Plesset (**MP2** keyword) and CASSCF (**CASSCF** keyword) theoretical procedures. Numeric second derivatives—which are much more time consuming—are available for other methods.

[†] The equilibrium geometries produced by electronic structure theory correspond to the spectroscopic geometry R_e, which assumes that there is no nuclear motion. Contrast this to the R_0 geometry, defined via the vibrationally-averaged nuclear positions.

Gaussian can also predict some other properties dependent on the second and higher derivatives of the energy, such as the polarizabilities and hyperpolarizabilities. These depend on the second derivative with respect to an electric field, and are included automatically in every Hartree-Fock frequency calculation.

To The Teacher: The Harmonic Oscillator

This chapter offers a number of opportunities for relating the text to topics in an elementary quantum mechanics course, including the following:

◆ Discuss how to compute vibrational frequencies using a simple harmonic oscillator model of nuclear motion.

◆ Present formal definitions of intensities and Raman depolarization ratios.

◆ Rationalize nonzero zero-point energies by reference to the harmonic oscillator model once again, and its energy:

$$h\nu \left(n + \frac{1}{2} \right)$$

The ground state corresponds to $n=0$, yielding a non-zero energy.

◆ Relate characterization of stationary points via the eigenvalues of the Hessian to the corresponding matrix under the harmonic oscillator problem.

Input for Frequency Jobs

Including the **Freq** keyword in the route section requests a frequency job. The other sections of the input file are the same as those we've considered previously.

Because of the nature of the computations involved, frequency calculations are valid *only* at stationary points on the potential energy surface. Thus, frequency calculations *must* be performed on optimized structures. For this reason, it is necessary to run a geometry optimization prior to doing a frequency calculation. The most convenient way of ensuring this is to include both Opt and Freq in the route section of the job, which requests a geometry optimization followed immediately by a frequency calculation. Alternatively, you can give an optimized geometry as the molecule specification section for a stand-alone frequency job.

A frequency job must use the same theoretical model and basis set as produced the optimized geometry. Frequencies computed with a different basis set or procedure *have no validity*. We'll be using the 6-31G(d) basis set for all of the examples and exercises in this chapter. This is the smallest basis set that gives satisfactory results for frequency calculations.

Note: The sample job files for this chapter do not generally include the optimization step. The molecule specifications in these input files have already been set to their optimized values.

Example 4.1: Formaldehyde Frequencies
file: e4_01

For our first example, we'll look at the Hartree-Fock frequencies for formaldehyde. Here is the route section from the input file:

```
# RHF/6-31G(d) Freq Test
```

The values of the variables were taken from an optimization job on formaldehyde.

Frequencies and Intensities

A frequency job begins by computing the energy of the input structure. It then goes on to compute the frequencies at that structure. *Gaussian* predicts the frequencies, intensities, and Raman depolarization ratios and scattering activities for each spectral line:

	1	2	3	4
	B1	B2	A1	A1
Frequencies ---	1336.0041	1383.6449	1679.5843	2028.0971
Red. masses ---	1.3689	1.3442	1.1039	7.2497
...				
IR Intensities ---	0.3694	23.1589	8.6240	150.1861
Raman Activities ---	0.7657	4.5170	12.8594	8.1124
Depolarizations ---	0.7500	0.7500	0.5908	0.3281

This display gives predicted values for the first four spectral lines for formaldehyde. The strongest line (IR) is line 4 at 2028.1 cm^{-1}.

Raw frequency values computed at the Hartree-Fock level contain known systematic errors due to the neglect of electron correlation, resulting in overestimates of about 10%-12%. Therefore, it is usual to scale frequencies predicted at the Hartree-Fock level by an empirical factor of 0.8929. Use of this factor has been demonstrated to produce very good agreement with experiment for a wide range of systems. Our values must be expected to deviate even a bit more from experiment because of our choice of a medium-sized basis set (by around 15% in all).

Computed values of the intensities should not be taken too literally. However, the relative values of the intensities for each frequency may be reliably compared.

Scaling Frequencies and Zero-Point Energies

Frequencies computed with methods other than Hartree-Fock are also scaled to similarly eliminate known systematic errors in calculated frequencies. The followng table lists the recommended scale factors for frequencies and for zero-point energies and for use in computing thermal energy corrections (the latter two items are discussed later in this chapter), for several important calculation types:[†]

	Scale Factor	
Method	Frequency	ZPE/Thermal
HF/3-21G	0.9085	0.9409
HF/6-31G(d)	0.8929	0.9135
MP2(Full)/6-31G(d)	0.9427	0.9646
MP2(FC)/6-31G(d)	0.9434	0.9676
SVWN/6-31G(d)	0.9833	1.0079
BLYP/6-31G(d)	0.9940	1.0119
B3LYP/6-31G(d)	0.9613	0.9804

As the table indicates, the optimal scaling factors for the frequencies themselves and for the zero-point energies and for use in computing thermal energy corrections are slightly different. However, it is also common practice to use the same factor for both of them (0.8929 in the case of Hartree-Fock). For example, the G2 high accuracy energy method scales computed HF/6-31G(d) zero-point energy corrections by 0.8929 (see Chapter 7).

You should be aware that the optimal scaling factors vary by basis set. For example, Bauschlicher and Partridge computed the B3LYP/6-311+G(3df,2p) ZPE/thermal energy correction scaling factor to be 0.989.[‡] Additional scaling factors have also been computed by Wong and by Scott and Radom.

Consult the references for detailed discussions of these issues.

[†] Most of the scale factors in this table are from the recent paper of Wong. The HF/6-31G(d) and MP2(Full) scale factors are the traditional ones computed by Pople and coworkers and cited by Wong. Note that the MP2 scale factor used in this book is the one for MP2(Full) even though our jobs are run using the (default) frozen core approximation. Scott and Radom computed the MP2(FC) and HF/3-21G entries in the table, but this work came to our attention only just as this book was going to press.

[‡] Their value is 0.980 for the 6-31G(d) basis set. Note that published scale factors often vary slightly from one another due primarily to differences in the molecule sets used to compute them.

Normal Modes

In addition to the frequencies and intensities, the output also displays the displacements of the nuclei corresponding to the normal mode associated with that spectral line. The displacements are presented as XYZ coordinates, in the standard orientation:

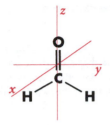

		Standard orientation:		
Center	Atomic		Coordinates (Angstroms)	
Number	Number	X	Y	Z
1	6	0.000000	0.000000	-0.542500
2	8	0.000000	0.000000	0.677500
3	1	0.000000	0.940000	-1.082500
4	1	0.000000	-0.940000	-1.082500

The carbon and oxygen atoms are situated on the Z-axis, and the plane of the molecule coincides with the YZ-plane.

Here is the first normal mode for formaldehyde:

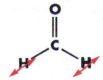

Atom	AN	X	Y	Z
1	6	0.17	0.00	0.00
2	8	-0.04	0.00	0.00
3	1	-0.70	0.00	0.00
4	1	-0.70	0.00	0.00

In the standard orientation, the X coordinates for all four atoms are 0. When interpreting normal mode output, the signs and relative values of the displacements for different atoms are more important than their exact magnitudes. Thus, for this normal mode, the two hydrogen atoms undergo the vast majority of the vibration, in the negative X direction. This means that they are moving perpendicular to the plane of the molecule. Although the values here suggest movement below the plane of the molecule, they are to be interpreted as motion in the opposite direction as well (in other words, as motion about the equilibrium positions). In our diagram, we illustrate the motion by showing the paths of the nuclei in both directions. Thus, the hydrogens are oscillating above and below the plane of the molecule in this mode. It produces a peak in the IR spectra at about 1189 cm^{-1}(which is 0.8929 times the value in the output).

The motion in the fourth normal mode is more complex:

```
Atom   AN      X        Y        Z
  1     6    0.00     0.00     0.58
  2     8    0.00     0.00    -0.41
  3     1    0.00    -0.46    -0.19
  4     1    0.00     0.46    -0.19
```

Here, the values of the displacement indicate that the oxygen and carbon atom move closer together, and the two hydrogen atoms also move toward one another, resulting in a decrease in the H-C-H bond angle. The actual vibration also occurs in the opposite directions, resulting in a stretching of the C-O bond, and the two hydrogens moving farther apart.

This mode corresponds to the IR peak associated with carbonyl stretch, used to identify the C-O double bond. Its predicted frequency is about 1810 (after scaling). This is in reasonable agreement with the experimental value of 1746. Using a larger basis set will improve this value. We'll discuss basis set effects in the next chapter.

Normal mode analysis provides a good example of information which is obtainable only through a theoretical calculation, since spectroscopic data does not directly indicate the specific type of nuclear motion producing each peak. Note that it is also possible to animate vibrational modes in some graphics packages.

Thermochemistry

All frequency calculations include thermochemical analysis of the system. By default, this analysis is carried out at 298.15 K and 1 atmosphere of pressure, using the principal isotope for each element type. Here is the start of the thermochemistry output for formaldehyde:

```
-------------------
- Thermochemistry -
-------------------
Temperature   298.150 Kelvin.  Pressure   1.00000 Atm.
Atom  1 has atomic number  6 and mass  12.00000
Atom  2 has atomic number  8 and mass  15.99491
...
Molecular mass:     30.01056 amu.
```

This section lists the parameters used for the thermochemical analysis: the temperature, pressure, and isotopes.

Gaussian predicts various important thermodynamic quantities at the specified temperature and pressure, including the thermal energy correction, heat capacity and entropy. These items are broken down into their source components in the output:

	E (Thermal)	CV	S
	KCAL/MOL	CAL/MOL-KELVIN	CAL/MOL-KELVIN
TOTAL	20.114	6.255	52.101
ELECTRONIC	0.000	0.000	0.000
TRANSLATIONAL	0.889	2.981	36.130
ROTATIONAL	0.889	2.981	15.921
VIBRATIONAL	18.337	0.294	0.049

thermal energy correction   constant volume molar heat capacity   entropy

To The Teacher: Connecting Thermochemistry to Statistical Mechanics

It is important that students be aware of how thermochemical properties arise from the energetics of vibrational frequencies. This connection is based upon partitioning the total energy of a macroscopic system among the constituent molecules. Nash's *Elements of Statistical Thermodynamics* provides an excellent discussion of the mathematical details of this transformation.

Changing Thermochemistry Parameters

You can specify a different temperature, pressure, and/or set of isotopes for the thermochemical analysis by specifying the **ReadIsotopes** option to the **Freq** keyword in the route section. Values for all parameters must then be specified in a separate input section following the molecule specification—and separated from it by a blank line.

Here is the general format for the **ReadIsotopes** input section:

temp pressure [*scale*]	*Temp. (ºK), pressure (atmospheres), and scale factor.*
isotope for atom 1	*Isotopes are specified as integers although the program*
isotope for atom 2	*will use the actual value.*
. . .	
isotope for atom N	

---

† The scale factor is optional. If included, it says to scale the frequencies before performing the thermochemical analysis. *Note that including the factor affects the thermochemistry output only* (including the ZPE); the frequencies printed earlier in the output remain unscaled. This parameter is the means by which scale factors are applied to thermal energy corrections.

All parameters other than the scale factor must be included, even if the default values are used.

Here is the thermochemistry parameters section of an input file for formaldehyde, requesting that the thermochemical analysis be done at 400 K, under 3 atmospheres of pressure, using the standard isotopes and without scaling:

```
400 3.0
12
16
1
1
```

Zero-Point Energy and Thermal Energy

Final predicted energies must always include a scaled zero-point or thermal energy correction.

The thermochemistry section of the output also gives the *zero-point energy* for this system. The zero-point energy is a correction to the electronic energy of the molecule to account for the effects of molecular vibrations which persist even at 0 K.

When comparing calculated results to thermodynamic quantities extrapolated to zero Kelvin, the zero point energy needs to be added to the total energy. As with the frequencies themselves, this predicted quantity is scaled to eliminate known systematic errors in frequency calculations. Accordingly, if you have not specified a scale factor via input to the **ReadIsotopes** option, you will need to multiply the values in the output by the appropriate scale factor (see page 64).

In order to predict the energy of a system at some higher temperature, a *thermal energy* correction must be added to the total energy, which includes the effects of molecular translation, rotation and vibration at the specified temperature and pressure. *Note that the thermal energy includes the zero-point energy automatically*; do not add both of them to an energy value.

When comparing energy results to experiments performed at particular temperatures, the thermal energy correction given in the output should be added to the total energy (this sum is also given in the output).[†] In order to apply the appropriate scale factor to a thermal energy correction, you *must* specify a scale factor via input to the **ReadIsotopes** option. The quantity reported in the output cannot simply be multiplied by the scale factor itself as it is composed of several terms, only some of which should be scaled.

[†] For a review of these thermodynamic terms, see Barrow and/or Nash.

Here is how the zero-point and thermal energy-corrected properties appear in the output from a frequency calculation:

```
Temperature   298.150 Kelvin.    Pressure   1.0000 Atm.
Zero-point correction=                          0.029201
Thermal correction to Energy=                   0.032054
Thermal correction to Enthalpy=                 0.032999
Thermal correction to Gibbs Free Energy=        0.008244
Sum of electronic and zero-point Energies=    -113.837130
Sum of electronic and thermal Energies=       -113.834277
Sum of electronic and thermal Enthalpies=     -113.833333
Sum of electronic and thermal Free Energies=  -113.858087
```

$$E_0 = E_{elec} + ZPE$$
$$E = E_0 + E_{vib} + E_{rot} + E_{transl}$$
$$H = E + RT$$
$$G = H - TS$$

The raw zero-point energy and thermal energy corrections are listed first, followed by the predicted energy of the system taking them into account. The output also includes corrections to and the final predicted values for the enthalpy and Gibbs free energy. All values are in Hartrees.

Polarizability and Hyperpolarizability

The other major properties computed by a frequency job are the polarizability and hyperpolarizability tensors. Normally, the polarizability is printed at the end of the output, just before the archive entry:

```
Exact polarizability:   6.478 0.000 12.919 0.000 0.000 17.641
Approx polarizability:  6.257 0.000 10.136 0.000 0.000 16.188
```

The tensor is given in lower-triangular format (i.e. α_{xx}, α_{xy}, α_{yy}, α_{xz}, α_{yz}, α_{zz}) in the standard orientation. The Approx polarizability line gives the results of the cruder polarizability estimate using sum-over-states perturbation theory, which is suggested by some older texts.

In a normal Hartree-Fock job, the hyperpolarizability tensor is given only in the archive entry, in the section beginning HyperPolar=. This tensor is also in lower tetrahedral order, but expressed in the input (Z-matrix) orientation. (This is also true of the polarizability tensor within the archive entry.)

If you begin the route section with **#P** rather than **#T**, then additional information is printed at various points in the job. One of these items is a display of the polarizability and hyperpolarizability tensors much earlier in the output, just prior to the frequency results:

```
Polarizability= 6.47820724D+00  5.07658124D-15  1.29193830D+01
                -5.41397131D-17 -1.33226763D-15  1.76406785D+01
HyperPolar=      2.32586107D-15  9.61495144D-15 -1.40039539D-15
                -5.91016464D-14 -3.29194932D+00 -2.38774194D-14
                -3.78952198D+01  9.31476424D-15  5.88564322D-14
                -3.65521797D+01
```

The tensors are again in lower triangular (tetrahedral) format, expressed here in the standard orientation.

Characterizing Stationary Points

Another use of frequency calculations is to determine the nature of a stationary point found by a geometry optimization. As we've noted, geometry optimizations converge to a structure on the potential energy surface where the forces on the system are essentially zero. The final structure may correspond to a minimum on the potential energy surface, or it may represent a saddle point, which is a minimum with respect to some directions on the surface and a maximum in one or more others. First order saddle points—which are a maximum in exactly one direction and a minimum in all other orthogonal directions—correspond to transition state structures linking two minima.

There are two pieces of information from the output which are critical to characterizing a stationary point:

✦ The number of imaginary frequencies.
✦ The normal mode corresponding to the imaginary frequency.

Imaginary frequencies are listed in the output of a frequency calculation as negative numbers. By definition, a structure which has n imaginary frequencies is an nth order saddle point. Thus, ordinary transition structures are usually characterized by one imaginary frequency since they are first-order saddle points.

If applicable, the program notes that there is an imaginary frequency present just prior to the frequency and normal modes output, and the first frequency value is less than zero. Log files may be searched for this line as a quick check for imaginary frequencies.

Here is a UNIX example:

```
% grep imagin job.log
 ******    1 imaginary frequencies (negative signs) ******
```

The equivalent VMS command would be:

```
$ Search Job.Log imagin
```

Under Windows, use the built-in search command in your preferred text editor to locate this line if present.

It is important to keep in mind that finding exactly one imaginary frequency does not guarantee that you have found the transition structure in which you are interested. Saddle points always connect two minima on the potential energy surface, but these minima may not be the reactants and products of interest. Whenever a structure yields an imaginary frequency, it means that there is some geometric distortion for which the energy of the system is lower than it is at the current structure (indicating a more stable structure). In order to fully understand the nature of a saddle point, you must determine the nature of this deformation.

One way to do so is to look at the normal mode corresponding to the imaginary frequency and determine whether the displacements that compose it tend to lead in the directions of the structures that you think the transition structure connects. The symmetry of the normal mode is also relevant in some cases (see the following example). Animating the vibrations with a chemical visualization package is often very useful. Another, more accurate way to determine what reactants and products the transition structure connects is to perform an IRC calculation to follow the reaction path and thereby determine the reactants and products explicity; this technique is discussed in Chapter 8.

The table on the next page summarizes the most important cases you will encounter when attempting to characterize stationary points.

Characterizing Stationary Points

If you were looking for ...	And the frequency calculation found ...	It means ...	So you should ...
A minimum	0 imaginary frequencies	The structure is a minimum.	Compare the energy to that of other isomers if you are looking for the global minimum.
A minimum	≥ 1 imaginary frequencies	The structure is a saddle point, not a minimum.	Continue searching for a minimum (try unconstraining the molecular symmetry or distorting the molecule along the normal mode corresponding to the imaginary frequency).
A transition state	0 imaginary frequencies	The structure is a minimum, not a saddle point.	Try using **Opt=QST2** or **QST3** to find the TS (see Chapter 3).
A transition state	1 imaginary frequency	The structure is a true transition state.	Determine if the structure connects the correct reactants and products by examining the imaginary frequency's normal mode or by performing an IRC calculation.
A transition state	> 1 imaginary frequency	The structure is a higher-order saddle point, but is not a transition structure that connects two minima.	**QST2** may again be of use. Otherwise, examine the normal modes corresponding to the imaginary frequencies. One of them will (hopefully) point toward the reactants and products. Modify the geometry based on the displacements in the other mode(s), and rerun the optimization.

Example 4.2: Characterizing Stationary Points

files: **e4_02a(0°)**
　　　e4_02b(180°)
　　　e4_02c (cis)
　　　e4_02d(TS)

We are interested in exploring the C_3H_5F potential energy surface. We will begin by running optimization and frequency jobs on these three isomers of 1-fluoropropene:

trans (0°)　　　　*trans (180°)*　　　　*cis (0°)*

All of the optimizations are successful. The frequency jobs for the two forms where the H-C-C-H dihedral angle is 0° produce no imaginary frequencies, and the cis form is lower in energy than the trans form by about 0.63 kcal/mole.

The frequency job on the middle structure produces one imaginary frequency, indicating that this conformation is a transition structure and not a minimum. But what two minima does it connect? Is it the transition structure for the cis-to-trans conversion reaction (i.e. rotation about the C=C bond)?

We look first at the energies of the three compounds:

Conformation	Energy
trans (0°)	-215.92046
trans (180°)	-215.91694
cis	-215.92147

The 180° trans structure is only about 2.5 kcal/mol higher in energy than the 0° conformation, a barrier which is quite a bit less than one would expect for rotation about the double bond. We note that this structure is a member of the C_s point group. Its normal modes of vibration, therefore, will be of two types: the symmetrical A' and the non-symmetrical A" (point-group symmetry is maintained in the course of symmetrical vibrations).

To investigate the status of this structure further, we next examine the frequency data and normal mode corresponding to the imaginary frequency:

```
                        1
                       A"
 Frequencies  --   -226.6781
 Red. masses  --      1.1175
 Frc consts   --      0.0338
 IR Inten     --      0.1566
 Raman Activ  --      2.8462
 Depolar      --      0.7500
 Atom AN     X        Y        Z
   1   6    0.00     0.00     0.00
   2   1    0.00     0.00     0.54
   3   6    0.00     0.00    -0.06
   4   1   -0.19    -0.42    -0.25
   5   1    0.19     0.42    -0.25
   6   1    0.00     0.00    -0.28
   7   6    0.00     0.00     0.08
   8   1    0.00     0.00     0.28
   9   9    0.00     0.00    -0.01
```

Note that the magnitude of the imaginary frequency is not very large (-226), indicating that the geometric distortion desired by the molecule is modest. The largest motion is in the three hydrogen atoms in the methyl group (consult the standard orientation to determine which atom is which).

This becomes even clearer when we examine the alternate version of this normal mode included later in the output, labeled as the eigenvector of the Hessian:

```
Eigenvalue 1 out of range, new value = 0.002670 Eigenvector:
                            1
          R1           0.00000
          R2           0.00000
          R3           0.00160
          R4          -0.00160
          ...
          A1           0.00000
          A2          -0.00316
          A3          -0.00305
          A4           0.00316
          A5           0.00305
          ...
          D1           0.41000
          D2           0.41598
          D3           0.41598
          D4           0.39778
          D5           0.40376
          D6           0.40376
          D7           0.02724
          ...
```

This table gives the displacements for the normal mode corresponding to the imaginary frequency in terms of redundant internal coordinates (several zero-valued coordinates have been eliminated). The most significant values in this list are for the dihedral angles D1 through D6. When we examine the standard orientation, we realize that such motion corresponds to a rotation of the methyl group.

Looking back at the frequency output once again, we note that its symmetry is A", indicating that this is a symmetry-breaking mode. The molecular structure has C_s symmetry, indicating that there is a single plane of symmetry (in this case, the plane of the carbon atoms). The structure wants to move down the PES to a lower-energy structure of equal or lower symmetry.

From all of this, we can deduce that this transition structure connects two structurally-equivalent minima, and that the path between them corresponds to a methyl rotation. This is not a very interesting transition structure.

We must look further in order to locate the transition structure linking the cis and trans forms of 1-propene. Since we are looking for a normal mode which suggests rotation about the C=C bond, then we can expect that its major motion will be in the dihedral angles involving those carbon atoms and the fluorine and hydrogen atoms.

Here is another transition structure that we located. An optimization and frequency calculation on it reveals that it too has one imaginary frequency, of significantly larger magnitude (-1517 vs. -226). Examining the normal mode reveals displacements in the dihedral angles involving the two carbons of interest, strongly suggesting that this is the transition structure that we seek (the output format for the eigenvector of the Hessian is slightly different when the program knows that it is searching for a transition structure):

```
Eigenvectors required to have negative eigenvalues:
         R1        R2        R3        R4        R5
  1   -0.00496   0.02656   0.00351   0.02361  -0.03319
         R6        R7        R8        A1        A2
  1    0.03211  -0.00007  -0.01430  -0.03200   0.00684
         A3        A4        A5        A6        A7
  1   -0.02217  -0.01426   0.07040  -0.01216   0.00888
         A8        A9       A10       A11       A12
  1   -0.43072   0.22027  -0.01413   0.00280   0.01156
         D1        D2        D3        D4        D5
  1   -0.05683  -0.03471  -0.04809   0.02073   0.04285
         D6        D7        D8        D9       D10
  1    0.02947   0.43757   0.39467   0.46699   0.42409
```

Examining the standard orientation for the molecule verifies that angles A8 through A10 and dihedral angles D7 through D10 involve the atoms in question.[†]

The predicted energy of this structure is approximately -215.76438 Hartrees, yielding a reaction barrier of about 86.6 kcal/mol. This value is more in line with expectations, although it is on the high side. Rotation of a double bond is a problem which often requires a higher level of theory than Hartree-Fock (for example, CASSCF) for accurate modeling.

We will continue exploring this potential energy surface in Exercise 4.6.

[†] You may wonder why so many coordinates apply to these same few atoms. Remember that we are using redundant internal coordinates.

Exercises

Exercise 4.1: Frequencies of Vinyl Alcohol Isomers

files: **4_01a (180°)**
　　　 4_01b (0°)

Run frequency calculations on the two vinyl alcohol isomers we considered in the last chapter. Optimize the structures at the RHF level, using the 6-31G(d) basis set, and perform a frequency calculation on each optimized structure. Are both of the forms minima? What effect does the change in structure (i.e., the position of hydrogen in the hydroxyl group) have on the frequencies?

Solution

Neither frequency job produces any imaginary frequencies, indicating that both structures are minima. A quick way to check for this is to search the output file for the string "imagin"; such a search indicates that there is no matching line in the file.

As we noted in Chapter 3, the 0° form has lower energy and is in fact the global minimum. The 180° form is a higher energy minimum elsewhere on the potential energy surface.

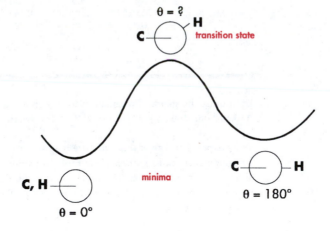

Based on the results for propene, we might guess that the transition structure is halfway between the two minima: the structure with a C-C-O-H dihedral angle of 90°. We would need to verify this with optimization and frequency calculations.

Here is the (unscaled) frequency data for the two forms of vinyl alcohol:

Peak	0° Isomer Freq.	Intensity	180° Isomer Freq.	Intensity
1	459	151	186	140
2	533	16	518	4
3	785	1	785	6
4	965	93	988	84
5	1048	14	1048	60
6	1128	17	1104	13
7	1234	230	1236	13
8	1447	5	1419	266
9	1468	5	1476	16
10	1595	24	1582	0.3
11	1879	198	1907	112
12	3334	8	3345	18
13	3404	6	3364	9
14	3433	20	3443	14
15	4096	54	4146	111

In most cases, the frequency and intensity of each peak are essentially equal; differences of up to about 50 cm^{-1} are not significant. The one noticeable shift comes with the first normal mode, which differs in frequency by about 272 cm^{-1}.

To understand this shift, we need to look at the displacements for the two forms:

Atom	AN	X	Y	Z
1	6	0.00	0.00	0.03
2	6	0.00	0.00	-0.04
3	1	0.00	0.00	0.25
4	1	0.00	0.00	-0.14
5	8	0.00	0.00	0.08
6	1	0.00	0.00	-0.14
7	1	0.00	0.00	-0.94

0° form

Atom	AN	X	Y	Z
1	6	0.00	0.00	0.04
2	6	0.00	0.00	-0.02
3	1	0.00	0.00	0.16
4	1	0.00	0.00	-0.09
5	8	0.00	0.00	-0.07
6	1	0.00	0.00	-0.14
7	1	0.00	0.00	0.97

180° form

Most of the movement occurs in the hydrogen attached to the oxygen atom, moving out of the plane of the molecule. This atom is positioned very differently in the two forms, and so it is not surprising that they generate substantially different vibrational frequencies in this normal mode. ■

To The Teacher: Additional Modes Discussion

A similar shift of peak between the two forms occurs in modes 7 and 8 (in the 0° form, peak 7 is quite strong while peak 8 is weak; these intensities are reversed for the 180° form). These modes are characterized by motion of several hydrogen nuclei. They could be used for further discussion of normal modes in this more complex system.

Exercise 4.2: Characterizing Planar Vinyl Amine

files: 4_02a
4_02b

Determine whether the vinyl amine structure we considered in the last chapter is a minimum or not. If it is not a minimum, characterize its nature and then locate the minimum and compute its frequencies.

Solution A frequency job on the optimized structure for planar vinyl amine will produce one imaginary frequency. This indicates that it is a transition state, not a minimum.

In order to find the minimum, we look at the normal mode associated with the imaginary frequency. Here are the displacements:

Atom	AN	X	Y	Z
1	6	0.00	0.00	0.02
2	6	0.00	0.00	0.02
3	1	0.00	0.00	-0.03
4	1	0.00	0.00	0.01
5	1	0.00	0.00	-0.01
6	7	0.00	0.00	-0.13
7	1	0.00	0.00	0.57
8	1	0.00	0.00	0.81

There is motion in the nitrogen atom and the hydrogens attached to it out of the plane of the molecule. This suggests that if we vary the structure of the NH_2 group, we will be able to locate the minimum. It turns out that the nitrogen atom exhibits pyramidalization in the optimized structure.

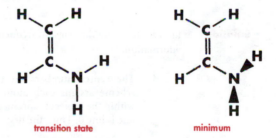

transition state   minimum

The frequency job on this structure will confirm that it is a minimum. We'll consider more of the results of this frequency calculation in the next exercise. ∎

Exercise 4.3: Vinyl Series Frequencies

files: 4_03a (C₂H₄)
$\quad\quad$**4_03b (C₂H₃F)**
$\quad\quad$**4_03c (C₃H₆)**

Perform frequency calculations on the members of the vinyl series listed below (lowest energy minima only):

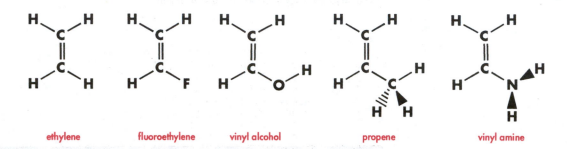

ethylene$\quad\quad$fluoroethylene$\quad\quad$vinyl alcohol$\quad\quad$propene$\quad\quad$vinyl amine

If you completed the previous exercises in this chapter, you've already run the jobs for vinyl alcohol and vinyl amine.

Once you've run all the jobs, describe the effect the substituent has on the vibrational mode associated with the C=C double bond in these systems.

Solution

In order to locate the relevant frequency for C=C stretch, you'll need three pieces of information:[†]

+ **The center numbers for the atoms of interest**. *Gaussian*'s numbering scheme assigns each atom the number corresponding to its input line within the molecule specification section, where the charge and multiplicity line is line 0. Thus, the first atom listed is center number 1, and so on.

+ The standard orientation for the molecule, and specifically **the coordinates of the atoms of interest**. Sometimes, the atomic numbers alone are enough to identify the atoms you want, but for larger systems, the center numbers will be needed to pick out specific atoms within the standard orientation. Their coordinates will enable you to characterize the expected components of the displacement for the motion under investigation.

+ **The frequency and normal mode displacement output**. Once you know the sort of displacement to expect, you can determine which normal mode corresponds to it and its associated frequency.

We'll go through this process in some detail for ethylene and propene and then summarize the results for the remaining systems.

_____

[†] You can also find the appropriate mode by animating each one in turn in a graphics program.

Here are the standard orientations for ethylene and propene:

ethylene

```
                     Standard orientation:
-----------------------------------------------------------------
Center      Atomic              Coordinates (Angstroms)
Number      Number         X              Y              Z
-----------------------------------------------------------------
   1           6         0.000000       0.000000       0.658480
   2           6         0.000000       0.000000      -0.658480
   3           1         0.000000       0.914361       1.225703
   4           1         0.000000      -0.914361       1.225703
   5           1         0.000000       0.914361      -1.225703
   6           1         0.000000      -0.914361      -1.225703
-----------------------------------------------------------------
```

propene

```
                     Standard orientation:
-----------------------------------------------------------------
Center      Atomic              Coordinates (Angstroms)
Number      Number         X              Y              Z
-----------------------------------------------------------------
   1           6         1.281948       0.164710       0.000000
   2           6         0.000000       0.473222       0.000000
   3           6        -1.130350      -0.516977       0.000000
   4           1         1.620546      -0.857728       0.000000
   5           1         2.045038       0.922802       0.000000
   6           1        -0.285763       1.513801       0.000000
   7           1        -0.763538      -1.537412       0.000000
   8           1        -1.762935      -0.383599       0.873865
   9           1        -1.762935      -0.383599      -0.873865
-----------------------------------------------------------------
```

It's easy to identify the carbons involved in the double bond in ethylene: atoms 1 and 2. In propene, things are slightly more complicated. In this case, the carbon which has three hydrogens attached to it is not involved in the double bond. We can identify this carbon atom as center number 3 by noting that it along with the final three hydrogen atoms all lie in the third quadrant (-X and -Y). Therefore the two carbons of interest are again atoms 1 and 2.

Here are plots of the positions of these carbon atoms in the two molecules:

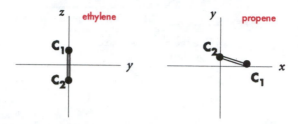

By examining the positions of the atoms, we can determine what type of displacements would occur when the C=C bond stretches. The carbons in ethylene must both move in the Z direction, since they are situated on the Z-axis, while those in propene must move primarily in the X direction.

We can now search the normal modes for each system, looking for ones which exhibit these types of displacements. In each case, there is only one mode with any significant displacements in the required coordinates.

Here are the modes associated with C=C stretch:

ethylene

	8		
	AG		
	1856.1319		
Atom AN	X	Y	Z
1 6	0.00	0.00	0.30
2 6	0.00	0.00	-0.30
3 1	0.00	0.38	-0.25
4 1	0.00	-0.38	-0.25
5 1	0.00	0.38	0.25
6 1	0.00	-0.38	0.25

propene

	15		
	A'		
	1880.7099		
Atom AN	X	Y	Z
1 6	0.35	-0.07	0.00
2 6	-0.40	0.03	0.00
3 6	0.06	0.01	0.00
4 1	-0.35	-0.36	0.00
5 1	-0.09	0.44	0.00
6 1	0.33	0.28	0.00
7 1	-0.18	-0.07	0.00
8 1	0.13	0.03	0.04
9 1	0.13	0.03	-0.04

In ethylene, both carbons have significant displacements in the Z direction (with opposite sign). In propene, their displacements are essentially in the X direction. In both cases, the hydrogens attached to these carbon atoms also move, as would be expected.

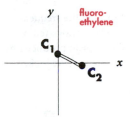

fluoro-
ethylene

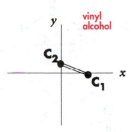

vinyl
alcohol

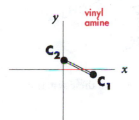

vinyl
amine

Here are the complete results for the vinyl series (the double-bonded carbons are center numbers 1 and 2 in all cases):

Vinyl Series (CH$_2$=CHR) C=C Stretch

System	Standard Orientation (C$_1$, C$_2$)	Expected Displacement	Scaled Frequency	Peak Number
Ethylene (R=H)	(0.00, 0.00, 0.66), (0.00, 0.00, -0.66)	Z	1652	8
Fluoroethylene (R=F)	(0.00, 0.43, 0.00), (1.17, -0.15, 0.00)	X, minor Y	1685	9
Propene (R=CH$_3$)	(1.28, 0.16, 0.00), (0.00, 0.47, 0.00)	X	1674	15
Vinyl Alcohol (R=OH)	(1.20, -0.10, 0.00), (0.00, 0.44, 0.00)	X, minor Y	1672	11
Vinyl Amine (R=NH$_2$)	(1.24, -0.20, 0.02), (0.07, 0.43, -0.01)	X, Y	1680	13

The frequencies for these systems fall into the expected range for C=C stretching (1690-1600 cm^{-1}). Replacing one of the hydrogens in ethylene with any substituent results in a frequency shift to a higher wave number, with the more electronegative groups producing the largest shifts. ■

To The Teacher: Interpreting Gas Phase Frequencies

Be sure to remind students that these frequencies are gas phase data and are thus not the same as the more-familiar solution spectra (we will treat solvated systems in Chapter 9). Even so, such gas phase calculations make excellent discovery-based exercises. For example, students may be asked to explain the substituent effects observed using basic chemistry knowledge.

Exercise 4.4: Carbonyl Stretch by Substituent

files: 4_04a (C₂H₄O)
4_04b (C₃H₅O)
4_04c (CNH₃O)
4_04d (C₃H₆O)
4_05e (C₂H₃ClO)
4_04f (C₃H₆O₂)

This exercise will investigate various carbonyl compounds. Examine the frequencies for the systems pictured below and determine the frequencies associated with carbonyl stretch in each case. In addition, locate the characteristic peak produced by the single hydrogen attached to the carbonyl for the applicable systems. (We looked at this mode in formaldehyde in Example 4.1.)

formaldehyde   acetaldehyde   acrolein   formamide

acetone   acetyl chloride   methyl acetate

Solution   The following table summarizes the results of the frequency jobs on these systems:

C=O Stretch for Carbonyl Series

System	Molecular Formula	Center #'s (C,O)	Standard Orientation (C,O)	Exp. Displ.	Scaled Freq.	Peak #
Formaldehyde	H₂CO	1,2	(0.00, 0.00, 0.00), (0.00, 0.00, 1.18)	Z	1805	4
Acetaldehyde	CH₃CHO	2, 6	(0.00, 0.46, 0.00), (-1.19, 0.40, 0.00)	X	1809	11
Acrolein	CH₂CHCHO	3, 4	(-0.15, -0.75, 0.00), (-1.20, -1.32, 0.00)	X, Y	1792	14
Formamide	HCONH₂	2, 3	(0.00, 0.42, 0.00), (1.18, 0.24, 0.00)	X	1780	9

C=O Stretch for Carbonyl Series

System	Molecular Formula	Center #'s (C,O)	Standard Orientation (C,O)	Exp. Displ.	Scaled Freq.	Peak #
Acetone	CH_3COCH_3	1, 2	(0.00, 0.00, 0.19), (0.00, 0.00, 1.38)	Z	1799	18
Acetyl Chloride	CH_3COCl	1, 4	(0.00, 0.52, 0.00), (-0.82, 1.35, 0.00)	X, Y	1850	12
Methyl Acetate	CH_3COOCH_3	1, 2	(0.00, 0.49, 0.00), (-1.15, 0.77, 0.00)	X	1797	21

After scaling, the predicted frequencies are generally within the expected range for carbonyl stretch (~1750 cm^{-1}). The table below reproduces our values, published theoretical values using the 6-31+G(d) basis set (this basis set includes diffuse functions), and the experimental values, arranged in order of ascending experimental frequency:

System	HF/6-31G(d)	HF/6-31+G(d)	Experiment
Acrolein	1792	1773	1723
Acetone	1799	1777	1737
Formamide	1780	1750	1740
Formaldehyde	1805	1787	1746
Acetaldehyde	1809	1789	1746
Methyl Acetate	1797	1771	1761
Acetyl Chloride	1850	1832	1822

This table provides an introduction to the basis set effects we'll discuss in the next chapter. Adding diffuse functions lowers the frequency by about 20-30 cm^{-1}. However, both sets of numbers are in reasonable agreement with the observed values, with the better theoretical values producing quite good agreement. However, even using the smaller basis set, we can successfully identify the carbonyl stretch.

The largest shifts in frequency occur for methyl acetate, where the hydrogens in formaldehyde are replaced by a methyl group and a methoxy group, and most strikingly in acetyl chloride, where the hydrogen atom is replaced by a chlorine atom and a methyl group.

We'll compare these gas phase frequencies to those for these systems in solution in Chapter 9.

Here are the results for the peaks associated with a lone hydrogen on the carbonyl group:

Carbonyl Hydrogen Peaks

System	Center Number	Scaled Frequency	Peak #
Acetaldehyde	7	2802	12
Acrolein	8	2813	15
Formamide	4	2859	10

The normal modes associated with these frequencies are characterized by motion limited to the hydrogen atom in question. The values of the frequencies are in reasonable agreement with observations which place this peak in the range 2745-2710 cm^{-1}, given our knowledge of basis set effects from the carbonyl stretch frequencies. ■

Advanced Exercise 4.5: Strained Hydrocarbons

files: 4_05a
4_05b

Perform frequency calculations for each of these strained hydrocarbon compounds:

bicyclo[1.1.1]pentane (C$_5$H$_8$)

prismane (C$_6$H$_6$)

cyclobutene (C$_4$H$_6$)

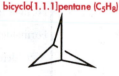

bicyclo[2.2.0]hex-1(4)-ene (C$_6$H$_8$)   [1.1.1]propellane (C$_5$H$_6$)

pentaprismane (C$_{10}$H$_{10}$)

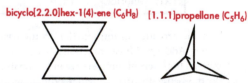
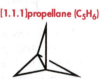

For the four smaller systems, determine how well the predicted frequencies compare to the experimental IR spectral data given below. Identify the symmetry type for the normal mode associated with each assigned peak.

System	Prominent IR Peaks (cm^{-1})
Cyclobutene	2955, 2916, 2933, 635
Bicyclo(2.2.0)hex-1(4)-ene	2933, 2966, 1226
Bicyclo[1.1.1]pentane	2976, 2973, 2878
[1.1.1]Propellane	611, 3020, 3079

For prismane and pentaprismane, predict the dominant IR peaks.

We've included several papers in the References section which perform theoretical and experimental studies of the IR and Raman spectra for these compounds. These compounds were among the earliest ab initio frequency studies of such systems. In addition, in the case of propellane, theoretical predictions of its energy and structure preceded its synthesis.

Solution   Here are the results of the frequency jobs:

System	Frequency Calc.	Frequency Scaled	Exp.	Symmetry	Intensity
Cyclobutene	3266	2906	2955	B_1	90.3
	3212	2859	2916	B_2	67.2
	3223	2868	2933	A_1	59.8
	726	647	635	B_1	43.9
Bicyclo(2.2.0)hex-1(4)-ene	3218	2864	2933	B_{2u}	136.9
	3224	2870	2933	B_{3u}	190.7
	3275	2915	2966	B_{1u}	171.1
	1362	1212	1226	B_{2u}	17.0
Bicyclo[1.1.1]pentane	3285	2923	2976	A_2''	150.3
	3282	2921	2973	E'	92.6
	3223	2868	2878	E'	90.4
[1.1.1]Propellane	625	558	611	A_2''	192.0
	3322	2956	3020	E'	32.0
	3406	3032	3079	E'	16.7

These results are in good agreement with the experimental values. Note that two different normal modes produce the doubly degenerate E' frequencies, and the intensity is the sum of the two.

Here are the strongest predicted peaks for prismane and pentaprismane:

System	Scaled Freq.	Intensity
Prismane	3022	56.8
	802	55.8
	3028	33.2
Pentaprismane	2935	185.9
	2934	176.0
	745	9.3

Remember that intensities can be compared qualitatively, but should not be taken too literally. When we examine the other frequencies for these compounds, we find that most of the normal modes are not IR active (the intensity is 0). ■

To The Teacher: Further Frequency Discussion

We've only scratched the surface of the frequency data for these compounds. More detailed treatments might include:

◆ Identifying the modes associated with motion of the carbon atoms (e.g. modes 6 and 13 for propellane).

◆ Isotopic substitution and its effect on the frequencies. For example, substituting deuterium for hydrogen in propellane produces different IR peaks.

Advanced Exercise 4.6: A 1,3 Hydrogen Shift on the C₃H₅F Potential Energy Surface

files: **4_06a (min.)**
4_06b (TS)

In this exercise, we continue our study of C_3H_5F potential energy surface begun in Example 4.2. Another sort of transformation that cis 1-fluoropropene can undergo is a 1,3 hydrogen shift, resulting in 3-fluoropropene (left):

Determine whether the structure on the right is the transition structure for this reaction based on an optimization and frequency calculation on it. What evidence can you provide for your conclusion?

Solution

The optimization of 3-fluoropropene leads to a minimum on the PES, indicated by the fact that the frequency calculation results in no imaginary frequencies.

The transition state optimization (**Opt=(TS,CalcFC)**) of the structure on the right converges in 12 steps. The UHF frequency calculation finds one imaginary frequency. Here is the associated normal mode:

```
Frequencies --  -2290.8426
Atom AN      X        Y       Z
   1   6    0.03    -0.02   -0.02
   2   1   -0.04    -0.08   -0.16
   3   6    0.01    -0.06    0.05
   4   6    0.04     0.04   -0.03
   5   9   -0.01     0.01   -0.02
   6   1    0.04    -0.03    0.05
   7   1    0.10     0.10    0.00
   8   1   -0.22    -0.20    0.02
   9   1   -0.63     0.54    0.40
```

The majority of the motion in this mode involves the shifting hydrogen atom, so it appears that this is the correct transition structure (this could be confirmed with an IRC calculation, as we'll discuss in Chapter 8). The large magnitude of the frequency (about -2291 unscaled) also indicates a substantial change in structure. Finally, the predicted energy barrier of about 120 kcal/mol is of the right order of magnitude. ∎

References

Frequency and ZPE Scale Factors

Hartree-Fock Frequencies: J. A. Pople, R. Krishnan, H. B. Schlegel, D. DeFrees, J. S. Binkley, M. J. Frisch, R. F. Whiteside, R. F. Hout, and W. J. Hehre, *Int. J. Quantum Chem., Symp.*, **15**, 269 (1981).

Hartree-Fock and MP2 Frequencies and ZPE: J. A. Pople, A. P. Scott, M. W. Wong and L. Radom, *Israel J. Chem.*, **33**, 345 (1993).

DFT Frequencies and ZPE: M. W. Wong, *Chem. Phys. Lett.*, in press (1996).

A. P. Scott and L. Radom, *J. Phys. Chem.*, submitted (1996).

B3LYP ZPE: C. W. Bauschlicher, Jr. and H. Partridge, *J. Chem. Phys.*, **103**, 1788 (1995).

IR Peak Locations

D. A. Skoog and D. M. West, *Principles of Instrumental Analysis*, 2nd. ed. (Saunders College, Philadelphia, 1980).

6-31+G(d) C=O Series Frequencies

M. W. Wong, K. B. Wiberg, and M. J. Frisch, *J. Chem. Phys,.* **95**, 8991 (1991).

Strained Hydrocarbon Frequencies

K. B. Wiberg and R. E. Rosenberg, *J. Phys. Chem.*, **96**, 8282 (1992).

K. B. Wiberg, M. G. Matturro, P. J. Okarma, M. E. Jason, W. P. Dailey, G. J. Burgmaier, W. F. Bailey, and P. Warner, *Tetrahedron*, **42**, 1895 (1985).

K. B. Wiberg, W. P. Bailey, F. H. Walker, S. T. Waddell, L. S. Crocker, and M. Newton, *J. Am. Chem. Soc.*, **107**, 7247 (1985).

K. B. Wiberg, R. E. Rosenberg, and S. T. Waddell, *J. Phys. Chem.*, **90**, 8294 (1992).

Statistical Mechanics Text

L. K. Nash, *Elements of Statistical Thermodynamics* (Addison-Wesley, 1968).

Thermochemistry Text

G. M. Barrow, *Physical Chemistry*, 5th edition (McGraw-Hill, New York, 1988), chapters 4-6.

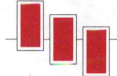

Part 2: Model Chemistries

Introduction

Real research studies with *Gaussian* involve not only larger molecules than the ones we've generally looked at so far, but also multiple calculations to thoroughly investigate systems of interest. Here is an example procedure that might be used to predict the total energy of a system:

A General Procedure for Predicting Total Energies

◆ Perform a low-level geometry optimization with a medium-sized basis set, for example, a Hartree-Fock or B3LYP Density Functional Theory calculation with the 6-31G(d) basis set. (For very large systems, a smaller basis set might be necessary.)

◆ Predict the zero point or thermal energy by running a frequency job at the optimized geometry, using the same method and basis set. (Note that these two steps may be run via a single *Gaussian* job via the **Opt Freq** keyword.)

◆ If it is computationally feasible, improve on the structure by using it as the starting point for a more accurate optimization (using a larger basis set and/or run at a higher level of theory).

◆ Run a very high level single point energy calculation—for example, MP4 or QCISD(T)—at the newly optimized structure, using a large basis set. Final energies should be computed at the most accurate model chemistry that is practical for the system in question. You may also choose to compute the energy using a high-accuracy compound method (discussed in Chapter 7).

Once these steps are complete, the energy can then be computed as the sum of the final single point energy and the zero point or thermal energy, as appropriate.

This hypothetical sequence of jobs should give you a sense of how a real study might proceed. We'll begin this part of the book by looking at each of the components of a model chemistry in more detail.

Model Chemistries

In the first chapter, we described a model chemistry as an unbiased, uniquely defined, and uniformly applicable theoretical model for predicting the properties of chemical systems. A model chemistry generally consists of the combination of a theoretical method with a basis set. Each such unique pairing of method with basis set represents a different approximation to the Schrödinger equation. Results for different systems generally may only be compared when they have been predicted via the same model chemistry. Different model chemistries may be compared and tested by comparing their results on the same systems to one another and to the results of experiments.

The chart below lists various model chemistries definable via traditional ab initio methods and standard basis sets:

| | Electron Correlation → | | | | | | |
	HF	MP2	MP3	MP4	QCISD(T)	...	Full CI
Minimal STO-3G							
Split valence 3-21G							
Polarized 6-31G(d)							
6-311G(d,p)							
Diffuse 6-311+G(d,p)							
High ang. momentum 6-311+G(2d,p)							
6-311++G(3df,3pd)							
...							
∞	HF Limit					...	Schrödinger Equation

(Basis Set — left margin label spanning the rows)

Each cell in the chart defines a model chemistry. The columns correspond to different theoretical methods and the rows to different basis sets. The level of correlation increases as you move to the right across any row, with the Hartree-Fock method at the extreme left (including no correlation), and the Full Configuration Interaction method at the right (which fully accounts for electron correlation). In general, computational cost and accuracy increase as you move to the right as well. The relative costs of different model chemistries for various job types is discussed in

Chapter 6 (page 122); the relative accuracies of various model chemistries is discussed in Chapter 7 (page 146). See Appendix A for a discussion of the approximation techniques used by the various methods.

The rows of the chart correspond to increasingly larger basis sets. The specific basis sets cited there serve as examples, illustrating the additional types of functions added as you move down any column. The bottom row of the chart represents a completely flexible basis set, and the cells in it correspond to the *basis set limit* for each specified theoretical method.

The cell in the lower right corner of the chart represents the exact solution of the Schrödinger equation, the limit toward which all approximate methods strive. Full CI using an infinitely flexible basis set is the exact solution.[†]

The first cell in the last row of the table represents the *Hartree-Fock limit*: the best approximation that can be achieved without taking electron correlation into account. Its location on the chart is rather far from the exact solution. Although in some cases, quite good results can be achieved with Hartree-Fock theory alone, in many others, its performance ranges from only fair to quite poor. We'll look at some these cases in Chapters 5 and 6.

Choosing a model chemistry almost always involves a trade-off between accuracy and computational cost. More accurate methods and larger basis sets make jobs run longer. We'll provide some specific examples of these effects throughout the chapters in this part of the book.

Terminology

We will designate model chemistries using this naming convention (which we have already used in earlier chapters without comment):

energy_method/energy_basis_set // geometry_method/geometry_basis_set

where the model to the left of the double slash is the one at which the energy is computed, and the model to the right of the double slash is the one at which the molecular geometry was optimized. For example, **RHF/6-31+G(d,p)//RHF/6-31G(d)** means that the energy calculation was performed using Hartree-Fock theory and the 6-31+G(d,p) basis set on a structure previously optimized with Hartree-Fock theory and the 6-31G(d) basis set. Similarly, **MP4/6-311+G(2d,p)//MP2/6-31G(d)** specifies an MP4 single point energy calculation using the 6-311+G(2d,p) basis set computed at the MP2/6-31G(d) geometry.

[†] Non-relativistic, Born-Oppenheimer.

Recommendations for Selecting Research Models

The following table summarizes some recommended research-level model chemistries for predicting total energies for molecular systems of various sizes (the details of the reasons behind these choices will unfold along with the chapters in this part of the book), arranged in order of increasing computational cost:

Model Chemistry	MAD[†]/Max. Error on G2 Molecule Set	Range of Applicability [# heavy atoms]	Relative Cost
AM1 // AM1	19.7/176.3	many hundreds	1
B3LYP/6-31G(d) // AM1	11.7/54.2	hundreds	2.5
B3LYP/6-31G(d) // HF/3-21G(d)	8.0/54.2	100	10
B3LYP/6-311+G(3df,2df,2p) // HF/6-31G(d)[‡]	~3.2/~21.2	50-75	40-50
B3LYP/6-311+G(3df,2df,2p) // B3LYP/6-31G(d)	2.7/12.5	50	50-100
CBS-4	2.0/7.0	25	80-100
CBS-Q	1.0/3.8	10	400-800
CBS-APNO	0.5/1.5	5	>5000

[†] Mean absolute deviation.   [‡] Larger, floppy molecules might need to be optimized with a smaller basis set.

The general strategy embodied by this table is to select the most accurate calculation that is computationally practical for a given size system. Note that for the lower-cost methods, you will also need to add diffuse functions and/or additional polarization functions on the hydrogen atoms as appropriate for the systems you are studying.

All models include zero-point corrections via frequency calculations at the optimized geometry and using the same method. The ranges of applicability are approximate and represent what is "practical" as of this writing: we are assuming that the combined calculations must take less than a week of CPU time on a high-end workstation such as an IBM RS/6000 or DEC AlphaStation 600. Users with significantly greater or fewer CPU resources will need to adjust the applicability ranges and/or model chemistries accordingly.

The relative accuracies of various model chemistries are discussed in more detail in Chapter 7 (page 146). Resource requirements for various models and calculation types are discussed in Chapter 6 (page 122). Recommended models for NMR calculations were discussed earlier in this work (pages 21 and 53).

Selecting Methods for Zero-Point and Thermal Energies

Zero-point and thermal energy corrections are usually computed with the same model chemistry as the geometry optimization. However, you may also choose to follow the common practice of always using the HF/6-31G(d) model chemistry for predicting zero-point and thermal energies (see page 149). Of course, such frequency calculations must follow a HF/6-31G(d) geometry optimization.

Chapter

5

Basis Set Effects

In This Chapter:

Split Valence Basis Sets

Polarized Basis Sets

Diffuse Functions

Pseudopotentials

A basis set is the mathematical description of the orbitals within a system (which in turn combine to approximate the total electronic wavefunction) used to perform the theoretical calculation. Larger basis sets more accurately approximate the orbitals by imposing fewer restrictions on the locations of the electrons in space. In the true quantum mechanical picture, electrons have a finite probability of existing anywhere in space; this limit corresponds to the infinite basis set expansion in the chart we looked at previously.

Standard basis sets for electronic structure calculations use linear combinations of gaussian functions to form the orbitals. *Gaussian* offers a wide range of pre-defined basis sets, which may be classified by the number and types of *basis functions* that they contain. Basis sets assign a group of basis functions to each atom within a molecule to approximate its orbitals. These basis functions themselves are composed of a linear combination of gaussian functions; such basis functions are referred to as *contracted functions*, and the component gaussian functions are referred to as *primitives*. A basis function consisting of a single gaussian function is termed *uncontracted*. These concepts are illustrated in detail in Advanced Exercise 5.5.

Minimal Basis Sets

Minimal basis sets contain the minimum number of basis functions needed for each atom, as in these examples:

H: 1s
C: 1s, 2s, $2p_x$, $2p_y$, $2p_z$

Minimal basis sets use fixed-size atomic-type orbitals. The STO-3G basis set is a minimal basis set (although it is not the smallest possible basis set). It uses three gaussian primitives per basis function, which accounts for the "3G" in its name. "STO" stands for "Slater-type orbitals," and the STO-3G basis set approximates Slater orbitals with gaussian functions.[†]

[†] Slater orbitals have been demonstrated to be more accurate than a similar number of gaussian functions for molecular orbital computations, but they are not as mathematically convenient to use. This is why it is preferable to gaussian functions even if larger numbers of functions are required.

Split Valence Basis Sets

$$c_1 \, \text{(orbital)} + c_2 \, \text{(orbital)} = \text{(orbital)}$$

The first way that a basis set can be made larger is to increase the number of basis functions per atom. *Split valence basis sets*, such as 3-21G and 6-31G,[†] have two (or more) sizes of basis function for each valence orbital. For example, hydrogen and carbon are represented as:

H: 1s, 1s'
C: 1s, 2s, 2s', $2p_x$, $2p_y$, $2p_z$, $2p_x'$, $2p_y'$, $2p_z'$

where the primed and unprimed orbitals differ in size.

The *double zeta* basis sets, such as the Dunning-Huzinaga basis set (D95), form all molecular orbitals from linear combinations of two sizes of functions for each atomic orbital. Similarly, *triple split valence* basis sets, like 6-311G, use three sizes of contracted functions for each orbital-type.

Polarized Basis Sets

$$\text{(orbital)} + c \, \text{(orbital)} = \text{(orbital)}$$

Split valence basis sets allow orbitals to change size, but not to change shape. Polarized basis sets remove this limitation by adding orbitals with angular momentum beyond what is required for the ground state to the description of each atom. For example, polarized basis sets add d functions to carbon atoms and f functions to transition metals, and some of them add p functions to hydrogen atoms.

So far, the only polarized basis set we've used is 6-31G(d). Its name indicates that it is the 6-31G basis set with d functions added to heavy atoms. This basis set is becoming very common for calculations involving up to medium-sized systems. This basis set is also known as 6-31G*. Another popular polarized basis set is 6-31G(d,p), also known as 6-31G**, which adds p functions to hydrogen atoms in addition to the d functions on heavy atoms.

[†] For details on basis set nomenclature, consult the *Gaussian 94 User's Reference*.

To The Teacher: Basis Set Details

The concept of polarization is often a difficult one to introduce. Students will typically ask, "Why do you need to include d function on a first row atom like carbon?" A good analogy for explaining this is the hybridization of orbitals discussed in Valence Bond Theory. For example, sp^3 orbitals are formed on carbon by mixing filled 2s orbitals and partially-filled 2p orbitals. A natural extension to this is allowing some small contribution from unfilled 3d orbitals as well. Similarly, diffuse functions (discussed in the next section of this chapter) can be thought of as the mixing in of 3s orbitals.

d polarization functions can consist of the 6 Cartesian types, which have added s character to the 5 pure types, or they can be the actual 5 pure types themselves:

Cartesian: $d_{x^2}, d_{y^2}, d_{z^2}, d_{xy}, d_{xz}, d_{yz}$
Pure: $d_{z^2-r^2}, d_{x^2-y^2}, d_{xy}, d_{xz}, d_{yz}$

Each polarized basis set includes which type is used as part of its definition (this is illustrated in Advanced Exercise 5.5). You may want to discuss the differences between the two. You can specify the use of one or the other type explicitly by including the **5D** or **6D** keyword in the route section (the keywords **7F** and **10F** similarly apply to all higher angular momentum basis functions).

Diffuse Functions

Diffuse functions are large-size versions of s- and p-type functions (as opposed to the standard valence-size functions). They allow orbitals to occupy a larger region of space. Basis sets with diffuse functions are important for systems where electrons are relatively far from the nucleus: molecules with lone pairs, anions and other systems with significant negative charge, systems in their excited states, systems with low ionization potentials, descriptions of absolute acidities, and so on.

The 6-31+G(d) basis set is the 6-31G(d) basis set with diffuse functions added to heavy atoms. The double plus version, 6-31++G(d), adds diffuse functions to the hydrogen atoms as well. Diffuse functions on hydrogen atoms seldom make a significant difference in accuracy.

Example 5.1: Methanol vs. Methoxide Anion Optimizations

file: e5_01

We ran geometry optimizations of methanol (gauche form) and methoxide anion using both the 6-31G(d) and 6-31+G(d) basis sets in order to determine the effects of diffuse functions on the predicted structures. Here are the results:

Methanol	6-31G(d)	6-31+G(d)	Experiment
CO bond	1.3966	1.4019	1.427±0.007
CH bond	1.0873	1.0865	1.096±0.01
OH bond	0.9463	0.9464	0.956±0.015
COH angle	109.406	110.346	108.9±2.0
HCH angle	108.4127	108.6555	109.3±0.75
OCH angle	112.008	111.691	

Methoxide anion	6-31G(d)	6-31+G(d)	6-311++G(3df,2pd)
CO bond	1.3107	1.3304	1.3223
CH bond	1.1332	1.121	1.1209
HCH angle	101.5713	103.4298	103.2904
OCH angle	116.537	114.9919	115.1097

Diffuse functions have very little effect on the optimized structure of methanol but do significantly affect the bond angles in negatively charged methoxide anion. We can conclude that they are required to produce an accurate structure for the anion by comparing the two calculated geometries to that predicted by Hartree-Fock theory at a very large basis set (which should eliminate basis set effects).

High Angular Momentum Basis Sets

Even larger basis sets are now practical for many systems. Such basis sets add multiple polarization functions per atom to the triple zeta basis set. For example, the 6-31G(2d) basis set adds two d functions per heavy atom instead of just one, while the 6-311++G(3df,3pd) basis set contains three sets of valence region functions, diffuse functions on both heavy atoms and hydrogens, and multiple polarization functions: 3 d functions and 1 f function on heavy atoms and 3 p functions and 1 d function on hydrogen atoms. Such basis sets are useful for describing the interactions between electrons in electron correlation methods; they are not generally needed for Hartree-Fock calculations.

Some large basis sets specify different sets of polarization functions for heavy atoms depending upon the row of the periodic table in which they are located. For example, the 6-311+(3df,2df,p) basis set places 3 d functions and 1 f function on heavy atoms in the second and higher rows of the periodic table, and it places 2 d functions and 1 f function on first row heavy atoms and 1 p function on hydrogen atoms. Note that quantum chemists ignore H and He when numbering the rows of the periodic table.

Example 5.2: PO Bond Distance
file: e5_02

The optimized bond length in PO will serve to illustrate the effect of larger basis sets. Here are the predicted values for several medium and large basis sets (all optimizations were run at the B3LYP level of theory):

Basis Set	Bond Length (Å)
6-31G(d)	1.4986
6-311G(d)	1.4914
6-311G(2d)	1.4818
6-311G(2df)	1.4796
6-311G(3df)	1.4758

The experimental bond length is 1.476. Both the triple zeta basis set and multiple polarization functions are needed to produce a very accurate structure for this molecule.

Basis Sets for Post-Third-Row Atoms

Basis sets for atoms beyond the third row of the periodic table are handled somewhat differently. For these very large nuclei, electrons near the nucleus are treated in an approximate way, via effective core potentials (ECPs). This treatment includes some relativistic effects, which are important in these atoms. The LANL2DZ basis set is the best known of these.

The following table summarizes the most commonly-used basis sets and provides some recommendations as to when each is appropriate:

Some Recommended Standard Basis Sets

Basis Set [Applicable Atoms]	Description	# Basis Functions		Default Function Types[†]
		1st row atoms	hydrogen atoms	
STO-3G [H-Xe]	Minimal basis set (stripped down in the interest of performance): use for more qualitative results on very large systems when you cannot afford even 3-21G.	5	1	**6D**
3-21G [H-Xe]	Split valence: 2 sets of functions in the valence region provide a more accurate representation of orbitals. Use for very large molecules for which 6-31G(d) is too expensive.	9	2	**6D**
6-31G(d) 6-31G* [H-Cl]	Adds polarization functions to heavy atoms: use for most jobs on up to medium/large sized systems. (This basis set uses the 6-component type d functions.)	15	2	**6D 7F**
6-31G(d,p) 6-31G** [H-Cl]	Adds polarization functions to the hydrogens as well: use when the hydrogens are the site of interest (for example, bond energies) and for final, accurate energy calculations	15	5	**6D 7F**
6-31+G(d) [H-Cl]	Adds diffuse functions: important for systems with lone pairs, anions, excited states.	19	2	**6D 7F**
6-31+G(d,p) [H-Cl]	Adds p functions to hydrogens as well: use when you'd use 6-31G(d,p) and diffuse functions are needed.	19	5	**6D 7F**
6-311+G(d,p) [H-Br]	Triple zeta: adds extra valence functions (3 sizes of s and p functions) to 6-31+G(d). Diffuse functions can also be added to the hydrogen atoms via a second +.	22	6	**5D 7F**
6-311+G(2d,p) [H-Br]	Puts 2 d functions on heavy atoms (plus diffuse functions), and 1 p function on hydrogens.	27	6	**5D 7F**
6-311+G(2df,2p) [H-Br]	Puts 2 d functions and 1 f function on heavy atoms (plus diffuse functions), and 2 p functions on the hydrogen atoms.	34	9	**5D 7F**
6-311++G(3df,2pd) [H-Br]	Puts 3 d functions and 1 f function on heavy atoms, and 2p functions and 1 d function on hydrogens, as well as diffuse functions on both.	39	15	**5D 7F**

[†] **6D** denotes Cartesian, 6-component d functions, **5D** and **7F** denote "pure," 5-component d functions and 7-component f functions, respectively.

Exercises

Exercise 5.1: HF Bond Length

file: **5_01**

The experimental bond length for the hydrogen fluoride molecule is 0.917Å. Determine the basis set required to predict this structure accurately. Perform your optimizations at the MP4 level of theory (electron correlation is known to be important for this system).

Solution

Here are the predicted values for several medium and large basis sets:

Basis Set	Bond Length (Å)
6-31G(d)	0.93497
6-31G(d,p)	0.92099
6-31+G(d,p)	0.94208
6-31++G(d,p)	0.92643
6-311G(d,p)	0.91312
6-311++G(d,p)	0.91720
6-311G(3df,3pd)	0.91369
6-311++G(3df,3pd)	0.91739

The values in red are within 0.01Å of the experimental value. Using the 6-31G basis set, including diffuse functions on the hydrogen atom, improves the result over that obtained with diffuse functions only on the fluorine atom, although the best result with this basis set is obtained with no diffuse functions at all.

All of the geometries predicted with the 6-311G basis set are quite accurate. Adding two sets of diffuse functions yields a more accurate structure. However, adding additional polarization functions does not significantly affect the results. 6-311++G(d,p) thus appears to achieve the basis set limit for this model chemistry. ■

Exercise 5.2: Periodic Trends in Transition Metal Complexes

file: **5_02**

In Chapter 3, we optimized the structure of chromium hexacarbonyl using two different basis sets. Now we will investigate the structures of $M(CO)_6$, where M is chromium, molybdenum and tungsten.

Optimize these three molecules at the Hartree-Fock level, using the LANL2DZ basis set. LANL2DZ is a double-zeta basis set containing effective core potential (ECP) representations of electrons near the nuclei for post-third row atoms. Compare the $Cr(CO)_6$ results with those we obtained in Chapter 3. Then compare the structures of the three systems to one another, and characterize the effect of changing the central atom on the overall molecular structure.

Solution

The $Cr(CO)_6$ geometry computed with the LANL2DZ basis set is very similar to the 3-21G geometry we obtained previously, and accordingly both produce good agreement with experiment.

Here are the results for the three compounds:

M	M-C bond (Å)	C-O bond (Å)	M-C-O (º)	C-M-C (º)
Cr	1.979	1.141	180	90, 180
Mo	2.105	1.143	180	90, 180
W	2.077	1.145	180	90, 180

All three structures have O_h symmetry and are very similar. The bond length from the central atom to the carbonyl group is slightly different in each compound, and it is longest for the molybdenum substituent. The internal structure of the carbonyl groups is essentially unchanged by substitution. ■

Advanced Exercise 5.3: Basis Set Effects on NMR Calculations (Benzene)

files: **5_03a** **(C_6H_6)**
      5_03b **(TMS)**

In Exercise 3.5, we predicted the NMR properties of benzene and calculated the relative shift for the carbon atom with respect to TMS. In this exercise, we will compare those results with ones computed using other basis sets.

Determine the effect of basis set on the predicted chemical shifts for benzene. Compute the NMR properties for both compounds at the B3LYP/6-31G(d) geometries we computed previously. Use the HF method for your NMR calculations, with whatever form(s) of the 6-31G basis set you deem appropriate. Compare your results to those of the HF/6-311+G(2d,p) job we ran in the earlier exercise. How does the basis set effect the accuracy of the computed ^{13}C chemical shift for benzene?

Solution   Here are the results of the various NMR calculations:

Model	Absolute Shielding Value		Relative Shift
	TMS	Benzene	
HF/6-31G(d) // B3LYP/6-31G(d)	195.120	72.643	122.5
HF/6-31G(d,p) // B3LYP/6-31G(d)	196.625	72.913	123.7
HF/6-31+G(d,p) // B3LYP/6-31G(d)	196.064	72.494	123.6
HF/6-31++G(d,p) // B3LYP/6-31G(d)	197.138	72.744	124.4
HF/6-311+G(2d,p) // B3LYP/6-31G(d)	188.788	57.620	131.2

Recall that the observed chemical shift is 130.9. For the B3LYP geometry, all of the computations using the 6-31G(d) basis set—however augmented—are substantially less accurate than the one using the 6-311+G(2d,p) basis set. ■

Advanced Exercise 5.4: Geometry of N,N-Dimethylformamide

file: 5_04

This exercise examines the effect of basis set on the computed equilibrium structure of N,N-Dimethylformamide.

Optimize the geometry of this system at the Hartree-Fock level, using the STO-3G minimal basis set and the 6-31G(d) basis set (augmented as appropriate). Run a frequency calculation following each optimization in order to confirm that you have found an equilibrium structure.

One important structural feature on which to focus is whether the nitrogen atom lies in the same plane as the three carbon atoms. Electron diffraction experiments have found the ground state to be slightly non-planar. You can determine the planarity of the structures you compute by examining the sum of the three C-N-C angles (for a planar molecule, the sum will be 360°) and by looking at the values of the C_2-N-C_4-O and C_3-N-C_4-H_6 dihedral angles (in a planar structure, both will be 0°).

Solution   Here are the results for the three jobs we ran:

Parameter	STO-3G	6-31G(d)	6-31++G(d,p)	Experiment
$R(O-C_4)$	1.218	1.197	1.200	1.224±.003
$R(C_4-N)$	1.410	1.349	1.356	1.391±.006
$R(C_3-N)$	1.463	1.442	1.444	1.453±.004
$R(C_2-N)$	1.465	1.446	1.448	1.453±.004
$R(O-H_6)$	2.054	1.996	1.998	2.4±.03

Parameter	STO-3G	6-31G(d)	6-31++G(d,p)	Experiment
A(N-C$_4$-H$_6$)	111.40	112.52	112.79	117.0±2.8
A(O-C$_4$-N)	124.36	125.94	125.91	123.5±0.6
A(O-C$_4$-H$_6$)	124.25	121.54	121.30	119.5±3.4
A(C$_4$-N-C$_2$)	119.90	120.61	120.83	120.8±0.3
A(C$_4$-N-C$_3$)	121.78	121.97	121.80	122.3±0.4
A(C$_2$-N-C$_3$)	118.32	117.43	117.36	113.9±0.5
Σ A(C-N-C)	360.00	360.01	359.99	357.0±1.2
D(C$_3$-N-C$_4$-H$_6$)	0.21	0.13	0.11	11±4
D(C$_2$-N-C$_4$-O)	-0.10	-0.05	-0.05	16±5
# Imaginary frequencies	1	0	0	
Is ground state planar?	no	yes	yes	no

All three optimizations result in very similar planar structures. The bond lengths are all in fairly good agreement with experiment with the exception of the O-H distance. The bond angle predictions are more erratic: some are reasonable while others have errors of several degrees. The dihedral angles are both predicted to be essentially zero in all three cases, consistent with a planar structure.

When we examine the frequency jobs, however, we see an important difference between the STO-3G job and the other two. The former finds one imaginary structure, indicating that the optimized structure is a transition structure not a minimum. When we examine the normal mode corresponding to the imaginary frequency, its motion involves moving the nitrogen atom out of the plane of the three carbon atoms, strongly suggesting that the ground state is slightly non-planar.

In contrast, the other two frequency calculations determine the corresponding optimized structure to be a minimum.

With these results, we see an example of a phenomenon that occurs from time to time: a less accurate model chemistry will produce a better answer than more accurate ones. In our case, fortuitous cancellation of errors at the HF/STO-3G levels leads to the correct identification of the planar conformation as a transition state. However, a more accurate model chemistry is needed to properly study this system. ∎

Advanced Exercise 5.5: Basis Set Definitions

file: 5_05

In this exercise, we examine how a basis set is defined in more detail.

Gaussian and other ab initio electronic structure programs use gaussian-type atomic functions as basis functions. Gaussian functions have the general form:

$$g(\alpha, \vec{r}) = cx^n y^m z^l e^{-\alpha r^2}$$

In this equation, α is a constant determining the size (radial extent) of the function. The exponential function is multiplied by powers (possibly 0) of x, y, and z, and a constant for normalization so that the integral of g^2 over all space is 1 (note that therefore c must also be a function of α).

The actual basis functions are formed as linear combinations of such primitive gaussians:

$$\chi_\mu = \sum_p d_{\mu p} g_p$$

where the coefficients $d_{\mu p}$'s are fixed constants within a given basis set.

Run a single-point energy calculation on methanol using the HF/6-31++G(d,p) model chemistry, including the **GFPrint** and **GFInput** keywords in the route section which request that the basis set information be included in the output file (in tabular and input format, respectively). Examine the basis set output and identify its main components.

Solution

The **GFPrint** output is best viewed on a terminal capable of supporting 132 columns. Here is the output for the carbon atom, divided in half horizontally and reformatted somewhat for reasons of space and clarity. Here is the left half of the table:

```
*************************************************************************
*            ATOMIC CENTER            *        ATOMIC ORBITAL
*************************************************************************
*                                     * FUNCTION    SHELL      SCALE
*   ATOM   X-COORD   Y-COORD  Z-COORD  * NUMBER      TYPE      FACTOR
*************************************************************************
*    C    -0.08715   1.23644  0.00000        1         S        1.00
*                                          2-  5       SP        1.00
*                                          6-  9       SP        1.00
*                                         10- 13       SP        1.00
*                                         14- 19       D         1.00
*-----------------------------------------------------------------------
```

This part of the table lists type and coordinates for the atom in question, along with the orbital type and orbital scaling factor for each basis function on this atom. Here we have a carbon atom described by 19 basis functions.

Details about the composition of each basis function are given in the right half of the table (we've included the function number column shown previously and eliminated zero-value entries):

```
**************************************************************************
          *          GAUSSIAN FUNCTIONS                                 *
**************************************************************************
 FUNCTION *                                                             *
  NUMBER  * EXPONENT      S-COEF        P-COEF        D-COEF      F-COEF *
**************************************************************************
       1  * 0.304752D+04 0.183474D-02                                   *
          * 0.457370D+03 0.140373D-01                                   *
          * 0.103949D+03 0.688426D-01                                   *
          * 0.292102D+02 0.232184D+00                                   *
          * 0.928666D+01 0.467941D+00                                   *
          * 0.316393D+01 0.362312D+00                                   *
   2-  5  * 0.786827D+01 -.119332D+00  0.689991D-01                     *
          * 0.188129D+01 -.160854D+00  0.316424D+00                     *
          * 0.544249D+00 0.114346D+01  0.744308D+00                     *
   6-  9  * 0.168714D+00 0.100000D+01  0.100000D+01                     *
  10- 13  * 0.438000D-01 0.100000D+01  0.100000D+01                     *
  14- 19  * 0.800000D+00                             0.100000D+01       *
----------------------------------------------------------------------- *
```

The columns to the right of the first vertical line of asterisks hold the exponents (α above) and the coefficients (the $d_{\mu p}$'s) for each primitive gaussian. For example, basis function 1, an s function, is a linear combination of six primitives, constructed with the exponents and coefficients (the latter are in the column labeled "S-COEF") listed in the table. Basis function 2 is another s function, comprised of three primitives using the exponents and S-COEF coefficients from the section of the table corresponding to functions 2-5. Basis function 3 is a p_x function also made up of three primitives constructed from the exponents and P-COEF coefficients in the same section of the table:

$$p_x \approx 0.07g_x(7.9, \vec{r}) + 0.32g_x(1.9, \vec{r}) + 0.74g_x(0.5, \vec{r})$$

The function $g_x(\alpha, \vec{r})$ is of the form $cxe^{-\alpha r^2}$ where c is a normalization constant also depending on α.

Basis functions 4 and 5 are p_y and p_z functions constructed in the same manner using the same exponents and coefficients.

Functions 6 through 9 are another set of uncontracted s and p functions, each composed of a single primitive, formed in the same way as functions 5 through 9.

Note that functions 1 through 9 form the heart of the 6-31G basis set: three sets of functions formed from six, three and one primitive gaussian.

Functions 10 through 13 comprise the diffuse s function (note the small value for the exponent α, which will fall off to zero at a much greater distance than the earlier gaussian functions). Functions 14 through 19 are d functions. This basis set uses six-component d functions: d_{x^2}, d_{y^2}, d_{z^2}, d_{xy}, d_{xz}, d_{yz}. They are constructed using the exponent and D-COEF coefficient from the final section of the preceding table.

Typically, the contracted functions themselves are also normalized.[†] This has two consequences:

✦ The coefficients specified for the component primitive gaussians are chosen so that the resulting constructed basis functions are normalized. This means that one coefficient in each set is effectively constrained so that this condition is fulfilled.

✦ The coefficients for uncontracted basis functions—consisting of only a single primitive—are usually 1.0. This is the case for functions 6 through 19 in the 6-31++G(d,p) example we have been examining.

The **GFInput** output gives exactly the same information in the format required for *Gaussian* general basis set input (see the discussion of the **Gen** keyword in the *Gaussian User's Reference* for more information). ■

Advanced Exercise 5.6: Comparing 6-31G(d) and 6-31G†

file: 5_06

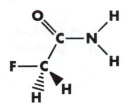

The 6-31G† basis set is defined as part of the Complete Basis Set model chemistry (described in detail in Chapter 7). This basis set attempts to remedy some deficiencies in the standard 6-31G(d) basis set.

Compare these two basis sets and note the differences between them for carbon, nitrogen, oxygen and fluorine (you can use **GFPrint** or **GFInput** with a system containing these elements; one example, fluoroacetamide, is illustrated at the left). What would you expect to be the advantages of the changes that you see?

[†] *Gaussian* will automatically scale input basis functions so that they are normalized.

Solution   The two basis sets differ in the value of the exponent on the d functions for these elements:

Basis Set	Exponent			
	C	N	O	F
6-31G(d)	0.8	0.8	0.8	0.8
6-31G†	0.626	0.913	1.292	1.75

6-31G(d) arbitrarily assigns an exponent of 0.8 to all four elements. The dagger basis set uses the exponents from the d functions in the 6-311G basis set (you can run an additional job to verify this), which have been individually optimized for each element.

The larger exponent on nitrogen, oxygen and fluorine has the effect of making the resulting valence function tighter in extent (it falls off more quickly as you move away from the nucleus). The arbitrary 0.8 value results in an orbital that is too diffuse for these elements, falling outside of the valence region at times. As the value indicates, this is especially true for fluorine. In fact, the 6-31G(d) basis set (and its variations) is known to have difficulties with some fluorine-containing compounds. You should keep this in mind when modeling such molecular systems. ■

References

Basis Set Concepts and Definitions   A. Szabo and N. S. Ostlund, *Modern Quantum Chemistry* (New York: Macmillan, 1982), §3.6, pp. 180-190.

N,N-Dimethylformamide   G. Schultz and I. Hargittai, *J. Chem. Phys.*, **97**, 4966 (1993).

NMR Calculations   J. R. Cheeseman, G. W. Trucks, T. A. Keith and M. J. Frisch, "A Comparison of Models for Calculating Nuclear Magnetic Resonance Shielding Tensors," *J. Chem. Phys.*, **104**, 5497 (1996).

6-31G† and 6-31G†† Basis Sets   G. A. Petersson, A. Bennett, T. G. Tensfeldt, M. A. Al-Laham, W. A. Shirley and J. Mantzaris, *J. Chem. Phys.*, **89**, 2193 (1988).

G. A. Petersson and M. A. Al-Laham, *J.Chem. Phys.*, **94**, 6081 (1991).

Selecting an Appropriate Theoretical Method

In this chapter, we will consider the other half of a model chemistry definition: the theoretical method used to model the molecular system. This chapter will serve as an introductory survey of the major classes of electronic structure calculations. The examples and exercises will compare the strengths and weaknesses of various specific methods in more detail. The final section of the chapter considers the CPU, memory and disk resource requirements of the various methods.

We will complete our consideration of model chemistries in Chapter 7, which describes compound methods for computing very accurate energies. It also includes a section discussing the relative accuracies of various model chemistries, as measured by their performance on the G2 set of test computations (see page 146).

Using Semi-Empirical Methods

Semi-empirical methods are characterized by their use of parameters derived from experimental data in order to simplify the approximation to the Schrödinger equation. As such, they are relatively inexpensive and can be practically applied to very, very large molecules. There are a variety of semi-empirical methods. Among the best known are AM1, PM3 and MNDO. *Gaussian* includes a variety of semi-empirical models, and they are also the central focus or present in many other programs including AMPAC, MOPAC, HyperChem and Spartan.

Semi-empirical methods are appropriate for a variety of modeling tasks, including the following:

◆ For very large systems for which they are the only computationally practical quantum mechanical methods.

◆ As a first step for large systems. For example, you might run a semi-empirical optimization on a large system to obtain a starting structure for a subsequent Hartree-Fock or Density Functional Theory optimization. We used this approach in Exercise 3.6.

◆ For ground state molecular systems for which the semi-empirical method is well-parametrized and well-calibrated. In general, semi-empirical methods have been developed to focus on simple organic molecules.

◆ To obtain qualitative information about a molecule, such as its molecular orbitals, atomic charges or vibrational normal modes. In some cases, semi-empirical methods may also be successfully used to predict energy trends arising from alternate conformations or substituent effects in a qualitative or semi-quantitative way (but care must be taken in this area).

Example 6.1: TPP Molecular Orbitals

file: e6_01

We will perform an AM1 calculation on tetraphenylporphin (TPP), pictured at right, in order to examine the four important molecular orbitals for this molecule: the second-highest and highest occupied MO's and the lowest and second-lowest unoccupied MO's (which we denote HOMO-1, HOMO, LUMO and LUMO+1, respectively).

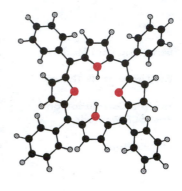

The orbitals we are interested in are the ones numbered 112 through 115, which are plotted below:

| HOMO–1 | HOMO | LUMO | LUMO+1 |

We can make the following comments about these orbitals

◆ The HOMO-1 is localized on the central rings and has no contribution from the phenyl rings. There are nodal planes running perpendicular to the viewing plane every 45 degrees. There is another nodal plane that is the molecular plane.

◆ The HOMO is quite delocalized and has contributions from the phenyl rings. Nitrogen p orbitals figure prominately at the center of this orbital, and these all in phase with one another (the positive lobes all line up).

◆ The LUMO is similar to the HOMO, but the lobes do not align. This appears more like an anti-bonding orbital.

◆ The LUMO+1 is very similar to the LUMO rotated by 90 degrees.

While orbitals may be useful for qualitative understanding of some molecules, it is important to remember that they are merely mathematical functions that represent solutions to the Hartree-Fock equations for a given molecule. Other orbitals exist which will produce the same energy and properties and which may look quite different. *There is ultimately no physical reality which can be associated with these images.* In short, individual orbitals are mathematical not physical constructs.

Limitations of Semi-Empirical Methods

Semi-empirical methods may only be used for systems where parameters have been developed for all of their component atoms. In addition to this, semi-empirical models have a number of well-known limitations. Types of problems on which they do not perform well include hydrogen bonding, transition structures, molecules containing atoms for which they are poorly parametrized, and so on. We consider one such case in the following example, and the exercises will discuss others.

Example 6.2: HF Dimer

file: e6_02

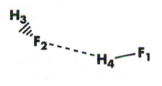

Here, we optimize the structure of the HF⋯HF complex. The following table lists the results for our AM1, PM3[†] and HF/6-31+G(d) optimizations as well as an MP2/6-311++G(2d,2p) tight-convergence optimization taken from the Gaussian Quantum Chemistry Archive:

Parameter	AM1	PM3	HF	MP2
$R(H\text{-}F)$	0.83	0.94	0.92	0.92
$R(H_4\text{-}F_2)$	2.09	1.74	1.88	1.84
$R(F\text{-}F)$	2.87	2.65	2.79	2.76
$A(F\text{-}H_4\text{-}F)$	159.3	159.8	168.3	170.6
$A(H_3\text{-}F\text{-}F)$	143.8	143.1	117.7	111.8

Both semi-empirical structures are quite far from the high-level results, especially with respect to the bond angles, although the AM1 bond lengths are also distorted. In contrast, the Hartree-Fock geometry is in reasonable agreement with the MP2 structure. Note that the Hartree-Fock optimization starting from the PM3 structure took 20 steps to converge (illustrating that semi-empirical structures are not always a good starting point for Hartree-Fock optimizations).

[†] Basis set keywords are not used for semi-empirical methods as they are inherent in the method's definition.

Electron Correlation and Post-SCF Methods

As we have seen throughout this book, the Hartree-Fock method provides a reasonable model for a wide range of problems and molecular systems. However, Hartree-Fock theory also has limitations. They arise principally from the fact that Hartree-Fock theory does not include a full treatment of the effects of *electron correlation*: the energy contributions arising from electrons interacting with one another. For systems and situations where such effects are important, Hartree-Fock results may not be satisfactory. The theory and methodology underlying electron correlation is discussed in Appendix A.

A variety of theoretical methods have been developed which include some effects of electron correlation. Traditionally, such methods are referred to as *post-SCF methods* because they add correlation corrections to the basic Hartree-Fock model. As of this writing, there are many correlation methods available in *Gaussian*, including the following:[†]

+ Møller-Plesset perturbation theory: energies through fifth-order (accessed via the keywords **MP2**, **MP3**, **MP4**, and **MP5**), optimizations via analytic gradients[‡] for second-order (**MP2**), third-order (**MP3**) and fourth-order (without triples: **MP4SDQ**), and analytic frequencies for second-order (**MP2**).

+ Quadratic CI energies, optionally including triples and quadruples terms (**QCISD**, **QCISD(T)**, and **QCISD(TQ)**) and optimizations via analytic gradients for **QCISD**.

+ Coupled Cluster methods, including doubles (energies and optimizations) or singles and doubles (energies only), and optional triples terms (**CCD**, **CCSD**, **CCSD(T)**).

+ Brueckner Doubles energies, optionally including triples and quadruples (**BD**, **BD(T)**, **BD(TQ)**).

All of these methods provide some improvement in the accurate description of molecules, but they vary quite a bit in terms of computational cost.

Methods based on Density Functional Theory also include some electron correlation effects (we'll consider them a bit later in this chapter). Of the traditional post-SCF methods, we'll be primarily using **MP2**, **MP4**, **QCISD** and **QCISD(T)** in this work.

[†] Consult the current *Gaussian User's Reference* for up-to-date information on method availability.

[‡] Numerical optimizations are available for methods lacking analytic gradients (first derivatives of the energy), but they are much, much slower. Similarly, frequencies may be computed numerically for methods without analytic second derivatives.

The Limits of Hartree-Fock Theory

Hartree-Fock theory is very useful for providing initial, first-level predictions for many systems. It is also reasonably good at computing the structures and vibrational frequencies of stable molecules and some transition states. As such, it is a good base-level theory. However, its neglect of electron correlation makes it unsuitable for some purposes. For example, it is insufficient for accurate modeling of the energetics of reactions and bond dissociation.

Example 6.3: HF Bond Energy

file: e6_03

There are many systems where electron correlation is essential for accurate predictions. One of the simplest is hydrogen fluoride, whose bond length we examined earlier. We calculate the bond energy by computing the energies of hydrogen and fluorine and then subtracting their sum from the energy of HF; this difference in energy must be accounted for by the H-F bond, which is present in the product but not in the reactants.

The following table lists the predicted bond energy of hydrogen fluoride computed with various methods using the 6-311++G(3df,3pd) basis set. We chose this basis set because it is near the basis set limit for this problem[†]; errors that remain can be assumed to arise from the method itself and not from the basis set.

| Method | Computed Energy | | | ΔE^{bond} |
	H atom	F atom	HF	kcal/mol
HF/STO-3G	-0.46658	-97.98651	-98.57082	73.9
HF	-0.49979	-99.40181	-100.05761	97.9
MP2		-99.60212	-100.33282	144.9
MP3		-99.61313	-100.33184	137.9
MP4(SDTQ)		-99.61731	-100.34306	141.8
QCISD		-99.61388	-100.33488	138.8
QCISD(T)		-99.61780	-100.34166	140.6
Experiment				141.2

We can compute all of the results except those in the first row by running just three jobs: **QCISD(T,E4T)** calculations on HF and fluorine and a Hartree-Fock calculation on hydrogen (with only one electron, the electron correlation energy is zero). Note that the **E4T** option to the **QCISD(T)** keyword requests that the triples computation be included in the component MP4 calculation as well as in the QCISD calculation (they are not needed or computed by default).

[†] We do not recommend using this basis set as a matter of course unless you have opulent CPU resources.

The experimental value for the H-F bond energy is 141.2 kcal-mol^{-1}. The Hartree-Fock value is in error by over 40 kcal-mol^{-1} (we've also included the HF/STO-3G values to indicate just how bad very low level calculations can be). However, both the MP4 and QCISD(T) values are in excellent agreement with experiment.

The computed MP2 bond energy is too large, with higher levels of correlation lowering it. MP2 often overcorrects the Hartree-Fock results, while higher levels of correlation return to the proper range. For this particular system, both a high level of theory and a large basis set are needed for accurate predictions.

The MP*n* Methods

Prior to the widespread usage of methods based on Density Functional Theory, the MP2 method was one of the least expensive ways to improve on Hartree-Fock and it was thus often the first correlation method to be applied to new problems. It can successfully model a wide variety of systems, and MP2 geometries are usually quite accurate. Thus, MP2 remains a very useful tool in a computational chemist's toolbox. We'll see several examples of its utility in the exercises.

There are problems for which MP2 theory fails as well, however. In general, the more unusual the electronic structure a system has, the higher level of theory that will be needed to model it accurately.

Higher-level MP orders are available for cases where the second-order solution of MP2 is inadequate. In practice, however, only MP4 sees wide use: MP3 is usually not sufficient to handle cases where MP2 does poorly, and it seldom offers improvements over MP2 which are commensurate with its additional computational cost. In contrast, although significantly more expensive that MP2, MP4 does successfully address many problems which MP2 cannot handle. We will examine some examples in the exercises.

For reasons similar to those for MP3, as well as its substantial computational cost, MP5 is also a rarely-used method.

Example: Convergence of the Møller-Plesset Orders

Nobes, Pople, Radom, Handy and Knowles have studied the convergence of the Møller-Plesset orders in some detail. They computed the energies of hydrogen cyanide, cyanide anion and cyano radical through order 24 as well as at the full Configuration Interaction level. Here are some of their results:

Method	HCN	CN⁻	CN
MP2	-91.82033	-91.07143	-91.11411
MP3	-91.82242	-91.06862	-91.12203
MP4	-91.82846	-91.07603	-91.13538
MP5	-91.83129	-91.07539	-91.14221
MP6	-91.83233	-91.07694	-91.14855
MP7	-91.83264	-91.07678	-91.15276
MP8	-91.83289	-91.07699	-91.15666
Full CI	-91.83317	-91.07706	-91.17006
$\Delta E < 0.001$ at	MP6	MP6	MP19
Full CI – MP4 (kcal-mol^{-1})	-2.96	-0.65	-21.76

These computations were performed using the STO-3G basis set for practicality reasons. While the absolute energies may be poor due to using such a small basis set, the trends across methods remain valid. For both HCN and CN⁻, the MP series converges fairly rapidly; we have noted the points at which the energy is within 0.001 Hartrees of the full CI value. However, for the CN radical, the same level of convergence is not achieved until MP19. This is a consequence of severe spin contamination in the Hartree-Fock reference determinant. We see the same effect in the difference between the full CI and MP4 results (the highest order which is practical for most systems). It is about 3 kcal-mol^{-1} for HCN and less than 1 kcal-mol^{-1} for the anion, but is over 21 kcal-mol^{-1} for CN.

Coupled Cluster and Quadratic Configuration Interaction Methods

The Coupled Cluster and QCI methods represent a higher-level treatment of electron correlation beyond MP4, usually providing even greater accuracy. Moreover, there are systems for which the Møller-Plesset orders converge rather slowly that these methods can successfully model. Coupled Cluster and QCI methods are very similar to one another. Both iteratively include the effects of single and double substitutions, effectively adding higher order terms than MP4, and can optionally include triples and quadruples. As of this writing, *Gaussian* includes its implementations of these methods via the **CCSD, CCSD(T), QCISD, QCISD(T)** and **QCISD(TQ)** keywords. We will be using the QCISD and QCISD(T) methods in this chapter.

Including triply excited configurations is often needed in order to obtain very accurate results with MP4, QCISD or CCSD (see Appendix A for some of the computational details). The following example illustrates this effect.

Example 6.4: Optimization of Ozone

file: e6_04

The structure of ozone is a well-known "pathological case" for electronic structure theory. Prior to the QCI and coupled cluster methods, it proved very difficult to model accurately. The following table summarized the results of geometry optimizations of ozone, performed at the MP2, QCISD and QCISD(T) levels using the 6-31G(d) basis set:

Parameter	MP2	QCISD	QCISD(T)	Experiment
R(O-O)	1.307	1.311	1.298	1.272
A(O-O-O)	113.2	114.6	116.7	116.8

When we speak of "accurate" geometries, we generally refer to bond lengths that are within about 0.01-0.02Å of experiment and bond and dihedral angles that are within about 1-2° of the experimentally-measured value (with the lower end of both ranges being more desirable). Only the QCISD(T) geometry can be termed accurate in the case of ozone (and its bond length is still a bit too long).

Density Functional Theory Methods

In the last few years, methods based on Density Functional Theory have gained steadily in popularity. The best DFT methods achieve significantly greater accuracy than Hartree-Fock theory at only a modest increase in cost (far less than MP2 for medium-size and larger molecular systems). They do so by including some of the effects of electron correlation much less expensively than traditional correlated methods.

DFT methods compute electron correlation via general *functionals*[†] of the electron density (see Appendix A for details). DFT functionals partition the electronic energy into several components which are computed separately: the kinetic energy, the electron-nuclear interaction, the Coulomb repulsion, and an exchange-correlation term accounting for the remainder of the electron-electron interaction (which is itself

---

[†] A *functional* is defined in mathematics as a function of a function. In Density Functional Theory, functionals are functions of the electron density (itself a function of coordinates in real space).

divided into separate exchange and correlation components in most actual DFT fomulations).

Traditional Functionals

A variety of functionals have been defined, generally distinguished by the way that they treat the exchange and correlation components:

- ✦ *Local* exchange and correlation functionals involve only the values of the electron spin densities. Slater and Xα are well-known local exchange functionals, and the local spin density treatment of Vosko, Wilk and Nusair (VWN) is a widely-used local correlation functional.

- ✦ *Gradient-corrected* functionals involve both the values of the electron spin densities and their gradients. Such functionals are also sometimes referred to as *non-local* in the literature. A popular gradient-corrected exchange functional is one proposed by Becke in 1988; a widely-used gradient-corrected correlation functional is the LYP functional of Lee, Yang and Parr. The combination of the two forms the B-LYP method (available via the **BLYP** keyword in *Gaussian*). Perdew has also proposed some important gradient-corrected correlation functionals, known as Perdew 86 and Perdew-Wang 91.

Hybrid Functionals

There are also several *hybrid functionals*, which define the exchange functional as a linear combination of Hartree-Fock, local, and gradient-corrected exchange terms; this exchange functional is then combined with a local and/or gradient-corrected correlation functional. The best known of these hybrid functionals is Becke's three-parameter formulation; hybrid functionals based on it are available in *Gaussian* via the **B3LYP** and **B3PW91** keywords. Becke-style hybrid functionals have proven to be superior to the traditional functionals defined so far, as the next example illustrates.

Example 6.5: CO$_2$ Structure and Atomization Energy

files: **e6_05a** (HF)
　　　e6_05b (SVWN)
　　　e6_05c (SVWN5)
　　　e6_05d (BLYP)
　　　e6_05e (B3LYP)
　　　e6_05f (B3PW91)
　　　e6_05g (MP2)

Atomization energies are often difficult to model accurately, and Hartree-Fock theory is seldom adequate. We will calculate the total atomization energy for carbon dioxide using a variety of DFT functionals by optimizing the structure of CO$_2$, performing a frequency calculation at the optimized structure in order to compute the zero-point energy, and then performing single point energy calculations for the carbon and oxygen atoms using tight SCF convergence (specified via **SCF=Tight**). The total atomization energy is then given by the formula: $D_0 = (E^C + 2E^O) - (E^{CO_2} + ZPE)$.

All jobs were run using the 6-31G(d) basis set. Our results are summarized in the following table, which also presents HF and MP2 values for comparison:

| Method | Carbon Dioxide | | | Carbon | Oxygen | D_0 | Δ(Exp) |
	R(C-O)	E	ZPE	E	E	(kcal-mol^{-1})	
HF	1.143	-187.63418	0.0114	-37.68086	-74.78393	234.7	147.2
SVWN	1.171	-187.61677	0.0116	-37.56616	-74.64334	472.1	-90.2
SVWN5	1.172	-187.18193	0.0116	-37.45370	-74.48842	464.2	-82.3
BLYP	1.183	-188.56306	0.0112	-37.83202	-75.04696	392.8	-10.9
B3LYP	1.169	-188.58094	0.0114	-37.84628	-75.06062	377.8	4.1
B3PW91	1.168	-188.50695	0.0115	-37.82569	-75.03133	381.0	0.9
MP2	1.180	-188.10775	0.0111	-37.73297	-74.88004	378.8	3.1
Exp.	1.162					381.9	

The carbon dioxide zero-point energies in the table are scaled, using the scaling factors listed on page 64.[†]

All of the predicted structures are at least reasonably good. The two hybrid functionals produce the best structures, in excellent agreement with the experimental geometry. The SVWN and SVWN5[‡] functionals both produce good structures, while the BLYP geometry is the least accurate.

When we consider the predicted atomization energy, however, we see vast differences among the functionals. Like Hartree-Fock theory, the SVWN and SVWN5 functionals are completely inadequate for predicting this system's atomization energy (which is not an atypical result). The BLYP value is also quite poor.

Only the values computed by the hybrid functionals and MP2 are at all reasonable, and the B3PW91 value is in excellent agreement with experimental observations. The MP2 and B3LYP values are only modestly outside of the desired accuracy of 2 kcal-mol^{-1}. In Chapter 7, we will consider methods which were developed to consistently produce such very accurate thermochemical results.

[†] We've somewhat arbitrarily used the SVWN scale factor for SVWN5 and the B3LYP scale factor for B3PW91, since no one has computed scale factors for those functionals as of this writing.

[‡] These two functionals differ in the form of the VWN correlation functional that they use. References in the literature to the LSDA functional usually refer to SVWN5, but some earlier references meant SVWN by LSDA. *Gaussian*'s **LSDA** keyword is a synonym for **SVWN**. However, other DFT programs refer to what *Gaussian* calls SVWN5 as LSDA. Check program documentation carefully when making comparisons of various "LSDA" functionals. For these reasons, we do not use the term LSDA at all.

Example 6.6: F_3^- Structure and Frequencies
file: e6_06

As a second example, we'll consider the structure and frequencies of the F_3^- anion. Tozer and Sosa studied this molecule at a variety of levels of theory, using the LANL2DZ basis set augmented with polarization and diffuse functions. We ran **Opt Freq** jobs using the SVWN5, BLYP and B3LYP functionals using the **D95V+(d)** basis set for all jobs (which is essentially the same basis set as that used by the original researchers). The following table summarizes the results of these calculations, as well as Tozer and Sosa's HF and MP2 results:

| Method | R | Frequencies | | |
		ω_1 Symm. Str.	ω_2 Bend	ω_3 Asymm. Str.
HF	1.646	501	315	522i
SVWN5	1.706	448	278	524
BLYP	1.777	390	255	477
B3LYP	1.728	425	268	441
MP2	1.733	392	251	699
Experiment		440 ± 10	260 ± 10	535 ± 20

All frequencies are scaled using the scaling factors listed in Chapter 4 (page 64).

The DFT and MP2 calculations produce very similar structures, although the BLYP bond length is again longer than those of the other functionals. Hartree-Fock theory predicts a bond length which is significantly shorter than the methods including electron correlation.

Hartree-Fock theory is quite poor at predicting the two lower frequencies; note also that it predicts an imaginary frequency for this structure (F_3^- is not a stable minimum at the Hartree-Fock level). MP2 does well only for the frequency corresponding to the bending mode. The SVWN5 frequencies are all in excellent agreement with the (rather approximate) experimental values, as are the B3LYP results for the lower two frequencies (B3LYP's prediction for the frequency corresponding to the symmetric stretching mode is somewhat low). The lower two BLYP frequencies follow the MP2 pattern and its highest frequency is also somewhat low, resulting in an overall vibrational spectrum which is only fair.

These SVWN5 results are somewhat fortuitous. Be careful not to overgeneralize from their agreement to experiment. We will see a different result in Exercise 6.7. Several other excerises will also include comparisons of DFT methods to Hartree-Fock theory, MP2 and other electron correlation methods.

Resource Usage

We've alluded to the fact that more accurate calculations come only at the expense of greater computational cost. In this section, we'd like to make that statement more concrete. We'll also look at memory requirements for jobs involving f and higher basis functions.

The table on the next page indicates the relationship between problem size and resource requirements for various theoretical methods. Problem size is measured primarily as the total number of basis functions (N) involved in a calculation, which itself depends on both the system size and the basis set chosen; some items depend also on the number of occupied and virtual (unoccupied) orbitals (O and V respectively), which again depend on both the molecular system and the basis set. The table lists both the formal, algorithmic dependence and the actual dependence as implemented in *Gaussian* (as of this writing), which may be somewhat better due to various computational techniques

The table indicates how resource usage varies by problem size. For example, it indicates that for direct MP2 energy calculations, CPU requirements scale roughly as the fourth power of the number of basis functions if the number of electrons stays the same. Using the table with timings from previous jobs (using the same method and executed on the same computer system) should enable you to estimate how long a potential job will run.

Resource Usage by Method and Job Type

Method	Formal			Actual	
	CPU	Memory	Disk	CPU	Disk
Conventional SCF	N^4	N^2	N^4	$N^{3.5}$	$N^{3.5}$
Direct SCF	N^4	N^2	—	$N^{2.7}$	N^2
MP2 Energies					
Conventional	ON^4	N^2	N^4	ON^4	N^4
Direct	ON^4	OVN	—	O^2N^3	N^2
Semi-Direct	ON^4	N^2	VN^2	O^2N^3	VN^2
MP2 Gradients					
Conventional	ON^4	N^2	N^4	ON^4	N^4
Direct	ON^4	N^3	—	O^2N^3	N^2
Semi-Direct	ON^4	N^2	N^3	O^2N^3	N^3
MP4, QCISD(T)	O^3V^4	N^2	N^4	O^3V^4	N^4
Full CI (CPU)	$((O+V)!/O!V!)^2$				

The following tables present timing information for single point energy calculations on CH_4 and C_5H_{12}, run at various levels of theory using a range of basis sets. All times are relative to the time used for the smallest job for each system (All jobs were run with *Gaussian 94*, using the default of 4 MW of memory for methane, 8 MW for pentane in general, with the two largest jobs requiring 16 MW). Timing ratios may vary depending on the computer architecture, but these sample values should give you a sense of the relative cost of various types of calculations.

Here are the results for CH_4 from an IBM RS/6000 Model 550:

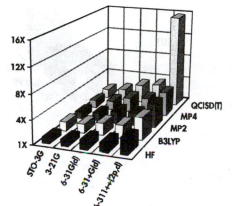

| Method | Basis Set [# basis functions] | | | | |
	STO-3G [9]	3-21G [17]	6-31G(d) [23]	6-31+G(d) [27]	6-311++G(2d,p) [55]
HF	1.0§	1.1	1.5	1.5	2.6
B3LYP	1.4	1.5	2.0	2.1	3.8
MP2	1.1	1.3	1.9	2.0	3.9
MP4	1.3	1.5	2.4	2.6	4.0
QCISD(T)	1.5	1.9	3.0	3.4	15.6

§ Job time: 11 seconds.

It may be somewhat surprising that there is so little variation in CPU time among the various jobs. However, most of these jobs are dominated by computational overhead since they are so small. Only the largest basis set jobs even approach typical research-sized problems. This table should serve as a caution against drawing performance conclusions from such small, "toy" jobs.

The performance data for C_5H_{12} is more representative of real-world problems (although this system is still on the small side). These jobs were all run on a Cray T-94 computer system[†]:

| Method | Basis Set [# basis functions] | | | |
	3-21G [69]	6-31G(d) [99]	6-31+G(d) [119]	6-311++G(2d,p) [219]
HF	1.0§	3.8	5.0	23.1
B3LYP	2.5	5.0	7.0	31.0
MP2	1.4	7.6	10.2	60.8
MP4	29.9	131.5	296.7	4066.2
QCISD(T)	63.3	220.9	558.3	8900.3

§ Job time: 6.4 seconds.

[†] The authors gratefully acknowledge Cray Research for providing the computer time to complete this study and thank John Carpenter and Carlos Sosa for their assistance.

The relative times in this chart are more typical of what you can expect from real-world calculations.

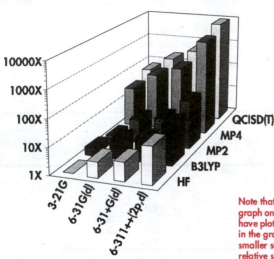

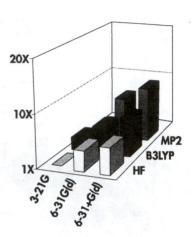

Note that the vertical scale in the graph on the left is *logarithmic*! We have plotted the smaller jobs again in the graph at the right, using a smaller scale, so you can see their relative sizes more clearly.

Exercises

Exercise 6.1: Butane-Iso-Butane Isomerization Energy

files: **6_01a (AM1)**
6_01b (PM3)
6_01c (HF)

Compute the isomerization energy between two forms of C_4H_{10}: iso-butane and n-butane using AM1, PM3 and HF/6-31G(d). How does each model chemistry compare with the observed energy difference (iso-butane minus n-butane) of -1.64 kcal-mol^{-1}?

Iso-butane

N-butane

We will provide you with the difference between the HF/6-31G(d) zero-point energy corrections for the two isomers, so you will not need to run frequency calculations:

ΔZPE(iso-butane – n-butane) = -0.00043 Hartrees = -0.27 kcal-mol^{-1}

The AM1 and PM3 energies do not need zero-point corrections.

Solution   We optimized the two structures at each model chemistry. The results of our AM1, PM3 and HF calculations are given in the table below, along with an MP2 calculation for reference:

Method	ΔE^{iso-n} kcal-mol^{-1}
AM1	+1.76
PM3	-0.47
HF/6-31G(d)	-0.63
MP2/6-31G(d)	-2.02
Experiment	-1.64

AM1 does not even get the correct sign for the energy difference. PM3 orders the isomers properly, but substantially underestimates the energy difference, and the Hartree-Fock value is only somewhat better. Electron correlation is needed to obtain even semi-quantitative results for this problem. ∎

Exercise 6.2: Rotational Barrier of N-Butane

files: **6_02a (semi)**
         6_02b (HF)

Calculate the rotational barrier between the anti and anticlinal forms of N-butane using the AM1 (or PM3 if you prefer) and HF/6-31G(d) model chemistries. Use the results for the anti form that you obtained in Exercise 6.1. Note that the anticlinal form is a transition structure; you will find the **Opt(TS,CalcFC)** keyword helpful in optimizing this structure.

anti isomer   anticlinal isomer

How well do your results agree with the experimental value of about 3.4 kcal-mol^{-1}? Since this observation is very approximate, we will not worry about zero-point energy corrections in this exercise.

Solution

These are the results we obtained from the various model chemistries:

Model	Rotational Barrier
AM1	1.53
PM3	1.67
HF/6-31G(d)	3.65
Experiment	~3.4

Semi-empirical methods were designed to treat ground state equilibrium geometries, so it is not surprising that they do not perform as well when modeling transition structures. In contrast, the Hartree-Fock value for the rotational barrier is in good agreement with experimental observations. ■

Exercise 6.3: Malonaldehyde Optimization

file: 6_03

Malonaldehyde provides one of the simplest examples of intramolecular hydrogen bonding. Its experimental structure is given in the following illustration (bond lengths are in black, and bond angles are in red):

H_8

128° | 1.091

H_7 1.348 C_3 1.454 H_9

1.089 C_2 119.4° C_4 1.094

106.6° 124.5° 123.0°

1.32 ‖ 1.234

O_1 O_5

0.969 H_6 1.68

What level of theory is required to produce an accurate structure for this molecule?

Solution   We'll begin with traditional electronic structure methods. Here are the results of optimizations we performed using the PM3, HF/6-311+G(d,p) and MP2/6-311+G(d,p) model chemistries:

Parameter	PM3	HF	MP2	Exp.
$R(O_1\text{-}H_6)$	0.968	0.953	0.993	0.969
$R(O_1\text{-}C_2)$	1.336	1.31	1.324	1.32
$R(C_2\text{-}C_3)$	1.356	1.342	1.367	1.348
$R(C_3\text{-}C_4)$	1.458	1.455	1.445	1.454
$R(C_4\text{-}O_5)$	1.225	1.202	1.242	1.234
$R(O_5\text{-}H_6)$	1.826	1.909	1.684	1.68
$R(C_2\text{-}H_7)$	1.095	1.076	1.087	1.089
$R(C_3\text{-}H_8)$	1.826	1.073	1.082	1.091
$R(C_4\text{-}H_9)$	1.100	1.093	1.102	1.094
$A(H_6\text{-}O_1\text{-}C_2)$	109.2	109.9	105.1	106.3
$A(C_2\text{-}C_3\text{-}H_8)$	120.2	119.3	119.9	128.1?
$A(C_2\text{-}C_3\text{-}C_4)$	121.8	121.3	119.4	119.4
$A(O_1\text{-}C_2\text{-}C_3)$	124.8	126.3	124.2	124.5
$A(C_3\text{-}C_4\text{-}O_5)$	121.5	124.1	123.2	123.0

Both the PM3 and Hartree-Fock geometries differ significantly from the experimental structure. This is most noticeable in the long hydrogen bonding distance ($O_5\text{-}H_6$) and the corresponding errors in the ring's internal bond angles.

In contrast, the MP2 structure is in excellent agreement with experiment. The one major discrepancy comes with the $C_2\text{-}C_3\text{-}H_8$ bond angle, but the reported experimental value is known to be quite uncertain.

file: 6_03x

We also ran an additional optimization using the B3LYP/6-31G(d) model chemistry, beginning from the optimized HF/6-311+G(d,p) structure (i.e., the same way we ran our MP2 job). The resulting geometry is in excellent agreement with the MP2 results (with a larger basis set). The average absolute deviation between the two is 0.0036Å for bond lengths and 0.34° for bond angles, while the B3LYP job takes less than 20% as long as the MP2 optimization. Thus, this hybrid functional successfully models the effects of electron correlation for this system. ∎

Exercise 6.4: Optimization of FOOF

file: 6_04

Historically, predicting the structure of F_2O_2 has been a challenge for successive electronic structure methods (it was a longstanding "pathological case"). The FOOF molecule has an unusually long O-F bond length, indicating a fairly weak interaction. FOOF is a case where MP2 does rather poorly, and a Coupled Cluster or Quadratic CI calculation is necessary. Gustavo Scuseria demonstrated the efficacy of CCSD(T) for this problem; the following table lists the predicted structures for a variety of levels of theory, including some of Scuseria's CCSD(T) results:

Parameter	HF/6-311+G(3df)	MP2/6-311+G(3df)	CCSD(T)/ 6-31G(d)	CCSD(T)/ TZ2P[§]	Experiment
R(O-O)	1.296	1.143	1.276	1.216	1.217±.001
R(O-F)	1.352	1.672	1.540	1.614	1.575±.001
A(F-O-O)	106.3	111.4	107.5	108.9	109.5±1.0
D(F-O-O-F)	85.1	89.3	86.8	87.8	87.5±1.0

[§] This basis set is essentially equivalent to 6-311G(2d).

The very large basis set we used does not enable either the HF or MP2 method to predict an accurate structure for FOOF. CCSD does pretty well using only the 6-31G(d) basis set and produces a structure in excellent agreement with experiment with the larger basis set.

How well does Density Functional Theory model this problem?

Solution

Clearly, a hybrid functional is the best choice for this problem. We ran B3LYP calculations using the 6-31G(d), 6-31+G(d) and 6-311G(2d) basis sets. Here are the results:

Parameter	B3LYP/6-31G(d)	B3LYP/6-31+G(d)	B3LYP/6-311G(2d)	Experiment
R(O-O)	1.266	1.238	1.241	1.217±.001
R(O-F)	1.497	1.531	1.515	1.575±.001
A(F-O-O)	108.3	109.2	108.7	109.5±1.0
D(F-O-O-F)	86.8	88.3	87.2	87.5±1.0

The B3LYP/6-31G(d) results are similar to the CCSD calculation using the same basis set. Adding diffuse functions to this basis set produces a substantial improvement in the predicted structure for the B3LYP method. Finally, the structure computed with the largest basis set is in good agreement with the experimental geometry. Thus, B3LYP is capable of successfully modeling the structure of this system. ■

Exercise 6.5: Acetaldehyde-Ethylene Oxide Isomerization Energy

files: **6_05a (A)**
      6_05b (EO)

Compute the isomerization energy between acetaldehyde and ethylene oxide at STP with the QCISD(T)/6-31G(d) model chemistry, and compare the performance of the various model chemistries. Use HF/6-31G(d) to compute the thermal energy corrections. Remember to specify the scaling factor via the **Freq=ReadIso** option. (Note that we have already optimized the structure of acetaldehyde.)

acetaldehyde   ethylene oxide

The experimental isomerization energy is 27.57 kcal-mol^{-1} (ethylene oxide minus acetaldehyde).

Solution

The predicted isomerization energy at various levels of theory are given in the following table:

Method	Energy		ΔE^{STP}
	Acetaldehyde	Ethylene Oxide	(kcal-mol^{-1})
Thermal Correction	0.05862	0.06004	
HF	-152.91597	-152.86736	31.4
MP2	-153.34454	-153.30161	27.8
MP4	-153.38411	-153.33888	29.3
QCISD	-153.37126	-153.32653	29.0
QCISD(T)	-153.38349	-153.33896	28.9
Experiment			27.57

The thermal corrections in the table are taken from the line labeled `Thermal correction to energy` in the *Gaussian* output.

All of the model chemistries predict acetaldehyde to the lower energy isomer. The methods including electron correlation all produce good estimates of the isomerization energy. However, it turns out that the MP2 value is fortuitously good; increasing the basis set size would produce a poorer result at the MP2 level. For the

MP4 and the two QCISD methods, the predicted isomerization energy would continue to converge toward the experimental value as the basis set size increases. ∎

Advanced Exercise 6.6: Spin Polarization in Heterosubstituted Allyl Radicals

files: **6_06a (R=O)**
     6_06b (R=CH$_2$)
     6_06c (R=Be)
     6_06d (R=Mg)
     6_06e (R=S)

In this exercise, we will be studying the spin polarization in a series of molecules of the form $CH_2=CH–XH_n{}^\bullet$. Our study will have two parts:

✦ First, we will determine the level of theory required to accurately model such compounds by performing several calculations on acetyl radical (R=O).

✦ Then, we will model several other compounds in this series using the appropriate model chemistry to examine the substituent effect on this molecular property.

Optimize the structure of acetyl radical using the 6-31G(d) basis set at the HF, MP2, B3LYP and QCISD levels of theory. We chose to perform an **Opt Freq** calculation at the Hartree-Fock level in order to produce initial force constants for the later optimizations (retrieved from the checkpoint file via **Opt=ReadFC**). Compare the predicted spin polarizations (listed as part of the population analysis output) for the carbon and oxygen atoms for the various methods to one another and to the experimental values of 0.7 for the C_2 carbon atom and 0.2 for the oxygen atom. Note that for the MP2 and QCISD calculations you will need to include the keyword **Density=Current** in the job's route section, which specifies that the population analysis be performed using the electron density computed by the current theoretical method (the default is to use the Hartree-Fock density).

Once you have determined the appropriate level of theory, predict the spin polarizations for these other substituents: CH_2, Mg, Be and S.

Solution

All of the geometry optimizations for acetyl radical produce similar structures. Here are the predicted spin densities (labeled "Total atomic spin densities" in the *Gaussian* output):

Method	C_1	C_2	O
HF	-0.615	1.091	0.651
MP2	0.127	0.994	0.023
B3LYP	-0.154	0.864	0.368
QCISD	-0.187	0.964	0.334
Experiment		0.7	0.2

Both the Hartree-Fock and MP2 predictions differ substantially from the observed values. The MP2 value for the C_1 carbon atom does not even have the right sign, and it underestimates the spin density on the oxygen atom. Spin contamination is a significant factor affecting the accuracy of both methods.

The B3LYP and QCISD values are in good agreement with one another and with the experimental observations. Both favor the resonance form with the radical centered mainly on the C_2 carbon. Therefore, we will use the B3LYP/6-31G(d) model chemistry for the remainder of this study.

Here are the results for the various compounds we are investigating:

Substituent	C_1	C_2	R
CH_2 (2.5)	-0.275	0.70	0.70
O (3.5)	-0.154	0.864	0.368
Be (1.5)	0.067	-0.019	0.938
Mg (1.2)	0.202	-0.034	0.806
S (2.5)	-0.192	0.521	0.714

The table gives the computed spin densities for each atom (the value in parentheses following the substituent is its electronegativity). The illustrations are Lewis dot structures showing the primary resonance form for each structure and indicating unpaired electrons and lone pairs.

In the allyl radical, the spin density is divided between the two terminal carbon atoms. In the four other compounds, the C_2 carbon atom retains an unpaired electron. For the Mg and Be cases, both the C_2 carbon atom and the substituent have an unpaired electron. In the Be compound, the spin density is localized mostly on the substituent atoms, while for the Mg compound, a bit more of the density remains near the C_1 carbon.

Both the oxygen and sulfur atoms have two lone pairs while the C_2 carbon has an unpaired electron, and in both cases the double bond shifts from the two carbon atoms to the carbon and the substituent. In acetyl radical, the electron density is centered primarily on the C_2 carbon, and the spin density is drawn toward the latter more than toward the former. In contrast, the density is more balanced between the two terminal heavy atoms with the sulfur substituent (similar to that in allyl radical) with a slight bias toward the sulfur atom. These trends can be easily related to the varying electronegativity of the heavy atom in the substituent.

We also plotted the electron spin polarization, by itself (top row) and projected onto the electron density isosurface for the molecules containing the CH_2, O and Be substituents (the orientation of the atoms in the plots is indicated at the left):

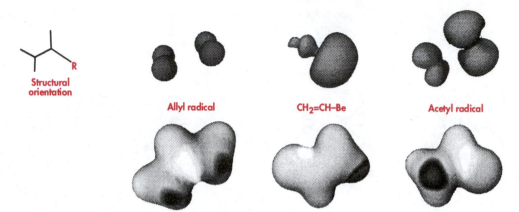

Structural orientation

Allyl radical CH_2=CH–Be   Acetyl radical

The first series of plots represent the limiting and perfectly balanced cases for the distribution of the electron density (positive values only are shown). These spin density plots show the excess density perfectly balanced between the two terminal heavy atoms for allyl radical, drawn toward the substituent for Be and pushed away from the substituent for acetyl radical.

The second set of illustrations show the spin density plotted on the electron density isosurface; the spin density provides the shading for the isodensity surface: dark areas indicate positive (excess α) spin density and light areas indicate negative (excess β) spin density. For example, in the allyl radical, the spin density is concentrated around the two terminal carbons (and away from the central carbon). In the Be form, it is concentrated around the substituent, and in acetyl radical, it is centered around the C_2 carbon atom.

The plots for Mg will be similar to the ones for the Be substituent, and the plots for sulfur will be intermediate between those of the allyl and acetyl radicals.

See the original paper by Wiberg and coworkers (listed in the references) for a more detailed discussion of the chemistry of these compounds. ∎

Advanced Exercise 6.7: $M^+F_3^-$ Structures and Frequencies

files: 6_07a (K)
6_07b (Na)
6_07c (Cs)

In this exercise, we will examine three alkali metal trifluorides: M=K, Na and Cs (drawn from the same study by Tozer and Sosa as Example 6.6). The structure can take on one of two forms, based on the angles θ and ϕ. When $\theta=\phi$, the resulting structure is T-shaped (left drawing below); if θ is significantly greater than ϕ, a distorted structure results (right):

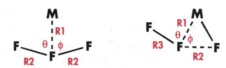

Experimental spectroscopic data for the three compounds is given in the table below:

M	Form	ω_1 MF...F_2 Str.	ω_2 Pert. Symm. Str.	ω_3 Pert. Asymm. Str.
Na	D	455, 460	*absent*	*absent*
K	T	*absent*	467	549
Cs	T	*absent*	*not IR active*	550

Note that the structural form of each compound is implied by the presence (T-shaped structure) or absence (distorted structure) of the perturbed asymmetric stretching mode at about 550 cm⁻¹.

The experimental spectra[†] are interpreted by Tozer and Sosa as follows: In the Na compound, the structure is of the form NaF...F_2, and it exhibits an absorption due to the complex at 455 cm⁻¹, with a 460 splitting (this mode is denoted ω_1). For the other two, T-shaped compounds, the two highest frequencies resemble perturbed forms of the symmetric and asymmetric F-F-F stretching modes that we saw in the F_3^- anion, which we denote ω_2 and ω_3. The Cs compound exhibits the asymmetric F_3 stretching (ω_3) at 550 cm⁻¹, while the K structure exhibits this vibration at 549 cm⁻¹ along with a weak absorption at 467 cm⁻¹. The latter may represent a weakly-active symmetric stretch (ω_2).

Predict the structure and frequencies for this compound using two or more different DFT functionals and the LANL2DZ basis set augmented by diffuse functions (this basis set also includes effective core potentials used to include some relativistic effects for K and Cs). How well does each functional reproduce the observed spectral data?

[†] The experimentalists observed other frequencies for these compounds which we will not consider here: in the Na compound at 495 cm⁻¹; in the K compound at 396 cm⁻¹; in the Cs compound at 313 cm⁻¹.

Diffuse functions must be added manually to **LANL2DZ** by adding the **ExtraBasis** keyword to the job's route section and including the **plus.gbs** file as its input via **@**:

```
#T method/LANL2DZ ExtraBasis ...

normal input file ...

@plus.gbs/N
```

The basis set file is stored in the *g9x/basis* subdirectory of the *Gaussian* tree. We have also placed a copy in the *explore/exercise* subdirectory. You'll need to specify the full pathname for the include file if you run the job from a different directory location.

Solution

Here are the results we obtained with the SVWN5, BLYP and B3LYP functionals, along with Tozer and Sosa's HF and MP2 results[†]. All frequencies are scaled, and we have limited our consideration to the frequencies of interest:

	Method	Structure Type	θ	φ	R1	R2	R3	ω_2 Pert. Symm. Str.	ω_3 Pert. Asymm. Str.
$K^+F_3^-$	Observed	T						467	549
	HF	D	164.7	14.3	4.759	2.625	1.342	*absent*	*absent*
	SVWN5	T	79.6	79.6	2.380	1.746	1.746	449	565
	BLYP	T	79.6	79.6	2.460	1.813	1.813	395	502
	B3LYP	T	80.1	80.1	2.434	1.762	1.762	428	503
	MP2	T	82.7	82.7	2.406	1.754	1.754	371	779
$Cs^+F_3^-$	Observed	T						*not IR active*	550
	HF	D	180.0	0.0	5.260	2.591	1.343	*absent*	*absent*
	SVWN5	T	81.8	81.8	2.744	1.742	1.742	*absent*	566
	BLYP	T	82.0	82.0	2.830	1.808	1.808	*absent*	504
	B3LYP	T	82.4	82.4	2.807	1.759	1.759	*absent*	503
	MP2	T	84.4	84.4	2.780	1.748	1.748	370	767

[†] Tozer and Sosa used a slightly different basis set: LANL2DZ for the alkali metals and LANL2DZ augmeted with diffuse and polarization functions for fluorine. In this table, their data is scaled using the scaling factors employed throughout this book.

$Na^+F_3^-$

Method	Structure Type	θ	ϕ	R1	R2	R3	ω_1 MF...F_2 Str.	ω_3 Pert. Asymm. Str.
Observed	D						455,460	*absent*
SVWN5	T	78.0	78.0	2.073	1.750	1.750	388	563
BLYP	T	75.8	75.8	2.077	1.823	1.823	363	489
B3LYP	D	100.9	63.9	2.139	1.872	1.672	403	*absent*
MP2	T	79.4	79.4	2.018	1.770	1.770	438	799

Hartree-Fock theory does quite a poor job of predicting the structures and frequencies for these compounds. It produces highly distorted structures in all three cases, and its computed frequencies bear little resemblance to the experimental observations. MP2 theory generally does better for the structures, although it fails to located a distorted structure for $Na^+F_3^-$. The frequencies computed at the MP2 level also vary widely from experiment.

For the Cs and K substituents, all three DFT functionals produce similar structures. All three functionals predict frequencies which are somewhat lower than the observed values but which reproduce the trends in the experimental data quite well. The SVWN5 frequencies tend to be higher than those computed by BLYP and B3LYP.

A difference between the B3LYP functional and the others is apparent for the Na substituent, however. Only B3LYP predicts a distorted structure for this compound (in line with the experimental implications); similarly, only the B3LYP spectrum is missing the band corresponding to the perturbed asymmetric stretching mode. The motion corresponding to its highest predicted frequency is of a perturbed symmetric stretching character. This mode is significantly different from that in the Cs and K compounds, and it represents a perturbed F-F stretch. Given the systematic underestimating of actual frequency values for these compounds by B3LYP, this computed frequency would correspond to a band significantly above the ~550 cm^{-1} range (making it a quite poor prediction for ω_2).

All in all, B3LYP performs best on this problem of all of the model chemistries we have considered. It provides good structural and qualitative frequency predictions, although its computed frequency values are only fair. ■

Advanced Exercise 6.8: Hyperfine Coupling Constants

file: 6_08

In this exercise, we will predict the isotropic hyperfine splitting in HNCN radical at a variety of levels of theory, which is a measure of the energy difference created by the spin of the electons at the nucleus interacting with the spin of the nucleus itself. Ian Carmichael has demonstrated that this problem tends to pose a severe challenge for even the higher order electron correlation methods.

Gaussian computes isotropic hyperfine coupling constants as part of the population analysis, given in the section labeled "Fermi contact analysis"; the values are in atomic units. It is necessary to convert these values to other units in order to compare with experiment; we will be converting from atomic units to MHz, using the following expressions:

$$b_F = \left(\frac{16\pi}{3}\right)\left(\frac{g}{2}\right)g_I K B_F$$

where g is the observed free-electron factor equal to 2.0023, K is a composite conversion factor equal to 47.705336 MHz, B_F is the atomic unit value computed by *Gaussian*, and g_I is the nuclear gyromagnetic ratio for the atom type in question.

g_I can be computed from the magnetic moment for the atom divided by the spin. Here are the values for the atoms in which we are interested:

Atom	Spin	Magnetic Moment
^1H	½	2.792670
^{13}C	½	0.7021
^{14}N	1	0.4036

Compute the isotropic hyperfine coupling constant for each of the atoms in HNCN with the HF, MP2, MP4(SDQ) and QCISD methods, using the D95(d,p) basis set. Make sure that the population analysis for each job uses the proper electron density by including the **Density=Current** keyword in the route section. Also, include the **5D** keyword in each job's route section(as was done in the original study).

Solution

The table below presents the results of our calculations, in atomic units and in MHz:

Atom	B_F (atomic units)				b_F (MHz)			
	HF	MP2	MP4(SDQ)	QCISD	HF	MP2	MP4	QCISD
H	-0.02698	0.00038	-0.00594	-0.01268	-120.58	1.72	-26.54	-56.66
C	-0.18948	0.04146	-0.01749	-0.06980	-212.91	46.59	-19.65	-78.43
N_1	0.17466	0.08524	0.08262	0.08676	56.41	27.53	26.68	28.02
N_2	0.13430	-0.06093	-0.01369	0.04222	43.38	-19.68	-4.42	13.63

There is rather poor agreement between the QCISD values and all of the lower levels of theory; this is a case where the successive MP orders converge rather slowly. Note that the QCISD values differ only a bit from Carmichael's QCISD(TQ) results. It turns out also that MP4(SDTQ) does not improve on the MP4(SDQ) values (accordingly, we chose the cheaper method for this exercise). ■

Advanced Exercise 6.9: Ozone Destruction by Atomic Chlorine
file: **6_09**

In the atmosphere, ozone is attacked by chlorine atoms primarily introduced via polutants. The destruction of ozone is self-sustaining via these reactions:

$$Cl + O_3 \rightarrow ClO + O_2$$
$$ClO + O_3 \rightarrow 2O_2 + Cl$$

In the second reaction, atomic chlorine is again produced by the reaction of the product of the first attack and another ozone molecule. We will consider the first of these reactions in this exercise.

Compute the enthalpy change for the destruction of ozone by atomic chlorine by subtracting the dissociation energies of O_2 and ClO from the dissociation energy for ozone. What model chemistry is required for accurate modeling of each phase of this process? The experimental values are given below (in kcal-mol^{-1}):

	D_0		
O_3	O_2	ClO	ΔH
142.2	118.0	63.6	-39.1

You'll need to run five calculations at each model chemistry: oxygen atom, chlorine atom, O_2, ClO and ozone (but don't forget that you can obtain lower-level energies from a higher-level calculation). Use the experimental geometries for the various molecules and the following scaled zero-point energy corrections:

+ ClO: R(Cl-O) = 1.56963, ZPE = 0.00602
+ O_2: R (O-O) = 1.20752, ZPE = 0.00406
+ Ozone: R(O-O) = 1.272, A(O-O-O) = 116.8, ZPE = 0.00170

Solution   Here are the results for a variety of theoretical methods and basis sets:

Method	D_0 O_3	D_0 O_2	ClO	ΔH
HF/6-31G(d)	-14.2	26.9	-1.8	-39.3
MP2/6-31G(d)	101.1	115.3	44.6	-58.7
MP4/6-31G(d)	96.1	105.1	43.0	-52.0
B3LYP/6-31G(d)	138.9	122.1	57.9	-41.2
QCISD(T)/6-31G(d)	108.4	103.0	45.3	-39.9
HF/6-31+G(d)	-15.6	26.1	-2.0	-39.7
MP2/6-31+G(d)	100.1	113.6	45.3	-58.8
MP4/6-31+G(d)	95.3	103.5	43.9	-52.1
B3LYP/6-31+G(d)	133.7	118.1	57.3	-41.7
QCISD(T)/6-31+G(d)	89.7	101.1	46.5	-58.0
HF/6-311+G(3df)	-7.1	31.1	4.9	-43.1
MP2/6-311+G(3df)	120.2	124.9	58.0	-62.7
MP4/6-311+G(3df)	117.2	117.3	56.7	-56.8
B3LYP/6-311+G(3df)	138.8	121.5	65.3	-47.9
QCISD(T)/6-311+G(3df)	127.3	113.5	58.6	-44.8
Experiment	**142.2**	**118.0**	**63.3**	**-39.1**

The short summary of these results is that none of these model chemistries is very accurate at modeling this process in toto. Some of them achieve good results on either the component dissociation energies or the final value of ΔH, but no method does well for all of them. Not even QCISD(T) at the very large 6-311+G(3df) basis set is adequate. A compound energy method is required to successfully address this problem. We will see such a solution in the next chapter. ■

References

HF Bond Dissociation Energy K. P. Huber and G. Herzberg, *Molecular Spectra and Molecular Structure IV. Constants of Diatomic Molecules* (Van Nostrand Reinhold Co., New York, 1979).

Resource Usage H. B. Schlegel and M. J. Frisch, "Computational Bottlenecks in Molecular Orbital Calculations," in *Theoretical and Computational Models for Organic Chemistry*, ed. S. J. Formosinho et. al., NATO-ASI Series C 339 (Kluwer Academic Pubs., The Netherlands, 1991), 5-33.

Convergence of MP Orders R. H. Nobes, J. A. Pople, L. Radom, N. C. Handy and P. J. Knowles, *Chem. Phys. Lett.*, **138**, 481 (1987).

H. B. Schlegel, *J. Phys. Chem.*, **92**, 3075 (1988).

Malonaldehyde M. J. Frisch, A. C. Scheiner, H. F. Schaefer, III and J. S. Binkley, *J. Chem. Phys.*, **82**, 4194 (1985).

FOOF G. E. Scuseria, *J. Chem. Phys.*, **94**, 442 (1991).

Heterosubstituted Allyl Radicals K. B. Wiberg, J. R. Cheeseman, J. W. Ochterski and M. J. Frisch, *J. Am. Chem. Soc.*, **117**, 6535 (1995).

F_3^- and $M^+F_3^-$ D. J. Tozer and C. P. Sosa, "The alkali metal trifluorides $M^+F_3^-$: How well can theory predict experiment?", *J. Chem. Phys.*, submitted (1996).

Hyperfine Splitting in HNCN *Theoretical*: I. Carmichael, *J. Phys. Chem.*, **99**, 6832 (1995); Prof. Carmichael also provided us with corresponding results for other theoretical methods by private communication.

Units Conversion: D. P. Chong, S. R. Langhoff and C. W. Bauschlicher, Jr., *J. Chem. Phys.*, **94**, 3700 (1991).

Magnetic Moments: M. Karplus and R. N. Porter, *Atoms & Molecules* (Benjamin/ Cummings Pub. Co, Menlo Park, CA, 1970), p. 544.

AM1 Semi-Empirical Method M. Dewar and W. Thiel, *J. Amer. Chem. Soc.* **99**, 4499 (1977).

L. P. Davis et. al., *J. Comp. Chem.* **2**, 433 (1981).

M. J. S. Dewar, M. L. McKee and H. S. Rzepa, *J. Am. Chem. Soc.* **100**, 3607 (1978).

M. J. S. Dewar, E. G. Zoebisch and E. F. Healy, "AM1: A New General Purpose Quantum Mechanical Molecular Model," *J. Amer. Chem. Soc.* **107**, 3902-3909 (1985).

M. J. S. Dewar and C. H. Reynolds, *J. Comp. Chem.* **2**, 140 (1986).

PM3 Semi-Empirical Method J. J. P. Stewart, *J. Comp. Chem.* **10**, 209 (1989).

J. J. P. Stewart, *J. Comp. Chem.* **10**, 221 (1989).

Chapter 7

High Accuracy Energy Models

In This Chapter:

**Relative Accuracies
of Various Model
Chemistries**

G1 and G2 Theory

**Complete Basis
Set (CBS) Methods**

In the last two chapters, we discussed the ways that computational accuracy varies by theoretical method and basis set. We've examined both the successes and failures of a variety of model chemistries. In this chapter, we turn our attention to models designed for modeling the energies of molecular processes very accurately.

Such models have been developed to achieve a target accuracy of ± 2 kcal-mol^{-1} with respect to experiment for quantities such as atomization energies and ionization potentials. This corresponds to about ± 0.1 eV or ± 0.003 Hartrees. Generally, it would take a very large QCISD(T) job to reach such a level, a job far larger than is practical computationally for any but the smallest molecules.

Instead, models like G2, CBS-4 and CBS-Q are compound methods consisting of a number of pre-defined component calculations whose results are combined in a specified manner. We'll consider the specific makeup of the most important compound methods after reviewing the computation of basic thermochemistry results and considering the accuracies of various traditional model chemistries.

Predicting Thermochemistry

The four major quantities on which we will focus are atomization energies, electron affinities, ionization potentials and proton affinities. We'll look at each of them in turn in this section. Note that all of them are conventionally defined to be greater than zero.

Atomization Energies

The atomization energy[†] is defined as the energy difference between a molecule and its component atoms. For example, the atomization energy of PH_2 may be computed as: $(E(P) + 2E(H)) – E(PH_2)$.

Example 7.1: Atomization Energy of PH₂
file: e7_01

We'll compute the atomization energy of PH_2 using B3LYP/6-31G(d) geometries and zero-point energy corrections (which we will scale by the usual factor of 0.9804) and B3LYP/6-31+G(d,p) energies. We must perform an optimization and frequency

---

[†] This computed quantity is also sometimes synonymously referred to as the total dissociation energy (D_0).

calculation for PH_2, and three single point energy calculations for the P atom, the H atom and the compound itself.

Here are the results we obtained (atomization energies in kcal-mol^{-1}):

Molecule	E	ZPE	AE
H	-0.50027		
P	-341.25930		
PH_2	-342.50942	0.01322	148.3
Experiment			144.7

The predicted atomization energy is 3.6 kcal-mol^{-1} higher than the experimental value, resulting in an error about twice as large as the target accuracy.

Electron Affinities

The electron affinity is defined as the energy released when an electron is added to a neutral molecule, computed as the energy difference between the neutral form and the anion. For example, the electron affinity of PH_2 may be computed as:
$E(PH_2) - E(PH_2^-)$.

Example 7.2: Electron Affinity of PH_2

file: e7_02

To compute this electron affinity, we need only run calculations on PH_2^- (since we can use the preceding PH_2 results). Here are the predicted energies and the resulting electron affinity:

Molecule	E	ZPE	EA	
			eV	kcal-mol^{-1}
PH_2^-	-342.55419	0.01245		
PH_2	-342.50942	0.01322	1.24	28.58
Experiment			1.26	29.06

The calculated electron affinity is about 0.02 eV too low (corresponding to a difference of about 0.5 kcal-mol^{-1}), in excellent agreement with experiment.

Ionization Potentials

The ionization potential is defined as the amount of energy required to remove an electron from a molecule, computed as the energy difference between the cation and the neutral molecule. For example, the ionization potential of PH_2 may be computed as: $E(PH_2^+) - E(PH_2)$

Example 7.3: Ionization Potential of PH₂
file: e7_03

We must run calculations on PH_2^+ in order to compute the ionization potential of PH_2. Here are the results:

Molecule	E	ZPE	IP eV	IP kcal-mol⁻¹
PH_2^+	-342.14416	0.01347		
PH_2	-342.50942	0.01322	9.95	229.36
Experiment			9.82	226.45

The computed ionization potential is -0.13 eV too high, corresponding to a difference of -2.9 kcal-mol⁻¹, a result which is similar in accuracy to the atomization energy.

Proton Affinities

The proton affinity is defined as the energy released when a proton is added to a system, computed as the energy difference between the system of interest and the same molecule with one additional proton (H^+). For example, the proton affinity of PH_3 is computed as: $E(PH_3) - E(PH_4^+)$.

Example 7.4: Proton Affinity of PH₃
file: e7_04

We compute the proton affinity for PH_3 by running two optimization plus frequency jobs, each followed by a single point energy calculation at the optimized geometry. Here are the results (proton affinities in kcal-mol⁻¹):

Molecule	E	ZPE	PA
PH_4^+	-343.45408	0.03470	
PH_3	-343.14691	0.02376	185.9
Experiment			187.1

This result, which differs from experiment by only 1.2 kcal-mol⁻¹, does achieve the desired level of accuracy.

Evaluating Model Chemistries

Calculation of thermochemical quantities like those we have just considered are a widely-used method for evaluating the accuracy of theoretical methods and models. In this section, we will look at the Gaussian-2 molecule set and then consider how well a variety of model chemistries perform on it. Note that our consideration of the G2 method itself will come later in this chapter.

The G2 Molecule Set (and Pitfalls in Its Interpretation)

The original paper defining the Gaussian-2 method by Curtiss, Raghavachari, Trucks and Pople tested the method's effectiveness by comparing its results to experimental thermochemical data for a set of 125 calculations: 55 atomization energies, 38 ionization potentials, 25 electron affinities and 7 proton affinities. All compounds included only first and second-row heavy atoms. The specific calculations chosen were selected because of the availability of high accuracy experimental values for these thermochemical quantities.

This molecule set has several strengths which make it valuable for evaluating the accuracy of a model chemistry:

✦ Thermochemical quantities are difficult to model very accurately (so good results really do imply a good method). Errors can generally be assumed to represent a worst-case scenario for the model, and actual results for "easier" properties may be better.

✦ The experimental results are well-accepted values with small errors.

✦ It includes compounds containing a range of different elements.

✦ It includes a significant number of molecules with unusual electronic states (for example, ions, open shell systems and hypervalent systems).

However, it is also important to recognize the weaknesses of the G2 molecule set when interpreting and extrapolating from the results for any particular model chemistry:[†]

✦ All of the molecules are quite small. Thus, one must be cautious when extrapolating either accuracy or performance results to significantly larger systems.

✦ Not all kinds of bonding are represented. For example, there are no ring systems within the molecule set, and there are no C-F bonds.

[†] One should also keep in mind that the G2 paper's authors never intended the molecule set to be a definitive test suite, and so they should not be held responsible for its shortcomings as one.

◆ Limiting the systems studied to first and second-row atoms makes extrapolating results for other types of systems—for example, those containing transition metals—somewhat problematic.

◆ The set is ultimately rather arbitrary since it was formed on the basis of the availability of very accurate experimental data. For example, not every possible thermochemical quantity even for small diatomic compounds of first and second-row elements is included.

This factor is most important when results are reported for only a subset of the entire collection of calculations. For example, some studies report results only for the atomization energies portion of the set. This subset of the calculations does not include some "difficult" molecules present for other thermochemical properties (e.g. PO, whose geometry can be challenging to model accurately), and so results for a subset can be more accurate than they would be for the entire set. This effect becomes more pronounced as overall method accuracy increases. Be cautious when general accuracy and applicability conclusions are drawn from such data.

Reported results for the G2 set can include some or all of the following statistics:

◆ The mean deviation from experiment: the average difference between the computed and experimental values. This statistic is not very meaningful since it allows positive and negative errors—underestimations and overestimations—to cancel one another. However, a large value usually indicates the presence of systematic errors.

◆ The mean absolute deviation from experiment (MAD): the average difference between the computed and experimental values ignoring the sign. This is a much better measure of how well a method performed across the calculation set.

◆ The standard deviation of the MAD gives a quantitative measure of how widely the data deviates from the mean.

◆ The root-mean-square error (RMS error) is a statistic closely related to the MAD for gaussian distributions. It provides a measure of the absolute differences between calculated values and experiment as well as the distribution of the values with respect to the mean.

◆ The largest errors in the computed values, specifically, the largest positive error (where the computed value is smaller than the experimental value) and the largest negative value (where the reverse is true). These errors give some sense of how badly a method may do when it models a problem poorly.

We will be focusing on the MAD, its standard deviation, and the maximum errors in each direction when we evaluate the relative accuracies of various model chemistries and composite methods in the course of this chapter.

Making Sense of the Numbers

As an example, consider a method with a MAD of 2.5, a standard deviation of the MAD of 3.1 and maximum errors of -18.3 and 21.2. These values indicate the following:

- ✦ The method differs from experiment by 2.5 kcal-mol^{-1} on average for the G2 set.

- ✦ About two-thirds of the G2 set results are within 3.1 kcal-mol^{-1} of the MAD. In other words, two-thirds of the results are within 5.6 kcal-mol^{-1} of the experimental values.

- ✦ The worst case errors on the G2 set are an overestimation of the experimental results by 18.3 kcal-mol^{-1} and an underestimation of the experimental result by 21.2 kcal-mol^{-1}.

Thus, we can conclude such a method is generally likely to be fairly accurate when computing these thermochemical quantities, but when it is wrong, it can be off by quite a lot. A method with smaller maximum errors is obviously preferable (since the errors in calculations on new and unknown systems are by definition uncertain).

Don't panic! This is not to imply that such a method may not be very useful and reliable for modeling other properties of molecular systems. For example, as we'll see in the next subsection, model chemistries that are known to be quite reliable for optimizing geometries can be quite poor at predicting absolute thermochemical properties.

Similarly, such a method could be quite accurate at predicting other molecular properties, vibrational frequencies, and a variety of relative energy values: energy differences to similar molecules, reaction energies, and so on. As we've noted before, calculating energy differences is much easier than computing absolute quantities such as bond energies since systematic errors in the method often cancel out across the systems being compared. If such problems are your focus, then comparing the relative performance of model chemistries you are considering—and which are affordable for your particular problem—may be more important than their absolute accuracy at predicting the thermochemistry of the G2 molecule set.

Relative Accuracies of Selected Model Chemistries

We are now in a position to examine the relative accuracies of a variety of different model chemistries by considering their performance on the G2 molecule set. The following table lists the mean absolute deviation from experiment, the standard deviation and the largest positive and negative deviations from experiment for each model chemistry. The table is divided into two parts: the first section lists results for single model chemistries, and the remaining sections present results derived from high-level chemistry calculations performed at a geometry optimized using a lower-level, less expensive model.

<table>
<tr><td rowspan="2">Model Chemistry</td><td rowspan="2">MAD</td><td rowspan="2">StdDev</td><td colspan="2">Largest Errors</td></tr>
<tr><td>Positive</td><td>Negative</td></tr>
<tr><td>B3LYP/6-311+G(2d,p) // B3LYP/6-311+G(2d,p)</td><td>3.1</td><td>3.0</td><td>13.6</td><td>-19.7</td></tr>
<tr><td>BLYP/6-311+G(2d,p) // BLYP/6-311+G(2d,p)</td><td>3.9</td><td>3.2</td><td>14.3</td><td>-15.9</td></tr>
<tr><td>BLYP/6-31+G(d,p) // BLYP/6-31+G(d,p)</td><td>3.9</td><td>3.2</td><td>15.2</td><td>-15.2</td></tr>
<tr><td>B3LYP/6-31+G(d,p) // B3LYP/6-31+G(d,p)</td><td>3.9</td><td>4.2</td><td>17.6</td><td>-33.8</td></tr>
<tr><td>B3LYP/6-31G(d) // B3LYP/6-31G(d)</td><td>7.9</td><td>9.5</td><td>12.2</td><td>-54.2</td></tr>
<tr><td>MP2/6-311+G(2d,p) // MP2/6-311+G(2d,p)</td><td>8.9</td><td>7.8</td><td>18.3</td><td>-39.2</td></tr>
<tr><td>MP2/6-31+G(d,p) // MP2/6-31+G(d,p)</td><td>11.4</td><td>8.1</td><td>15.6</td><td>-44.0</td></tr>
<tr><td>PM3 // PM3</td><td>17.2</td><td>14.0</td><td>49.6</td><td>-69.9</td></tr>
<tr><td>SVWN5/6-311+G(2d,p) // SVWN5/6-311+G(2d,p)</td><td>18.1</td><td>19.8</td><td>81.0</td><td>-10.1</td></tr>
<tr><td>AM1 // AM1</td><td>18.8</td><td>16.9</td><td>47.8</td><td>-95.5</td></tr>
<tr><td>SVWN/6-311+G(2d,p) // SVWN/6-311+G(2d,p)</td><td>24.9</td><td>19.2</td><td>89.3</td><td>-10.4</td></tr>
<tr><td>HF/6-31+G(d,p) // HF/6-31+G(d,p)</td><td>46.7</td><td>40.6</td><td>10.1</td><td>-179.8</td></tr>
<tr><td>HF/6-31G(d) // HF/6-31G(d)</td><td>51.0</td><td>41.2</td><td>11.5</td><td>-184.2</td></tr>
<tr><td>HF/3-21G(d) // HF/3-21G(d)</td><td>58.4</td><td>50.1</td><td>19.5</td><td>-215.2</td></tr>
<tr><td>HF/STO-3G // HF/STO-3G</td><td>93.3</td><td>66.3</td><td>101.3</td><td>-313.9</td></tr>
<tr><td>B3LYP/6-311+G(3df,2df,2p) // B3LYP/6-31G(d)</td><td>2.7</td><td>2.6</td><td>12.5</td><td>-9.3</td></tr>
<tr><td>B3LYP/6-311+G(2d,p) // B3LYP/6-31G(d)</td><td>3.2</td><td>3.0</td><td>13.6</td><td>-20.1</td></tr>
<tr><td>B3LYP/6-31+G(d,p) // B3LYP/6-31G(d)</td><td>4.0</td><td>4.2</td><td>17.6</td><td>-33.9</td></tr>
<tr><td>MP2/6-311+G(2d,p) // B3LYP/6-31G(d)</td><td>8.9</td><td>7.8</td><td>29.7</td><td>-39.2</td></tr>
<tr><td>HF/6-311+G(2d,p) // B3LYP/6-31G(d)</td><td>46.6</td><td>40.5</td><td>9.1</td><td>-174.6</td></tr>
<tr><td>MP2/6-31+G(d,p) // HF/6-31G(d)</td><td>11.8</td><td>8.2</td><td>20.9</td><td>-43.2</td></tr>
<tr><td>HF/6-311+G(2d,p) // HF/6-31G(d)</td><td>46.1</td><td>40.0</td><td>8.8</td><td>-173.8</td></tr>
<tr><td>HF/6-31+G(d,p) // HF/6-31G(d)</td><td>46.6</td><td>40.7</td><td>10.0</td><td>-179.9</td></tr>
<tr><td>B3LYP/6-311+G(2d,p) // HF/3-21G(d)</td><td>3.2</td><td>3.0</td><td>13.8</td><td>-21.2</td></tr>
<tr><td>B3LYP/6-31G(d) // HF/3-21G(d)</td><td>8.0</td><td>9.4</td><td>9.4</td><td>-54.2</td></tr>
<tr><td>B3LYP/6-31G(d) // AM1</td><td>10.5</td><td>11.3</td><td>14.7</td><td>-54.2</td></tr>
<tr><td>HF/6-31+G(d,p) // AM1</td><td>49.4</td><td>43.1</td><td>8.0</td><td>-206.1</td></tr>
<tr><td>HF/6-31G(d) // AM1</td><td>54.2</td><td>43.1</td><td>8.6</td><td>-207.2</td></tr>
</table>

The entries in this first section of the table perform geometry optimizations and compute zero-point energy corrections and final total energy values with the same model chemistry.

The entries in the remaining sections of the table perform the final higher-level total energy calculation at a geometry optimized at a lower level of theory. Zero-point energy corrections were computed with the same model as the optimized geometry.

This same data is plotted in the chart on the following page. The mean absolute deviation and standard deviation are plotted as points with error bars, and the shaded blocks plot the largest positive and negative-magnitude errors.

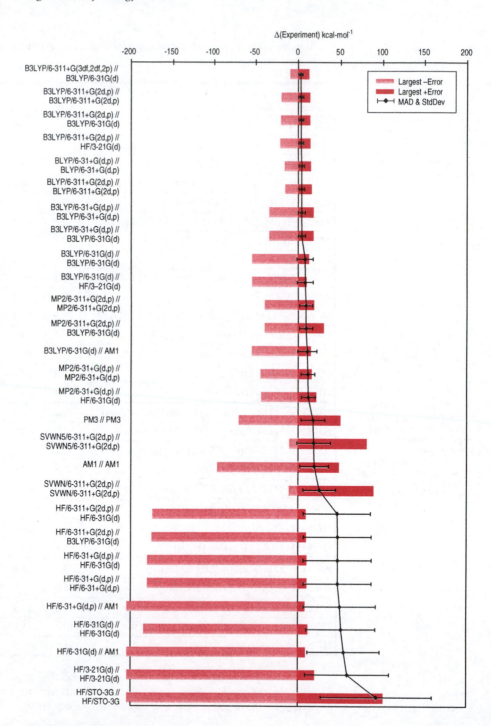

Some notes on methodology:

[1] SCF stability calculations were performed for every molecule at every model chemistry to ensure that the lowest energy electronic state of the proper type was used.

[2] All ab initio and DFT zero-point energies were scaled by the scale factors cited in Chapter 4. Semi-empirical zero-point energies were not scaled.

[3] The PM3//PM3 and AM1//AM1 models cited do not include ZPE corrections (in the full study, these models were run with and without zero-point corrections, and the results were only trivially different).

[4] Semi-empirical methods predict a non-zero energy for H+. This value was computed and taken into account in the calculation of proton affinities.

Models are arranged in the plot in order of decreasing MAD, and thus decreasing overall accuracy.

Don't be overly alarmed by the large maximum errors for many model chemistries and the rather poor results in general. It is not surprising that these methods are very inaccurate at predicting thermochemical data. It is because of the known shortcomings of existing methods that the compound methods to be discussed in the next section were developed.

We can make a number of observations about these results:

✦ The most accurate method is B3LYP/6-311+G(3df,2df,2p) // B3LYP/6-31G(d). Note that this is not the most expensive method, however.

✦ More generally, this data confirms that the common practice of running a high-level single point energy calculation at a geometry computed with a cheaper method is just as good than performing all calculations at the higher level of theory. Using geometries computed with more expensive models do not necessarily lead to more accurate final results.

✦ A corollary of the previous point is that additional basis functions are not as important for optimizing geometries as they are for predicting total energies. For example, B3LYP/6-31+G(d,p) // B3LYP/6-31G(d) performs as well on the G2 molecule set as B3LYP/6-31+G(d,p) // B3LYP/6-31+G(d,p).

✦ The semi-empirical methods have better MAD's than the Hartree-Fock-based methods, indicating that their parametrization has accounted for some of the effects of electron correlation. However, their maximum errors are very large. Semi-empirical methods are especially poor at predicting ionization potentials and proton affinities.

✦ Energies computed with the B3LYP functional are surprisingly insensitive to the geometry optimization level. The B3LYP/6-311+G(2d,p)// HF/3-21G(d) results are just as good as those computed at the B3LYP/6-31G(d) geometries, and a similar trend is seen when B3LYP/6-31G(d) final single point energy calculations are used.

The data suggest the following recommendations for selecting methods:

✦ If you can afford it, use B3LYP/6-31G(d) for geometries and zero-point corrections and B3LYP with the largest practical basis set for energy calculations.

✦ Some researchers prefer to use HF/6-31G(d) zero-point energy and thermal corrections. For some very large systems, performing a Hartree-Fock optimization and frequency calculation followed by a B3LYP/6-31G(d) optimization may be more cost effective than computing the B3LYP/6-31G(d) frequencies.

✦ When the B3LYP/6-31G(d) model chemistry is too expensive for the geometry optimization and frequency calculation, often the best tradeoff is using HF/3-21G(d) geometries and zero-point corrections, saving CPU cycles for the final B3LYP energy calculation.

✦ When AM1 geometries are all that are practical for a molecular system, using the B3LYP functional for a single point energy calculation will still often significantly improve the accuracy of the final energy.

For a much more detailed discussion of this study, consult the paper listed in the references.

Compound Methods

A variety of compound methods have been developed in an attempt to accurately model the thermochemical quantities we have been considering. These methods attempt to achieve high accuracy by combining the results of several different calculations as an approximation to a single, very high level computation which is much too expensive to be practical. We will consider two families of methods: the Gaussian-*n* methods and the Complete Basis Set (CBS) methods.

Gaussian-1 and Gaussian-2 Theories

The Gaussian-1 and Gaussian-2 theories are general procedures for computing the total energies of molecules at their equilibrium geometries (they are known as G1 and G2 for short). Both consist of several component calculations whose results are then combined in a pre-defined way.

We'll examine the steps involved in computing an energy with the G1 procedure in some detail in order to give you a feel for these types of methods. We will describe each component calculation in turn, including the values to be computed from the results. Note that for all calculations, either restricted or unrestricted methods are used, as appropriate for the system of interest.

Step 1.   Produce an initial equilibrium structure at the Hartree-Fock level using the 6-31G(d) basis set. Verify that it is a minimum with a frequency calculation and predict the zero-point energy (**ZPE**). This quantity is scaled by 0.8929.

Step 2. Beginning with the final optimized structure from step 1, obtain the final equilibrium geometry using the full MP2 method—requested with the **MP2(Full)** keyword in the route section—which includes inner shell electrons.[†] The 6-31G(d) basis set is again used. This geometry is used for all subsequent calculations.

Step 3. Compute a base level energy, which we will denote E^{base}, using MP4/6-311G(d,p) at the optimized geometry from step 2. Various corrections will be made to this energy in subsequent steps. *Note that this energy is obtained from the job run for Step 6.*

Step 4. Correct the base energy by including diffuse functions on a second energy calculation by computing the MP4/6-311G+(d,p) energy. Subtract the base energy E^{base} from this energy to obtain ΔE^{+}.

Step 5. Correct the base energy with higher polarization functions on heavy atoms by computing the MP4/6-311G(2df,p) energy. Subtract E^{base} from this energy to obtain ΔE^{2df}. If ΔE^{2df} is positive (meaning the additional polarization functions produced a higher energy than resulted without them), set this term to zero.

Step 6. Correct the base energy for residual correlation effects (to counteract known deficiencies of truncating perturbation theory at fourth order) by computing the QCISD(T)/6-311G(d,p) energy. Subtract E^{base} from this energy to produce ΔE^{QCI}.

Step 7. Correct the energy from step 6 for remaining basis set deficiencies by empirically estimating the remaining correlation energy between spin-paired electrons with the formula:

$$\Delta E^{HLC} = -0.00019n_\alpha + -0.00595n_\beta,$$

where n_α is the number of alpha electrons, and n_β is the number of beta electrons in the molecule. This term is known as the higher level correlation.

By convention, n_α must be greater than n_β for a system with an odd number of electrons. Also, this counting should ignore the core electrons in the molecule (these are treated in step 6). *Gaussian* will indicate the number of electrons of each type. Look for the line containing NOB in the output from the single point energy calculation in step 3:

```
NROrb= 19 NOA= 5 NOB= 4 NVA= 14 NVB= 15
```

The number of alpha electrons is NOA, and the number of beta electrons is

---

[†] G1 theory also predates frozen core gradients, which is why the **Full** option is specified.

NOB. The energy corrected in this way is the G1 value for the electronic energy, denoted E_e.

We can now compute the G1 energy:

$$E^{G1} = E^{base} + \Delta E^+ + \Delta E^{2df} + \Delta E^{QCI} + \Delta E^{HLC} + ZPE$$

The quantity E^{G1} is essentially an approximation to an energy calculated directly at QCISD(T)/6-311+G(2df,p).[†] Replacing this one very large calculation with four smaller ones is much faster. The components of a G1 calculation are summarized in steps 1 through 7 of the following table:

Components of G1 and G2 Total Energies

Step	Job	Result	Notes
1	HF/6-31G(d) Opt Freq	ZPE	Scale by 0.8929.
2	MP2(Full)/6-31G(d) Opt	*geometry*	Start from HF results; use this geometry for all later jobs.
3	MP4/6-311G(d,p)[†]	E^{base}	Base level energy.
4	MP4/6-311+G(d,p)	ΔE^+	= Energy - E^{base}
5	MP4/6-311G(2df,p)	ΔE^{2df}	= Energy - E^{base} (set to 0 if > 0).
6	QCISD(T)/6-311G(d,p)[†]	ΔE^{QCI}	= Energy - E^{base}
7	*Any job*	ΔE^{HLC}	= $-0.00019 n_\alpha + -0.00595 n_\beta$
8	MP2/6-311+G(3df,2p)	Δ^{G2}	= Energy - $E^{Step5(MP2)}$ - $E^{Step4(MP2)}$ + $E^{Step3(MP2)}$
9	*Any job*	Δ^{HLC}	= $+0.00114 n_\beta$

[†] These quantities are computed in a single job.

G2 Theory

Gaussian-2 theory adds some additional corrections to the G1 final result. The major term is a correction at the MP2 level, described in the next step:

Step 8.   Perform an MP2/6-311+G(3df,2p) energy calculation. Use this energy to correct the G1 energy according to the formula:

$$\Delta^{G2} = (\Delta^{+2df} - \Delta^+ - \Delta^{2df}) + \Delta^{3d2p}$$

The parenthesized term corrects for the assumption in G1 theory that the 2df and diffuse function corrections were additive. It is formed by

---

[†] This additivity assumption has been tested by Carpenter and coworkers, who computed the quantities in the entire G2 set at the QCISD(T)/6-311+G(3df,2p) level. They obtained a MAD of 1.17 kcal-mol[-1] from experiment (vs. 1.21 for G2), and an average absolute difference from the G2 values of 0.3 kcal-mol[-1]. See the paper listed in the references for full details.

computing the MP2-level +2df correction and then subtracting the separate MP2-level diffuse function and 2df corrections from it.[†]

The final term computes the correction for a third set of f functions on heavy atoms and a second set of p functions on the hydrogen atoms.[‡]

Note that all of the required MP2 energies can be extracted from the previously-run MP4 jobs in steps 3 through 5. Thus, after algebraic manipulation,[§] the final formula is:

$$\Delta^{G2} = E^{Step8} - E^{Step5(MP2)} - E^{Step4(MP2)} + E^{Step3(MP2)}$$

Step 9. G2 theory makes a modification to the higher-level correction of G1 theory by adding $0.00114n_\beta$ into the final energy calculation (which we denote Δ^{HLC}).[*]

The G2 energy can now be computed as $E^{G2} = E^{G1} + \Delta^{G2} + \Delta^{HLC}$.

Example 7.5: G2 Proton Affinity of PH₃

file: e7_05

We'll compute the proton affinity of PH_3 at the G2 level. G2 energies can be computed automatically in *Gaussian* via the **G2** keyword. Here is the output from a G2 calculation (which appears at the conclusion of the final component job step):

Temperature=	298.150000	Pressure=	1.000000
E(ZPE)=	0.034647	E(Thermal)=	0.037639
E(QCISD(T))=	-342.959149	E(Empiric)=	-0.024560
DE(Plus)=	-0.000757	DE(2DF)=	-0.023352
G1(0 K)=	-342.973171	G1 Energy=	-342.970179
G1 Enthalpy=	-342.969234	G1 Free Energy=	-342.992286
E(Delta-G2)=	-0.007122	E(G2-Empiric)=	0.004560
G2(0 K)=	-342.975733	G2 Energy=	
G2 Enthalpy=	-342.971796	G2 Free Energy=	-342.994849
DE(MP2)=	-0.027479		
G2MP2(0 K)=	-342.971982	G2MP2 Energy=	-342.968989
G2MP2 Enthalpy=	-342.968045	G2MP2 Free Energy=	-342.991097

[†] The relevant formulas are: Δ^{+2df} = E(MP2/6-311+G(2df,p)) - E(MP2/6-311G(d,p)); Δ^+ = E(MP2/6-311+G(d,p)) - E(MP2/6-311G(d,p)); Δ^{2df} = E(MP2/6-311G(2df,p)) - E(MP2/6-311G(d,p)).

[‡] Δ^{3d2p} = E(MP2/6-311+G(3df,2p)) - E(MP2/6-311+G(2df,p))

[§] Note that the E(MP2/6-311+G(2df,p)) energies cancel when we add Δ^{G2} and Δ^{3d2p}, so this job never needs to be run. How's that for sleight of hand?

[*] Alternatively, one can modify the ΔE^{HLC} formula to be: $-0.00019n_\alpha + -0.00481n_\beta$.

The components of the final G2 energy are listed as well as the computed value (in red). Note that the G1 energy is also given, as well as the value predicted by the G2(MP2) method, a related procedure to G2 designed to be less expensive.[†]

Here are the results we obtained for the proton affinity of PH_3:

	G1	G2	G2(MP2)	Exp.
PH_3	-342.67362	-342.67611	-342.67131	
PH_4^+	-342.97018	-342.97274	-342.96899	
PA (kcal-mol^{-1})	186.10	186.14	186.80	187.1
Δ(Exp)	1.00	0.96	0.30	
CPU seconds	682.4	829.1	607.5	

The values are in excellent agreement with experiment, well under the desired 2 kcal-mol^{-1} limit. This table also lists the CPU requirements for this problem.

The following table summarizes the accuracy of the various methods we have considered for the G2 molecule set:

Model	MAD	Max. Error
G1	1.53	7.4
G2	1.21	4.4
G2(MP2)	1.58	6.3

G2 theory is the most accurate and also the most expensive. G2(MP2) probably represents the best compromise between cost and accuracy among these three methods. Note that the performance differences between G2 and the other methods become more pronounced as molecule size increases. At the conclusion of the next section, we will compare these model chemistries with the CBS family of methods.

Complete Basis Set Methods

The Complete Basis Set (CBS) methods were developed by George Petersson and several collaborators. The family name reflects the fundamental observation underlying these methods: the largest errors in ab initio thermochemical calculations result from basis set truncation.

[†] In the G2(MP2) method, the several basis set extension corrections added to G1 are replaced by a single MP2-level correction: $\Delta^{MP2} = E(MP2/6\text{-}311+G(3df,2p)) - E(MP2/6\text{-}311G(d,p))$.

As in G2 theory, the total energy is computed from the results of a series of calculations. The component calculations are defined on the basis of the following principles and observations:

✦ The successive contributions to the total energy generally decrease with order of perturbation theory, while the computational expense increases rapidly. For example, in order to compute the dissociation energy for O_2 to within 1 millihartree (about 0.64 kcal-mol^{-1}), the SCF energy must be correct to six figures, the MP2 contribution must be correct to three figures, and contributions from higher orders of correlation need only be correct to two figures. The CBS models take advantage of these complimentary trends by using progressively smaller basis sets as the level of theory increases.

✦ The CBS models use the known asymptotic convergence of pair natural orbital expansions to extrapolate from calculations using a finite basis set to the estimated *complete basis set limit*. See Appendix A for more details on this technique.

CBS models typically include a Hartree-Fock calculation with a very large basis set, an MP2 calculation with a medium-sized basis set (and this is also the level where the CBS extrapolation is performed), and one or more higher-level calculations with a medium-to-modest basis set. The following table outlines the components of the CBS-4 and CBS-Q model chemistries:

Components of CBS Methods

Energy Component	CBS-4	CBS-Q
Optimized geometry	HF/3-21G(d)	MP2/6-31G(d)
ZPE (scale factor)	HF/3-21G(d) (0.91671)	HF/6-31G† (0.91844)
SCF energy	HF/6-311+G(3d2f,2df,p)	HF/6-311+G(3d2f,2df,2p)
2nd order correlation	MP2/6-31+G†	MP2/6-311+G(3d2f,2df,2p)
CBS extrapolation	≥5 configurations	≥10 configurations
Higher order correlation	MP4(SDQ)/6-31G	MP4(SDQ)/6-31+G(d(f),d,f) QCISD(T)/6-31+G†
Additional empirical corrections	1 and 2-electron higher-order corrections (size-consistent), spin contamination	2-electron higher-order correction (size-consistent), spin contamination, core correlation for sodium

CBS-4 is the less expensive of these two methods. It begins with a HF/3-21G(d) geometry optimization; the zero-point energy is computed at the same level. It then uses a large basis set SCF calculation as a base energy, and an MP2/6-31+G† calculation with a CBS extrapolation to correct the energy through second order. A

MP4(SDQ)/6-31+(d,p) calculation is used to approximate higher order contributions. This model also includes some additional empirical corrections.

The CBS-Q model starts with a geometry optimization at the MP2 level of theory; the zero-point energy is computed at the HF level. It then uses a large basis set MP2 calculation as a base energy, and a CBS extrapolation to correct the energy through second order. Two additional calculations are used to approximate higher order contributions: MP4(SDQ)/6-31+(d,p) (with extra polarization functions on sulfur, phosphorous and chlorine) to approximate the higher order correlation effects, and QCISD(T)/6-31+G† for still higher order effects. This model also has empirical corrections for spin contamination and a size-consistent higher-order correction.

There are other defined CBS methods, including the very accurate and very expensive CBS-APNO, but we will be focusing on CBS-4 and CBS-Q.

Example 7.6: CBS-4 and CBS-Q Proton Affinities of PH₃

file: e7_06

We will use the CBS-4 and CBS-Q methods to compute the proton affinity of PH_3. The computed CBS energy is given at the conclusion of the final component job step. Here are the results we obtained:

	CBS-4	CBS-Q	Exp
PH_3	-342.68354	-342.67548	
PH_4^+	-342.98512	-342.97227	
PA (kcal-mol^{-1})	189.25	186.24	187.1
Δ(Exp)	-2.15	0.86	
CPU seconds	356.7	708.7	

Both methods produce good results for this problem. The CBS-4 value is all the more remarkable when the method's computational efficiency is taken into consideration.

Here are the overall results for the CBS and G2 model chemistries we have considered on the G2 molecule set, as well as some sample relative performance data:

Model	MAD	|Max. Error|	Sample Relative CPU Times		
			PH_3	F_2CO	SiF_4
CBS-4	1.98	7.0	1.0	1.0	1.0
G2(MP2)	1.58	6.3	2.4	10.3	11.5
CBS-Q	1.01	3.8	2.8	8.4	12.7
G2	1.21	4.4	3.2	25.9	59.1

CBS-4 achieves a MAD under 2 kcal-mol^{-1} for substantially less computational cost than any other method (and these cost differentials will increase with problem size). CBS-Q achieves better results than G2 and is also significantly less expensive.

The following table and graph summarize the accuracies of the methods we have considered in this chapter.

The model chemistries in this table are arranged in ascending order of mean absolute deviation. The other columns give the standard deviation of the MAD and the absolute value of the maximum error with respect to experiment for each model chemistry.

This same data is plotted on the following page. The darkest portion of each bar indicates the MAD. The middle portion corresponds to the standard deviation; about two-thirds of the actual absolute deviations fall within the first two segments of the bar. The final lightest portion of each bar indicates the maximum absolute deviation from experiment for that model chemistry. (All values greater than 50 kcal-mol^{-1} are truncated just beyond that level).

Model Chemistry	MAD	Standard Deviation	Absolute Max. Error
CBS-Q	1.0	0.8	3.8
G2	1.2	0.9	5.1
G2(MP2)	1.5	1.2	6.2
G1	1.6	1.4	9.2
CBS-4	2.0	1.5	7.0
B3LYP/6-311+G(3df,2df,2p) // B3LYP/6-31G(d)	2.7	2.6	12.5
B3LYP/6-311+G(2d,p) // B3LYP/6-311+G(2d,p)	3.1	3.0	19.7
B3LYP/6-311+G(2d,p) // B3LYP/6-31G(d)	3.2	3.0	20.1
B3LYP/6-311+G(2d,p) // HF/3-21G(d)	3.2	3.0	21.2
BLYP/6-31+G(d,p) // BLYP/6-31+G(d,p)	3.9	3.2	15.2
BLYP/6-311+G(2d,p) // BLYP/6-311+G(2d,p)	3.9	3.2	15.9
B3LYP/6-31+G(d,p) // B3LYP/6-31+G(d,p)	3.9	4.2	33.8
B3LYP/6-31+G(d,p) // B3LYP/6-31G(d)	4.0	4.2	33.9
B3LYP/6-31G(d) // B3LYP/6-31G(d)	7.9	9.5	54.2
B3LYP/6-31G(d) // HF/3-21G(d)	8.0	9.4	54.2
MP2/6-311+G(2d,p) // B3LYP/6-31G(d)	8.9	7.8	39.2
MP2/6-311+G(2d,p) // MP2/6-311+G(2d,p)	8.9	7.8	39.2
B3LYP/6-31G(d) // AM1	10.5	11.3	54.2
MP2/6-31+G(d,p) // MP2/6-31+G(d,p)	11.4	8.1	44.0
MP2/6-31+G(d,p) // HF/6-31G(d)	11.8	8.2	43.2
PM3 // PM3	17.2	14.0	69.9
SVWN5/6-311+G(2d,p) // SVWN5/6-311+G(2d,p)	18.1	19.8	81.0
AM1 // AM1	18.8	16.9	95.5
SVWN/6-311+G(2d,p) // SVWN/6-311+G(2d,p)	24.9	19.2	89.3
HF/6-311+G(2d,p) // HF/6-31G(d)	46.1	40.0	173.8
HF/6-311+G(2d,p) // B3LYP/6-31G(d)	46.6	40.5	174.6
HF/6-31+G(d,p) // HF/6-31G(d)	46.6	40.7	179.9
HF/6-31+G(d,p) // HF/6-31+G(d,p)	46.7	40.6	179.8
HF/6-31+G(d,p) // AM1	49.4	43.1	206.1
HF/6-31G(d) // HF/6-31G(d)	51.0	41.2	184.2
HF/6-31G(d) // AM1	54.2	43.1	207.2
HF/3-21G(d) // HF/3-21G(d)	58.4	50.1	215.2
HF/STO-3G // HF/STO-3G	93.3	66.3	313.9

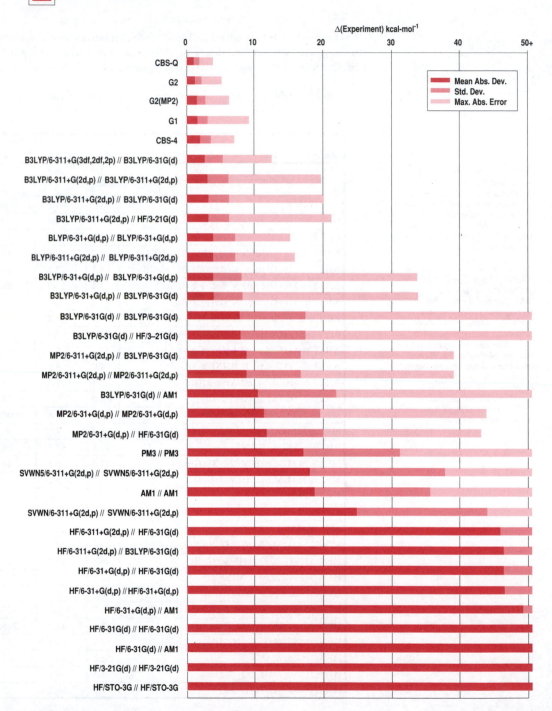

Exercises

Exercise 7.1: CBS-4 Thermochemistry

files: **7_01a (AE)**
7_01b (IP)
7_01c (PA)
7_01d (EA)

Compute the atomization energy, ionization potential and proton affinities for water as well as the electron affinity for OH. Use the CBS-4 method for all calculations (the keyword is **CBS-4**).

Solution Here are the results we obtained as well as the corresponding experimental values:

Molecule	Energy
H	-0.50194
O	-74.99147
H_2O	-76.34574
H_2O^+	-75.87605
H_3O^+	-76.60408
OH	-75.65500
OH^-	-75.72523

	eV		kcal-mol^{-1}		
	CBS-4	Exp	CBS-4	Exp	Δ
AE(H_2O)	9.54	9.51	219.90	219.3	-0.6
EA(OH)	1.91	1.83	44.09	42.2	-1.9
IP(H_2O)	12.78	12.62	294.74	291.0	-3.7
PA(H_2O)	7.03	7.13	162.11	164.5	2.4

CBS-4 does very well for the atomization energy and electron affinity computations and fairly well for the other two calculations. ■

Advanced Exercise 7.2: Ozone Destruction by Atomic Chlorine Revisited

files: **7_02a (G2)**
7_02b. (CBS-4)
7_02c (CBS-Q)

This exercise completes the study we began in exercise 6.9. Compute the enthalpy change for the destruction of ozone by atomic chlorine by subtracting the dissociation energies of O_2 and ClO from the dissociation energy for ozone. Use the G2, CBS-4 and CBS-Q model chemistries, and the experimental geometries given in exercise 6.9 as starting points.

Solution   Here are the results that we obtained:

Method	Ozone	O_2	Oxygen	ClO	Chlorine
G2	-225.17155	-150.14585	-74.98061	-534.75372	-459.67521
CBS-4	-225.18302	-150.16970	-74.99147	-534.75362	-459.67432
CBS-Q	-225.18558	-150.16035	-74.98562	-534.76794	-459.68148

| | D_0 | | | | |
	O_3	O_2	ClO	ΔH	CPU (secs.)
G2	144.1	115.9	61.4	-33.1	6172.6
CBS-4	130.9	117.2	55.1	-41.4	1109.4
CBS-Q	143.5	118.7	63.3	-38.4	3384.4
Experiment	142.2	118.0	63.3	-39.1	

The top table gives the predicted total energies for each molecule, and the bottom table lists the computed dissociation energies and ΔH. All three model chemistries do pretty well on all three phases of the process, with G2 and CBS-Q generally modeling it very accurately. The CBS-Q values are the most accurate, and they take only about half as long to compute as G2 theory. CBS-4 performs well for O_2 and for the overall ΔH at substantially less cost: about one sixth the cost of G2 and one third the cost of CBS-Q. ■

References

G1 and G2 Theory   *G1*: J. A. Pople, M. Head-Gordon, D. J. Fox, K. Raghavachari, and L. A. Curtiss, *J. Chem. Phys*, **90**, 5622 (1989).

G2: L. A. Curtiss, K. Raghavachari, G. W. Trucks, and J. A. Pople, *J. Chem. Phys.*, **94**, 7221 (1991).

G2(MP2): L. A. Curtiss, K. Raghavachari and J. A. Pople, *J. Chem. Phys.*, **98**, 1293 (1993).

Testing Additivity Assumptions: L. A. Curtiss, J. E. Carpenter, K. Raghavachari and J. A. Pople, *J. Chem. Phys.*, **96**, 9030 (1992).

CBS Methods   J. W. Ochterski, G. A. Petersson and J. A. Montgomery, Jr., *J. Chem. Phys.*, **104**, 2598 (1996).

Comparing CBS and G2 Methods   J. W. Ochterski, G. A. Petersson and K. B. Wiberg, *J. Am. Chem. Soc.*, 117, 11299 (1995).

Allyl Cation Charges	J. B. Foresman, M. W. Wong, K. B. Wiberg, and M. J. Frisch, "A Theoretical Investigation of the Rotational Barrier in Allyl and 1,1,3,3-Tetramethylallyl Ions," *J. Am. Chem. Soc.*, 115, 2220 (1993).
Charge Assignment Schemes	*CHelpG*: C. M. Breneman and K. B. Wiberg, *J. Comp. Chem.*, 11, 361 (1990).
	Merz-Kollman-Singh: U. C. Singh and P. A. Kollman, *J. Comp. Chem.*, 5, 129 (1984).
	B. H. Besler, K. M. Merz, Jr., and P. A. Kollman, *J. Comp. Chem.*, 11, 431 (1990).
	Natural Population Analysis: A. E. Reed and F. Weinhold, *J. Amer. Chem. Soc.*, 102, 7211 (1980).
	A. E. Reed, R. B. Weinstock, and F. Weinhold, *J. Chem. Phys.*, 78, 4066 (1983).
	A. E. Reed and F. Weinhold, *J. Chem. Phys.*, 81, 1736 (1983).
	J. E. Carpenter and F. Weinhold, *J. Mol. Struct. (Theochem)*, 169, 41 (1988).
MP2 vs. HF Charges	K. B. Wiberg, C. M. Hadad, T. J. LePage, C. M. Breneman, and M. J. Frisch, *J. Phys. Chem.*, 96, 671 (1992).
Comparing Charge Methods	K. B. Wiberg and P. R. Rablen, *J. Comp. Chem.*, 14, 1504 (1993).
Atoms in Molecules Analysis	R. F. W. Bader, *Atoms in Molecules: A Quantum Theory* (Oxford, Oxford Univ. Press, 1990).
	J. Cioslowski and S. T. Mixon, *J. Am. Chem. Soc.*, 114, 4382 (1992).
	J. Cioslowski and S. T. Mixon, *J. Am. Chem. Soc.*, 113, 4142 (1991).
Accuracies of Model Chemistries	J. B. Foresman, Æ. Frisch, J. W. Ochterski and M. J. Frisch, *in preparation*.

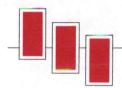

Part 3: Applications

Chapter

8

Studying Chemical Reactions and Reactivity

In This Chapter:

Potential Energy Surface Scans

IRC Calculations

Isodesmic Reactions

In this chapter, we will focus on using electronic structure theory to study chemical reactions. We will begin by examining plots of the electron density in order to assess what information may be gleaned from them. Next, we will review and expand on our earlier discussion of computing activation barriers in Chapter 4. Then, we will go on to discuss more sophisticated techniques for modeling chemical reactions, and we will conclude this chapter by discussing the modeling of isodesmic reactions and their use in predicting heats of formation for unknown systems.

In the course of our explorations, we will introduce two new types of calculations:

✦   Potential energy surface scans.
✦   Reaction path following (using intrinsic reaction coordinates).

Interpreting the Electron Density

Visualizing the electron density or the electrostatic potential can be a useful first step in exploring the reactivity of a molecular system.

Example 8.1: Electron Densities of Substituted Benzenes

files: **e8_01a (Cl)**
e8_01b (NO$_2$)

Isomeric orientation in electrophilic aromatic substitution is a well-studied topic in organic chemistry. Here we visualize the electron density of various compounds as an aid to understanding this phenomon.

The nitration of nitrobenzene and of chlorobenzene are known to occur via the same mechanism: the ring is initially attacked by NO$_2^+$, yielding a cation intermediate for each isomer. When the nitration process is fully complete, the distribution of the various isomers of the final product varies greatly for the two compounds:

System	ortho	meta	para
C$_6$H$_4$NO$_2$Cl	29%	1%	70%
C$_6$H$_4$N$_2$O$_4$	7%	88%	1%

We will examine the meta and para cation intermediates for the two substances.

para forms

Cl

chlorobenzene
intermediates

meta forms

nitrobenzene
intermediates

The plots on the next page illustrate an isodensity surface (δ=0.0001) for the two isomers of each cation intermediate molecule, as well as seven slices through the electron density. The structures were optimized using the B3LYP/6-31G(d) model chemistry, and the electron densities were computed at the HF/6-31G(d) level of theory. The slices on the far left in each row represent the "center" of the density, approximately corresponding to the plane of the carbon ring. The slices to their right begin 12.5% of the "thickness" of the density below that plane (toward the hydrogen atom on the attacking nitro group), and each successive illustration steps about 2.5% farther away from the central plane. The four sets of illustrations were plotted at exactly the same relative locations with respect to the plane of the molecule

The darkest regions in the slices indicate the greatest electron density. The meta form of nitrated chlorobenzene and the para form of nitrated nitrobenzene retain the resonance structure to a much greater degree throughout the extent of the electron density. In contrast, the density in the less-favored conformations becomes more localized on the substituent as one moves outward from the plane of the carbon atoms.

As this example illustrates, plots such as these can be useful for providing a qualitative understanding of the electron density and its relationship to reactivity, but you would be wise to use and interpret them with care. It is all too easy to unintentionally manipulate such illustrations to create the effect that one expects to observe. For example, any one slice or isosurface of the electron density can be used to argue for a given viewpoint. It is important to examine and visualize the entire volumetric data set before reaching conclusions based on it. [†]

Computing Enthalpies of Reaction

Example 8.2: Hydration Reactions
file: e8_02

Let's consider the hydration reaction: $H^+ + H_2O \rightarrow H_3O^+$. Our goal is to compute $\Delta H^{298\ddagger}$ for the reaction. It can be calculated using these expressions:

$$\Delta H^{298} = \Delta E^{298} + \Delta(PV)$$

$$\Delta E^{298} = \Delta E_e^0 + \Delta(\Delta E_e)^{298} + \Delta E_v^0 + \Delta(\Delta E_v)^{298} + \Delta E_r^{298} + \Delta E_t^{298}$$

[†] See the Gaussian, Inc. white paper , "Visualizing Results from *Gaussian*" for more discussion of the relevant techniques and issues.

[‡] Actually, 298.15 K.

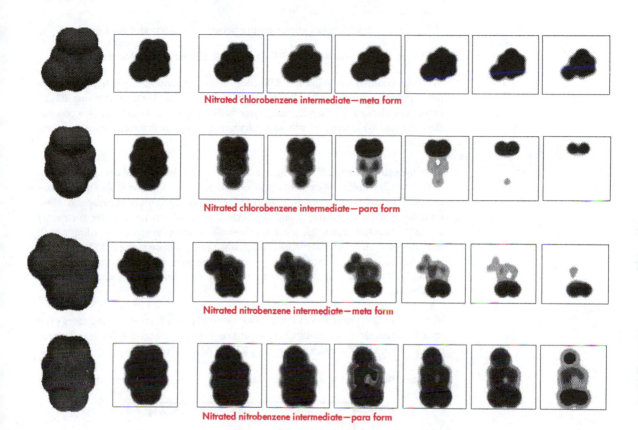

Nitrated chlorobenzene intermediate—meta form

Nitrated chlorobenzene intermediate—para form

Nitrated nitrobenzene intermediate—meta form

Nitrated nitrobenzene intermediate—para form

Example 8.2 Continued

The terms in these expressions are defined as follows:

ΔE_e^0 — Energy difference between products and reactants at 0 K.

$\Delta (\Delta E_e)^{298}$ — Change in the electronic energy difference between 0 K and 298 K. This term is negligible for these reactions and will be ignored.

ΔE_v^0 — Difference between the zero-point energies of the products and reactants (0° K).

$\Delta (\Delta E_v)^{298}$ — Change in the vibrational energy difference between 0 K and 298 K.

ΔE_r^{298} — Difference in the rotational energies of products and reactants.

ΔE_t^{298} Translational energy change between products and reactants.

$\Delta(PV)$ PV work term = −RT since 1 mole of gas is lost in the reactions.

ΔE_e^0 is obtained by taking the difference of the total energies predicted in single point energy calculations for the reactants and products. We'll be running B3LYP energy calculations with a reasonably large basis set—6-311+G(2df,2p)—to produce these values. We'll need to run one calculation for each distinct molecule in the reaction.

All of the other ΔE and $\Delta(PV)$ terms are combined into the thermal energy correction to the enthalpy predicted by frequency calculations. Therefore, we'll also need to run an optimization plus frequency calculation for each component of the reaction. Now, we could run the frequencies using the method and basis set we want for the energy and get both results in a single job, but this would be too expensive. Accordingly, we'll run a distinct job for each molecule, computing the frequency at the B3LYP/6-31G(d) level, which is accurate enough for predicting the zero-point and thermal energy terms. We'll use the geometries computed in this step for the high accuracy energy calculations.

Note that we don't need to run any calculations on H^+ at all. Its electronic energy is 0 since it has no electrons, and its only other non-zero energy term is the translational energy term ΔE_t^{298}, which is equal to $\frac{3}{2}RT = 0.889$ kcal mol^{-1}.

Here are the results for our reaction (energy in hartrees, scaled thermal energy in kcal-mol^{-1}):

Molecule	E_e^0	Thermal Corr. to H^{298}	
		Hartrees	kcal-mol^{-1}
H^+	0.0		0.889
H_2O	-76.46241	0.02452	15.39
H_3O^+	-76.73422	0.03753	23.55

ΔH^{298} = -163.3 kcal mol^{-1}

Experiment = -165.3±1.8 kcal mol^{-1}

The computed value for ΔH^{298} is in excellent agreement with the experimental value. We'll look at two similar hydration reactions in Exercise 8.1.

Studying Potential Energy Surfaces

Theoretical predictions of potential energy surfaces and reaction paths can sometimes yield quite surprising results. In this section, we'll consider an example which illustrates the general approach toward and usefulness of studying potential energy surfaces in detail.

Consider rotational isomerism in allyl cation:

One suggested path between the two forms is via a perpendicular transition structure having C_s symmetry. A plausible way to begin an investigation of this reaction is to attempt to locate a saddle point on the potential energy surface corresponding to this hypothesized transition structure. A Hartree-Fock/6-311++G(d,p) calculation succeeds in finding such a transition structure. However, higher level computations using MP2 and QCISD with the same basis set fail to locate a similar stationary point. Instead, these optimizations proceed to a C_s minimum (not a saddle point and thus not a transition structure) in which the hydrogen of the central carbon has migrated to the terminal carbon. This new minimum lies approximately 10 kcal-mol^{-1} above the equilibrium structure on the potential energy surface.

These results suggest another route for isomerization, involving three steps:

✦ An initial hydrogen shift from the central carbon to the terminal carbon, forming a methyl group (I→II);

✦ Methyl rotation of the three hydrogens (III);

✦ A second hydrogen migration from the methyl group back to the central carbon (IV, which is equivalent to I');

Subsequent calculations at the MP2 level locate the two transition structures like those suggested. In this case, Intrinsic Reaction Coordinate (IRC) calculations were used to confirm that these transition structures do in fact connect the minima in question; we'll look at this kind of calculation in detail later in this chapter.

Hartree-Fock theory produces a "phantom" transition structure in this case. The potential energy surface defined by the RHF/6-311++G(d,p) model chemistry does contain this saddle point, but it is absent from those predicted by higher levels of theory. One explanation for this discrepancy is the underestimation of the barrier to localize positive charge on a terminal carbon at the Hartree-Fock level, resulting in the "path" involving methylene rotation being lower in energy than the one resulting from proton migration.

Potential Energy Surface Scans

A potential energy surface scan allows you to explore a region of a potential energy surface. A normal scan calculation performs a series of single point energy calculations at various structures, thereby sampling points on the potential energy surface.[†] When you request a scan, you specify the variable(s) in the molecular structure which are to vary and the range of values which they should take on.

In *Gaussian*, potential energy surface scans are automated. Here is a sample input file for a simple potential energy surface scan:

```
#T UMP4/6-311+G(d,p) Scan Test

CH PES Scan

0 2
C
H 1 R

R 0.5 40 0.05
```

This input file requests a potential energy surface scan for CH by including the **Scan** keyword in the route section. The variables section of the molecule specification uses an expanded format:

name initial-value [*number-of-points increment-size*]

When only one parameter follows a variable name, that variable is held fixed throughout the entire scan. When all three parameters are included, that variable will be allowed to vary during the scan. Its initial value will be set to *initial-value*; this value will increase by *increment-size* at each of *number-of-points* subsequent points.

When only one variable is allowed to vary, the scan begins at the structure where the specified variable is equal to *initial-value*. At each subsequent point, *increment-size* is added to the current value for the variable. The process is repeated until *number-of-points* additional points have been completed.

[†] A *relaxed* PES scan similarly samples points on the potential energy surface and performs a geometry optimization of the remaining non-scanned coordinates at each one. Such a scan is requested by using the **Opt=AddRedundant** keyword and including the **S** code on one or more variables in the **AddRedundant** input section. See the *Gaussian User's Reference* for details.

When more than one variable is allowed to vary, then all possible combinations of their values will be included. For example, the following variable definitions will result in a total of 20 scan points:

```
R  1.0 4 0.1
A 60.0 3 1.0
```

There are five values of R and four values of A, and the program will compute energies at all 20 structures corresponding to the different combinations of them.

The results of a potential energy surface scan appear following this heading within *Gaussian* output:

```
Summary of the potential surface scan:
```

All of the available levels of theory appear in the table of results. For example, a scan run at the MP2 level will also include the Hartree-Fock energies at each point.

You can plot the results of the scan to get a picture of the region of the potential energy surface that you've explored. By doing so, you may be able to determine the approximate location of the minimum energy structure. However, potential energy surface scans do not include a geometry optimization.

We'll look at examples of potential energy surface scan calculations in Exercise 8.2.

Reaction Path Following

As we noted in Chapter 4, successfully completing a transition structure optimization does not guarantee that you have found the right transition structure: the one that connects the reactants and products of interest. One way to determine what minima a transition structure connects is to examine the normal mode corresponding to the imaginary frequency, determining whether or not the motion tends to deform the transition structure as expected. Sometimes, it can be hard to tell for certain. In this section, we will discuss a more precise method for determining what points on a potential energy surface are connected by a given transition structure.

An IRC calculation examines the reaction path leading down from a transition structure on a potential energy surface. Such a calculation starts at the saddle point and follows the path in both directions from the transition state, optimizing the geometry of the molecular system at each point along the path. In this way, an IRC calculation definitively connects two minima on the potential energy surface by a path which passes through the transition state between them.

When studying a reaction, the reaction path connects the reactants and the products through the transition state. Note that two minima on a potential energy surface may have more than one reaction path connecting them, corresponding to different transition structures through which the reaction passes. From this point on, we will use the term reaction path to designate the intrinsic reaction path predicted by the IRC procedure, which can be qualitatively thought of as the lowest energy path, in mass-weighted coordinates, which passes through that saddle point.

Reaction path computations allow you to verify that a given transition structure actually connects the starting and ending structures that you think it does. Once this fact is confirmed, you can then go on to compute an activation energy for the reaction by comparing the (zero-point corrected) energies of the reactants and the transition state.

Running IRC Calculations

In *Gaussian*, a reaction path calculation is requested with the **IRC** keyword in the route section. Before you can run one, however, certain requirements must be met. An IRC calculation begins at a transition structure and steps along the reaction path a fixed number of times (the default is 6) in each direction, toward the two minima that it connects. However, in most cases, it will not step all the way to the minimum on either side of the path.

Here is the procedure for running an IRC calculation:

✦   Optimize the starting transition structure (discussed in Chapter 3).

✦   Run a frequency calculation on the optimized transition structure. This is done for several reasons:

   ❖   To verify that the first job did in fact find a transition structure.
   ❖   To determine the zero-point energy for the transition structure.
   ❖   To generate force constant data needed in the IRC calculation.

✦   Perform the IRC calculation (requested with the **IRC** keyword). This job will help you to verify that you have the correct transition state for the reaction when you examine the structures that are downhill from the saddle point. In some cases, however, you will need to increase the number of steps taken in the IRC in order to get closer to the minimum; the **MaxPoints** option specifies the number of steps to take in each direction as its argument. You can also continue an IRC calculation by using the **IRC=(ReStart,MaxPoints=**n**)** keyword, setting n to some appropriate value (provided, of course, that you have saved the checkpoint file).

The various components of an IRC study are often run as a single, multi-step job.

To accurately predict the barrier for the reaction, you may need to perform some additional computations in order to collect all required data. This may include one or more of the following additional jobs:

✦   A high level, large basis set energy calculation on the optimized transition structure.

✦   Optimizations of the reactants and products, followed by frequency calculations and high level energy calculations (to produce zero-point energies and high quality total energies, respectively).

The entire process can then be repeated for a different reaction path, starting from a different saddle point, in order to explore other possible ways to move from reactants to products.

Exploring a Potential Energy Surface

We'll now use *Gaussian*'s reaction path following facility to explore the H_2CO potential energy surface. There are many minima on this surface—including formaldehyde, hydroxycarbene (HCOH: cis and trans), and H_2 + CO—each corresponding to different reactant/product combinations. For now, we will consider only these two reactions:

Molecular Dissociation of Formaldehyde

We'll consider the molecular dissociation reaction first (upper illustration). We want to determine the transition structure and to predict the activation energy for the reaction. In order to do so, we'll need the following information:

✦ Zero-point-corrected energies for formaldehyde, hydrogen molecule, and carbon monoxide.

✦ The geometry of the transition structure and its zero-point corrected energy.

We will model this reaction at the HF/6-31G(d) level. We can draw upon previous calculations for some of this data. The following table lists these results:

Molecule	SCF Energy	ZPE	Total Energy
H_2	-1.12683	0.00968	-1.11716
CO	-112.73788	0.00508	-112.73280
Thus, H_2 + CO = -113.84996			
H_2CO	-113.86633	0.02668	-113.83966

To compute the energy of the transition structure, we'll need to perform the following set of calculations:

✦ An optimization of the transition structure geometry (yields the SCF energy).
✦ A frequency calculation (yields the zero-point energy).
✦ An IRC calculation (indicates the two minima connected by the saddle point).

Optimizing the Transition Structure

Example 8.3: CH₂O → H₂ + CO IRC
file: **e8_03**

For our initial geometry for the transition structure, we'll detach one hydrogen from the carbon and increase the O-C-H bond angle.[†] We specified the **Opt=(TS,CalcFC)** keyword in the route section, requesting an optimization to a transition state. The **CalcFC** option is used to compute the initial force constants, a technique which is generally helpful for transition state optimizations. We've also included the **Freq** keyword so that a frequency calculation will automatically be run at the optimized geometry.

The optimization job converges quickly, computing an SCF energy of -113.69352 hartrees at the final point. The final structure is close to the starting molecule specification.

Verifying the Optimized Structure

The results of the frequency calculation confirm that the optimized structure is a transition structure, producing one imaginary frequency. The predicted zero-point energy is 0.01774 (after scaling), yielding a total energy of -113.67578 hartrees.

Running the IRC Calculation

We will also use the results of the frequency job in the IRC calculation we'll do next. This job will enable us to verify that this transition structure connects the two minima that we think it does, and we use the keyword **IRC** to request it. By default, the calculation takes 6 steps in each direction, where each step corresponds to a geometry optimization. However, the calculation will stop searching in a given direction once its convergence criteria are met, and an IRC calculation does not necessarily step all the way down to the minimum.

An IRC calculation requires both an optimized transition structure and the corresponding force constants in order to do its work. The two most common ways of providing force constants are:

[†] Here is our actual molecule specification input:
```
0,1
O
C,1,1.13
H,2,1.1,1,164.0
H,3,1.3,2,90.0,1,0.
```

◆ Retrieving them from the checkpoint file from a previous frequency calculation (**IRC=RCFC**).

◆ Computing them at the start of the IRC calculation (**IRC=CalcFC**).

IRC calculations produce a table summarizing their results just before exiting. Here is the table for our calculation:

Farthest points reached on each side of the TS

```
--------------------------------------------------------------------
           SUMMARY OF REACTION PATH FOLLOWING:
           (Int. Coord:  Angstroms, and Degrees)
--------------------------------------------------------------------
                ENERGY    RX.COORD      X1        Y1        Z1
        1     -113.72238  -0.59920   -0.12955   0.00000  -0.67890
        2     -113.71426  -0.49922   -0.12815   0.00000  -0.67871
        ...
       12     -113.71641   0.49933   -0.11657   0.00000  -0.67703
       13     -113.72583   0.59933   -0.11574   0.00000  -0.67702
                 X2         Y2         Z2        X3        Y3
        1     -0.07668    0.00000    0.46594   -0.07299   0.00000
        2     -0.08318    0.00000    0.46435   -0.03184   0.00000
       12     -0.13961    0.00000    0.44769    0.41469   0.00000
       13     -0.14420    0.00000    0.44590    0.46084   0.00000
                 Z3         X4         Y4        Z4
        1      1.52435    1.41289    0.00000   1.06418
        2      1.52252    1.42688    0.00000   1.08209
       12      1.50917    1.46844    0.00000   1.26710
       13      1.51247    1.46389    0.00000   1.28489
```

The entries in the table are arranged in order of increasing reaction coordinate or distance along the reaction path (the reaction coordinate is a composite variable spanning all of the degrees of freedom of the potential energy surface). The energy and optimized variable values are listed for each point (in this case, as Cartesian coordinates). The first and last entries correspond to the final points on each side of the reaction path.

Here are the two structures our calculation produced,[†] along with the transition structure from which the IRC began:

† We obtained the values for these geometrical parameters by reading the Cartesian coordinates produced by the IRC calculation into our favorite molecular visualization package.

In structure I (numbered 1 in the IRC output), we find a formaldehyde-like structure, although the O-C-H bond angles are distorted from the equilibrium geometry. However, we can identify the minimum along this side of the path as formaldehyde.

In structure II (numbered 13 in the IRC output), the C-H bond has lengthened with respect to the transition structure (1.23 versus 1.09Å), while the C-O bond length has contracted slightly. Both changes are what would be expected as formaldehyde dissociates to form carbon monoxide and hydrogen molecule.[†]

Predicting the Activation Energies

Since the IRC has verified that this transition structure does connect the reactants and products for this reaction, we can now compute the activation energies for the reaction:

System	Energy (*hartrees*)	Activation Energy (*kcal mol^{-1}*)
Transition State	-113.67578	
Reactants: H_2CO	-113.83966	102.8 (*forward*)
Products: $H_2 + CO$	-113.84996	109.3 (*reverse*)

These values suggest that the barriers in both directions for the reaction are essentially equal.

Note that the final energy of the products in an IRC calculation may not equal the sum of the energies of the isolated molecules. An IRC terminates when the energy reaches a minimum for the molecular complex, a level which is slightly above the sum of the isolated product molecules.

The 1,2 Hydrogen Shift Reaction

We will use a similar procedure to investigate the second reaction, where formaldehyde transforms into the trans form of hydroxycarbene:

[†] Some chemical visualization programs even plot this structure as two distinct molecules.

The zero-point corrected energy for the trans hydroxycarbene structure is -113.75709 hartrees at the RHF/6-31G(d) level of theory.

Finding the Transition Structure

Example 8.4: CH₂O → HCOH IRC
file: e8_04

First, we perform an optimization of the transition structure for the reaction, yielding the planar structure at the left. A frequency calculation on the optimized structure confirms that it is a first-order saddle point and hence a transition structure, having a zero-point corrected energy of -113.67941 hartrees. The frequency calculation also prepares for the IRC computation to follow.

Following the Reaction Path

Here are the structures at the two ends of the IRC path as well as that of the transition structure for comparison:

Parameter	I	II	TS
C-O bond length (Å)	1.25	1.29	1.27
C-H bond length (Å)	1.1, 1.4	1.1, 1.13	1.1, 1.23
O-H distance (Å)	1.0	1.4	1.17
O-C-H bond angle (°)	113.8, 43.6	118.0, 72.3	116.0,56.3
H-C-H bond angle (°)	157.4	169.7	172.2
C-O-H bond angle (°)	74.0	49.8	59.7

In structure I, the O-C-H bond angle (with the hydrogen closest to the oxygen atom) is decreasing, moving the hydrogen closer to the oxygen. Continuing in this direction will result in the hydrogen detaching completely from the carbon and becoming fully bonded to the oxygen, leading to trans hydroxycarbene.

In structure II, on the other hand, the same O-C-H bond angle is increasing. Continuing down this path will eventually result in formaldehyde as the hydrogen moves away from the oxygen and toward its final position on the opposite side of the carbon atom.

Predicting the Activation Energies

Since we have verified that the transition structure connects the reactants and products, we can now compute the activation energy for the reaction. The results we obtained are listed in the following table:

System	Energy (hartrees)
Formaldehyde	-113.83966
trans Hydroxycarbene	-113.75709
Transition State	-113.67941
Forward Reaction Activation Energy	100.6 kcal mol^{-1}
Reverse Reaction Activation Energy	48.7 kcal mol^{-1}

These results predict that the hydroxycarbene to formaldehyde reaction will proceed significantly more easily than the forward reaction. However, for this problem, electron correlation is needed for good quantitative values. For example, the MP4/6-31G(d,p) level predicts a value of 86.6 kcal mol^{-1} for the activation energy of the forward reaction.

The following diagram illustrates the results we've computed so far for the H$_2$CO potential energy surface:

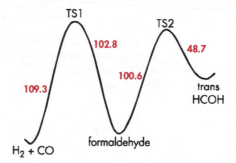

We'll continue our study of the H$_2$CO potential energy surface in Exercise 8.3.

A Final Note on IRC Calculations

We'll close this section with the following reminder from Shaik, Schlegel and Wolfe, describing both the usefulness and the limitations of the IRC method:

> Although intrinsic reaction coordinates like minima, maxima, and saddle points comprise geometrical or mathematical features of energy surfaces, considerable care must be exercised not to attribute chemical or physical significance to them. Real molecules have more than infinitesimal kinetic energy, and will not follow the intrinsic reaction path. Nevertheless, the intrinsic reaction coordinate provides a convenient description of the progress of a reaction, and also plays a central role in the calculation of reaction rates by variational state theory and reaction path Hamiltonians.
>
> [pp. 50-51]

Isodesmic Reactions

An *isodesmic* reaction is one in which the total number of each type of bond is identical in the reactants and products. Here is a simple example:

In this reaction, there are twelve single bonds and one (C-O) double bond in both the reactants and products. Because of this conservation of the total number and types of bonds, very good results can be obtained relatively inexpensively for isodesmic reactions due to the cancellation of errors on the two sides of the reaction. In other words, comparing very similar systems enables us to take maximum advantage of cancellation of error.

Isodesmic reactions may be studied in themselves. For example, energy differences may be compared between the reactants and products in order to predict ΔH. In addition, isodesmic reactions may be used to predict the heats of formation for compounds of interest by predicting ΔH for the reaction and then computing the desired heat of formation by removing the known heats of formation for the other compounds from this quantity. We will look at an example of each type in this section.

Example 8.5: ΔH for an Isodesmic Reaction
file: e8_05

We will compute ΔH for the reaction illustrated at the start of this section, using the following procedure:

✦ Optimize the structures at HF/6-31G(d).
✦ Compute the frequencies at each optimized geometry using the same method to obtain the zero point energy corrections.
✦ Calculate the energy at B3LYP/6-311+G(3df,2p).

We will use these values to compute E^0 for each system, and then take the difference of products and reactants to obtain ΔH. Here are our results for the individual molecules:

System	E	ZPE	E^0
Ethane	-79.86142	0.07286	-79.78856
Acetaldehyde	-153.89170	0.05474	-153.83695
Methane	-40.53678	0.04364	-40.49314
Acetone	-193.23038	0.08214	-193.14824

These values result in a calculated value for ΔH of -9.95 kcal-mol^{-1}, indicating that the reaction is exothermic. This value is in excellent agreement with the experimental value of -9.9±0.3 kcal-mol^{-1}.

Example 8.6: Predicting the Heat of Formation of CO₂ via an Isodesmic Reaction
file: e8_06

In this example, we will use an isodesmic reaction to predict the heat of formation of carbon dioxide. Here is the reaction we will consider: $CO_2 + CH_4 \rightarrow 2H_2CO$ (there is often more than one isodesmic reaction that may be constructed to predict a heat of formation of interest). This is a bond formation/separation reaction, which is often a good choice for this purpose.

The types and number of bonds are the same for the products and reactants, so this is an isodesmic reaction. We can compute the heat of formation for CO_2 in this way:

$$\Delta H^{calc} = 2E^0(H_2CO) - (E^0(CO_2) + E^0(CH_4))$$
$$\Delta H_f(CO_2) = -(\Delta H^{calc} - \Delta H_f^{exp}(CH_4) + 2\Delta H_f^{exp}(H_2CO))$$

The experimental heats of formation for methane and formaldhyde are -16.0 and -25.0 kcal-mol^{-1}, respectively (both at 0 K).

We will use the same model chemistries as in the preceding example. Accordingly, we can use the results for methane from the preceding example, as well as earlier optimization and frequency computations for formaldehyde. Here are the results of our computations for this isodesmic reaction (same procedure as for Example 8.5):

System	E	˙ ZPE	E^0	ΔH_f^{exp}
CO_2	-188.65935	0.01164	-188.64771	?
Formaldehyde	-114.54878	0.02668	-114.52210	-25.0
Methane	-40.53678	0.04364	-40.49314	-16.0

The values lead to a computed value for ΔH of 60.64 kcal-mol^{-1} for the reaction, and a predicted value of -94.64 kcal-mol^{-1} for ΔH_f for carbon dioxide. This value is in excellent agreement with the experimental value of -93.96 kcal-mol^{-1}.

Limitations of Isodesmic Reactions

Isodesmic reactions can be very useful for modeling systems and reactions. However, this approach is not without its limitations as well, which include the following:

✦ Good experimental values must be available for all but one reaction component. The predicted heat of formation is no more accurate than the least accurate of the experimental values used to compute it.

✦ This technique cannot be applied to activation barriers.

✦ This technique cannot be applied to reactions which do not happen to be isodesmic (for example, destruction of ozone by atomic chlorine).

✦ Different isodesmic reactions will predict different values for the same heat of formation. Thus, this technique does not produce a uniquely defined value for the heat of formation; it is *not* a model chemistry and cannot be systematically evaluated quantitatively. This effect is illustrated in the following example.

Example 8.7: Limitations of Isodesmic Reactions
file: e8_07.com

We will compute the heat of formation for ethane using these two different isodesmic reactions (studied at MP2/6-31G(d) // HF/6-31G(d)):

propane + $H_2 \rightarrow$ ethane + methane   ethane + $H_2 \rightarrow$ 2 methane

We will also compute the heat of formation for SiF_4 using these reactions (studied at MP2/6-311G(d,p) // HF/6-31G(d)):

$SiH_4 + 2F_2 \rightarrow 2H_2 + SiF_4$ $SiH_4 + 4HF \rightarrow 4H_2 + SiF_4$
$SiF_3H + HF \rightarrow SiF_4$ $SiF_2H_2 + 2HF \rightarrow 2H_2 + SiF_4$
$SiFH_3 + 3HF \rightarrow 3H_2 + SiF_4$ $SiH_4 + 4F_2 \rightarrow SiF_4 + 4HF$

Here are our results:

System	ΔH_f^{exp}	E
Propane	-25.0±0.1	-118.552
Ethane	-20.0±0.1	-79.415
H_2	0.0	-1.131, -1.147
Methane	-17.8±0.1	-40.284
F_2	0.0	-199.147
HF	-65.1	-100.255
SiH_3F	-90.0±5.0	-390.482
SiH_4	8.0	-291.337
SiF_4	-386.0±0.3	-687.950
SiF_3H	-287.0±5.0	-588.797
SiF_2H_2	N/A	

Reaction	ΔH	Calc. ΔH_f	Δ^{exp}
propane + $H_2 \rightarrow$ ethane + methane	-10.16	-17.361	-2.64
ethane + $H_2 \rightarrow$ 2 methane	-13.342	-22.258	2.26
$SiH_4 + 2F_2 \rightarrow 2H_2 + SiF_4$	-383.98	-375.983	-10.02
$SiH_4 + 4HF \rightarrow 4H_2 + SiF_4$	-114.10	-366.588	-19.41
$SiF_3H + HF \rightarrow SiF_4 + H_2$	-28.406	-380.506	-5.49
$SiFH_3 + 3HF \rightarrow SiF_4 + 3H_2$	-90.81	-376.112	-9.89
$SiH_4 + 4F_2 \rightarrow SiF_4 + 4HF$	-653.78	-385.379	-0.62
$SiF_2H_2 + 2HF \rightarrow SiF_4 + 2H_2$	N/A	N/A	N/A

Although both predictions of ΔH_f(ethane) are in reasonable agreement with experiment, they differ from one another by almost 5 kcal-mol^{-1}. Such a large difference for a simple hydrocarbon system—the sort of species isodesmic reactions are purported to treat well—suggests caution when applying this technique.

The five predictions for ΔH_f(SiF_4)—we were not able to model the reaction involving SiF_2H_2 due to the lack of an experimental ΔH_f for that compound—also differ from one another quite substantially. Although one of them produces excellent agreement with experiment, the others differ from the observed value by up to ~20 kcal-mol^{-1}. Note also that some of the experimental ΔH_f values for these silicon compounds have large uncertainties.

Exercises

Exercise 8.1: Hydration Reactions

files: 8_01a (Li⁺)
8_01b (H₂O)
8_01c (dimer)

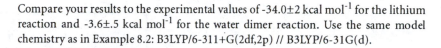

Compute ΔH for these hydration reactions:

$$Li^+ + H_2O \rightarrow H_2OLi^+ \text{ at } 298.15 \text{ K}$$
$$H_2O + H_2O \rightarrow (H_2O)_2 \text{ at } 373 \text{ K}$$

Compare your results to the experimental values of -34.0±2 kcal mol⁻¹ for the lithium reaction and -3.6±.5 kcal mol⁻¹ for the water dimer reaction. Use the same model chemistry as in Example 8.2: B3LYP/6-311+G(2df,2p) // B3LYP/6-31G(d).

Note that you will need to compute the thermochemistry of water at both 298.15 and 373 K. Here is the structure of an input file which will allow you to do so without having to run two separate frequency jobs:

```
%Chk=water                          Save the checkpoint file from this job.
#T RHF/6-31G(d) Freq=ReadIso        Normal route section.
...                                 Remainder of input.
--Link1--                           Start a second job step.
%Chk=water                          Identify the checkpoint file.
%NoSave                             Discard the checkpoint file after this job.
#T RHF/6-31G(d) Geom=Check          Route section for the second job.
   Freq=(ReadFC,ReadIso) Guess=Read Test
...                                 Other input lines..
373.0 1.0 0.9135                    Second temperature, pressure and scale factor.
16                                  Standard isotopes..
1
1
```

Solution

Here are the results for the lithium reaction (E values in hartrees, and thermal correction to the enthalpy in kcal-mol⁻¹):

Molecule	E	Thermal Corr. To H^{298}
Li^+	-7.28492	0.889
H_2O	-76.46241	15.39
H_2OLi^+	-83.80400	17.86

These values predict a value of -34.0 kcal mol⁻¹ for ΔH^{298}. This value is in excellent agreement with experiment (-34.0±2.0 kcal mol). Note that we didn't need to run a frequency job on Li^+, but rather computed the enthalpy correction as $\frac{3}{2}$ RT (just a translational component).

Optimizing water dimer can be challenging in general, and DFT methods are known to have difficulty with weakly-bound complexes. When your optimization succeeds, make sure that you have found a minimum and not a transition structure by verifying that there are no imaginary frequencies. In the course of developing this exercise, we needed to restart our initial optimization from an improved intermediate step and to use **Opt=CalcAll** to reach a minimum.

Here are the results for the water dimer reaction:

Molecule	E	Thermal Corr. To H^{373}
H_2O	-76.46241	16.00
$(H_2O)_2$	-152.93149	33.26

The computed value of ΔH^{373} is -2.9 kcal mol^{-1}, which again agrees very well with the experimental value of -3.6±0.5 kcal mol^{-1}. ■

Exercise 8.2: Bond Dissociation

files: 8_02a **(CH)**
8_02b **(CH$_4$)**

In this exercise, you will explore the bond rupture process by performing a potential energy surface scan. Run potential energy surface scans for these molecules, gradually increasing one of the C-H bond lengths, using the specified model chemistries:

System	Model Chemistry	Bond Length Range
CH	UMP4/6-311+G(d,p)	0.5 - 2.5 Å
CH$_4$	RQCISD(T)/6-311++G(d,p) *and* UQCISD(T,E4T)/6-311++G(d,p)	.75 - 3.15 Å

The **E4T** option to the **UQCISD** method keyword tells *Gaussian* to run the component MP4 calculations at the MP4(SDTQ) level, rather than the default of MP4(SDQ). When you set up the QCISD(T) calculations for methane, include the additional option **IOP(2/16=1)** in the route section (which says to ignore any symmetry changes during the scan) and also include **Guess=(Always,Mix)** for the unrestricted case; **Mix** requests that the HOMO and LUMO be mixed so as to destroy alpha-beta and spatial spin symmetries (this option is also useful for producing unrestricted wave functions for singlet systems), and **Always** says to recompute a new guess wavefunction at each point.

We ran a 40-point scan for CH and two 24-point scans for methane. Users with slower computer systems might want to decrease these values.

Examine the results of these potential energy surface studies in these ways:

◆ Make a plot of bond distance versus energy for the restricted and unrestricted method scans of methane for the HF, MP2, MP4, and QCISD(T) levels.

◆ For each system, plot the bond distance versus energy for each of the reported levels of theory. For CH, this will mean plotting the HF, MP2, MP3, and full MP4 (i.e., MP4(SDTQ)) energies at each point. For methane, include the HF, MP2, MP3, full MP4, QCISD, and QCISD(T) levels.

◆ Using these plots, describe the importance of the following factors when studying bond dissociation:

❖ Restricted versus unrestricted method computations.
❖ Electron correlation (how well does Møller-Plesset perturbation theory converge for these problems?)
❖ The triples contribution to the QCISD level.

Include the energy at the optimized equilibrium geometry in the unrestricted method plots, which is given for each method in the following table:

	R(C-H)	HF	MP2	MP3	MP4SDTQ	QCISD	QCISD(T)
CH	1.1266	-38.27811	-38.36399	-38.38218	-38.38777		
CH$_4$	1.0944	-40.20888	-40.37959	-40.39866	-40.40599	-40.40203	-40.40638

Solution   Here is the plot of the energies at each point for the various levels of theory for CH:

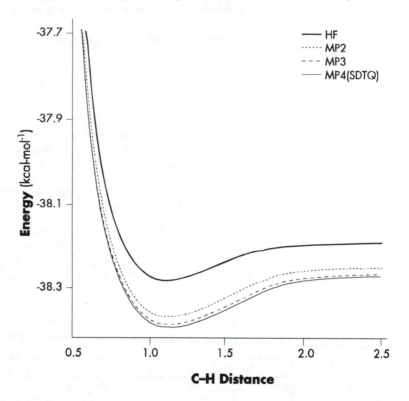

The UHF curve is much higher than those for the correlation methods; Hartree-Fock theory does a relatively poor job of describing this process. The MP2 curve is somewhat higher than those for the MP3 and MP4(SDTQ) levels, which appear to have converged.

Here is the plot for methane:

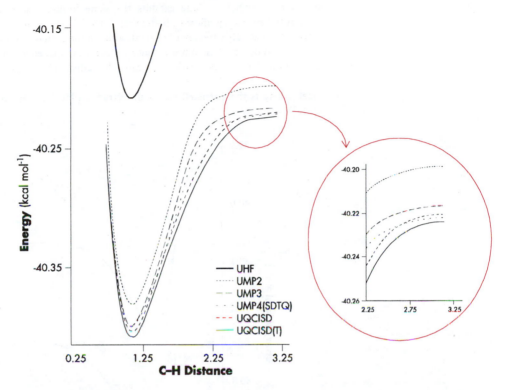

Once again, Hartree-Fock theory produces significantly higher energies than the correlation methods (the rest of its curve is off the chart in the preceding plot). MP2 theory diverges from the other correlated methods throughout the entire curve. The other correlation methods produce very similar curves for bond lengths near the equilibrium structure. They begin to diverge in the intermediate region between the equilibrium and dissociated states. In this region, each successively higher level of Møller-Plesset perturbation theory decreases the energy. (The MP orders converge slowly due to severe spin contamination).

The importance of the triples contribution with QCISD theory is clearly illustrated in the enlargement. The QCISD curve is very near the MP4 curve. The authors of the paper from which this exercise is drawn emphasized the importance of the single and triples to the MP4 level, but nevertheless concluded that MP4(SDTQ) was not an adequate representation of the potential energy surface in the intermediate region since it converged very slowly as the bond length increased to infinity. We can conclude that QCISD alone exhibits the same limitations, and that QCISD(T) appears to perform significantly better than MP4(SDTQ) in this respect. This suggests that both the iterative treatment of single and double excitations and the inclusion of triple excitations are vital to producing a realistic potential energy surface as the bond dissociates. (The QCI calculations are much less affected by spin contamination.)

Finally, here is the restricted versus unrestricted plot for methane, at the HF and QCISD(T) levels:

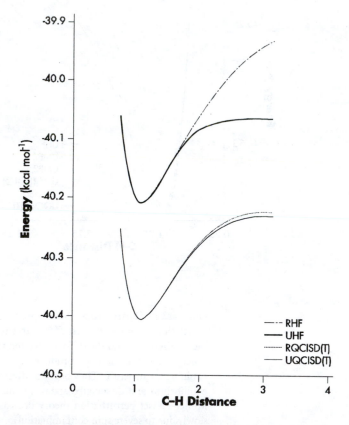

The two plots diverge only in the region of the potential energy surface where bond breaking occurs. At the Hartree-Fock level, the restricted method does not correctly describe bond dissociation. Instead, it predicts increasing energy as the bond length increases, and never properly breaks the bond. This plot illustrates the importance of using unrestricted theory for studying bond breaking processes when using low levels of theory, even when the system has an even number of electrons. These effects are much less intense at the higher levels of theory. ■

Exercise 8.3: H₂CO Potential Energy Surface
file: 8_03

In this exercise, we'll conclude our investigation of the H₂CO potential energy surface.

We have already considered two reactions on the H₂CO potential energy surface. In doing so, we studied five stationary points: three minima—formaldehyde, trans hydroxycarbene, and carbon monoxide plus hydrogen molecule—and the two transition structures connecting formaldehyde with the two sets of products. One obvious remaining step is to find a path between the two sets of products.

Determine the reaction path connecting trans hydroxycarbene and $H_2 + CO$. Predict the activation energy, referring to the values for the SCF and zero-point energies for the products and reactants summarized at the conclusion of this problem. This reaction occurs via a two step process:

$$\text{trans HCOH} \leftrightarrow \text{cis HCOH} \leftrightarrow H_2 + CO$$

Perform this study at the HF/6-31G(d) level. The following data provides some of the energetic data you will need for this exercise:

Molecule	SCF Energy	ZPE[†]
H_2	-1.12683	0.00968
CO	-112.73788	0.00508
HCOH (trans)	-113.78352	0.02643
HCOH (cis)	-113.77449	0.02590

[†] Already scaled by 0.9135.

Solution

This study will require these steps for each of the two reactions:

✦ Finding the transition structure.
✦ Verifying that the stationary point is a transition structure, and computing its zero-point energy.
✦ Determining which minima this transition structure connects.

A plausible initial structure for the hydroxycarbene trans to cis transition structure is one in which the hydrogen atom bonded to the oxygen has moved halfway between its position in the two structures. This corresponds to a 90° dihedral angle (the cis form has a 0° dihedral angle, and the trans form's angle is 180°). We used **Opt=QST3** to locate the transition structure, giving the two forms of HCOH and this initial structure to the program as input. It is illustrated at the left.

We next run an IRC calculation, which produces these two final points on the path:

∠ HCOH=118.3°   ∠ HCOH=61.2°

We can easily identify both structures by the value of the dihedral angle. In the one on the left, the dihedral angle has increased to 118.3°, indicating that this side of the path is leading to the trans form. Indeed, if we look at all of the points in the reaction path, we see that the dihedral angle steadily increases on this side of the transition structure, and steadily decreases on the opposite side. From the latter, we can conclude that the right structure is tending toward the cis form. Thus, we have confirmed that this transition structure does in fact connect the cis and trans isomers of hydroxycarbene.

Following a similar procedure, we locate and verify the transition structure connecting cis hydroxycarbene and the two dissociated species. Here is the transition structure and the two structures at the end of the reaction path computed by the IRC calculation:

Variable	TS	I	II
R(C-O)	1.23	1.26	1.20
R(C-H)	1.48	0.98	1.43
R(O-H)	1.11	1.36	1.57
A(H-O-C)	97.1	82.6	67.6
A(C-O-H)	72.1	99.5	94.6

Structure 1 is clearly tending toward cis hydroxycarbene. The other endpoint exhibits quite large bond distances between both hydrogens and the associated heavy atom. The hydrogens themselves are close enough to be bonded. This structure is a point on the path to H_2 + CO.

We can now compute the activation energies:

Molecule	SCF Energy	ZPE
H$_2$	-1.12683	0.00968
CO	-112.73788	0.00508
HCOH (trans)	-113.78352	0.02643
HCOH (cis)	-113.77449	0.02590
trans/cis TS	-113.73830	0.02235
cis/diss. TS	-113.65588	0.01559

Reaction	Activation Energies	
	Forward	Reverse
trans ↔ cis	25.8	20.5
cis ↔ H$_2$ + CO	68.0	131.6

These values suggest that the two hydroxycarbene isomers convert into one another very easily. The barrier to molecular dissociation of the cis form is significant, however, and so this structure probably does not dissociate directly, but rather first converts to the trans isomer, which is subsequently transformed into formaldehyde, which dissociates to carbon monoxide and hydrogen gas. The article from which this study was drawn computes the activation energy for the trans to cis reaction as 28.6 kcal- mol^{-1} at RMP4(SDQ)/6-31G(d,p) (it does not consider the other reactions).

Here is an updated version of our illustration of the RHF/6-31G(d) H$_2$CO PES:

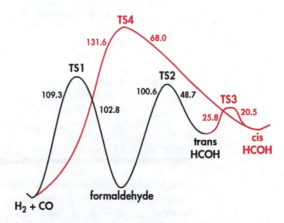

Exercise 8.7 will consider a much more complex potential energy surface. ∎

Exercise 8.4: Atomic Charge Analysis

file: **8_04**

This exercise will examine other ways of computing charges other than Mulliken population analysis. Since atomic charge is not a quantum mechanical observable, all methods for computing it are necessarily arbitrary. We'll explore the relative merits of various schemes for partitioning the electron density among the atoms in a molecular system.

Compute the charge distributions for allyl cation using the following methods:

- ✦ Mulliken population analysis (the default procedure)
- ✦ Natural population analysis (keyword: **Pop=NPA**)
- ✦ Electrostatic potential-derived charges using the CHelpG scheme of Breneman (keyword: **Pop=CHelpG**)
- ✦ Electrostatic potential-derived charges using the Merz-Kollman-Singh scheme (keyword: **Pop=MK**)

Run the jobs at the MP2/6-31G(d) level. You should be aware that this is the practice adopted by researchers who include charge distribution analysis in publications.

In order to save computation time, set up the second and subsequent jobs to extract the electron density from the checkpoint file by using the **Geom=Checkpoint** and **Density=(Checkpoint,MP2)** keywords in the route section. You will also need to include **Density=MP2** for the first job, which specifies that the population analysis should be performed using the electron density computed at the MP2 level (the default is to use the Hartree-Fock density).

Solution

Here are the Mulliken charges for this system:

```
Total atomic charges:
                1
   1  C   -0.117948
   2  H    0.301526
   3  C   -0.184767
   4  C   -0.184767
   5  H    0.304392
   6  H    0.288586
   7  H    0.304392
   8  H    0.288586
Sum of Mulliken charges=    1.00000
```

The Mulliken scheme places the negative charge more or less evenly on the three carbons, and splits the positive charge among the hydrogens. Mulliken population analysis computes charges by dividing orbital overlap evenly between the two atoms involved.

NBO Population Analysis

Natural population analysis is carried out in terms of localized electron-pair "bonding" units. Here are the charges computed by natural population analysis (the essential output is extracted):

```
******************Gaussian NBO Version 3.1*******************
      N A T U R A L   A T O M I C   O R B I T A L   A N D
      N A T U R A L   B O N D   O R B I T A L   A N A L Y S I S
******************Gaussian NBO Version 3.1*******************
Analyzing the MP2 density
...
Summary of Natural Population Analysis:
                                        Natural Population
                   Natural      ---------------------------------
 Atom No           Charge        Core    Valence  Rydberg    Total
 --------------------------------------------------------------
   C   1          -0.34614      1.99903  4.30125  0.04585   6.34614
   H   2           0.29596      0.00000  0.70181  0.00223   0.70404
   C   3           0.01453      1.99914  3.94980  0.03653   5.98547
   C   4           0.01453      1.99914  3.94980  0.03653   5.98547
   H   5           0.26378      0.00000  0.73427  0.00195   0.73622
   H   6           0.24678      0.00000  0.75073  0.00249   0.75322
   H   7           0.26378      0.00000  0.73427  0.00195   0.73622
   H   8           0.24678      0.00000  0.75073  0.00249   0.75322
 ==============================================================
 * Total * 1.00000            5.9973  15.87267  0.13001 22.00000
...
Natural Population
 --------------------------------------------------------------
   Core                        5.99732 ( 99.9553% of    6)
   Valence                    15.87267 ( 99.2042% of   16)
   Natural Minimal Basis      21.86999 ( 99.4090% of   22)
   Natural Rydberg Basis       0.13001 (  0.5910% of   22)
 --------------------------------------------------------------
...
 Atom No    Natural Electron Configuration
 --------------------------------------------------------------
   C   1    [core]2s( 1.03)2p( 3.27)3s( 0.01)3p( 0.02)3d( 0.02)
   H   2          1s( 0.70)
   C   3    [core]2s( 1.12)2p( 2.83)3p( 0.02)3d( 0.02)
   C   4    [core]2s( 1.12)2p( 2.83)3p( 0.02)3d( 0.02)
   H   5          1s( 0.73)
   H   6          1s( 0.75)
   H   7          1s( 0.73)
   H   8          1s( 0.75)
```

The scheme assigns charges very differently, placing most of the negative charge on one carbon atom. Its more detailed analysis also includes the number of core electrons, valence electrons, and Rydberg electrons, located in diffuse orbitals. It also partitions the charge on each atom among the atomic orbitals.[†]

CHelpG Electrostatic Potential-Derived Charges

Electrostatic potential-derived charges assign point charges to fit the computed electrostatic potential at a number of points on or near the van der Waals surface. This sort of analysis is commonly used to create input charges for molecular mechanics calculation.

There are three major schemes for selecting the points: CHelp, CHelpG, and Merz-Kollman-Singh. The CHelpG scheme of Breneman produces these charges:

```
*******************************************************************
Electrostatic Properties Using The MP2 Density
*******************************************************************
...
Charge= 1.00000 Dipole= 0.0000 0.0000 -0.5753 Tot= 0.5753
                1
    1  C   -0.103415
    2  H    0.169967
    3  C    0.166042
    4  C    0.166042
    5  H    0.161798
    6  H    0.138884
    7  H    0.161798
    8  H    0.138884
```

This scheme also assigns the negative charge to the middle carbon atom.

[†] If the NBO program (*Gaussian* Link 607) is used to produce published results, then it should be cited as well. The reference is: NBO Version 3.1, E. D. Glendening, A. E. Reed, J. E. Carpenter, and F. Weinhold.

MKS Electrostatic Potential-Derived Charges

Here are the results using the Merz-Kollman-Singh scheme, which fits the electrostatic potential to points selected on a set of concentric spheres around each atom:

```
****************************************************************
Electrostatic Properties Using The MP2 Density
****************************************************************
...
Charge= 1.00000 Dipole= 0.0000 0.0000 -0.5841 Tot= 0.5841
            1
  1   C    -0.091216
  2   H     0.183731
  3   C     0.101199
  4   C     0.101199
  5   H     0.186162
  6   H     0.166382
  7   H     0.186162
  8   H     0.166382
```

This scheme also places the negative charge on the middle carbon. However, its partitioning of the positive charge is more uniform than that of CHelpG. ∎

Exercise 8.5: Group Charges
file: 8_04

Compute the group charges for the CH and CH_2 groups with each method for allyl cation using each of the methods from the previous exercise.

Solution

Here are the results:

	Mulliken	NPA	CHelpG	MKS
CH	+.18	−.05	−.10	+.09
CH$_2$	+.41	+.52	+.47	+.45

There is much greater agreement among the methods when it comes to the group charges than there was for the charges on each individual atom. The methods agree that the CH2 has the majority of the positive charge. NPA and CHelpG assign a very small negative charge to the CH group while MKS and Mulliken analysis assign a small positive charge to this group. ∎

Advanced Exercise 8.6: Atoms in Molecules Charges and Bond Orders

file: 8_06

The *theory of atoms in molecules* of R. F. W. Bader and coworkers provides another, more sophisticated approach to atomic charges and related properties. Jerzy Cioslowski has drawn on and extended this theory, and he is responsible for the AIM facility in *Gaussian*.

The theory of atoms in molecules defines chemical properties such as bonds between atoms and atomic charges on the basis of the topology of the electron density ρ, characterized in terms of ρ itself, its gradient $\nabla\rho$, and the Laplacian of the electron density $\nabla^2\rho$. The theory defines an atom as the region of space enclosed by a *zero-flux surface*: the surface such that $\nabla\rho\cdot\mathbf{n}=0$, indicating that there is no component of the gradient of the electron density perpendicular to the surface (n is a normal vector). The nucleus within the atom is a local maximum of the electron density.

Atoms defined in this way can be treated as quantum-mechanically distinct systems, and their properties may be computed by integrating over these atomic basins. The resulting properties are well-defined and are based on physical observables. This approach also contrasts with traditional methods for population analysis in that it is independent of calculation method and basis set.

The AIM facility in *Gaussian* can be used to predict a variety of atomic properties based on this theory. We will use it to compute atomic charges and bond order for the allyl cation.

Run an **AIM=BondOrders** calculation for allyl cation at the MP2/6-31G(d) model chemistry. What are the predicted atomic charges and bond orders for this molecule?

Solution

The relevant output from the AIM facility is given on the next page (note that the three portions we have extracted are from separate sections of the AIM output). We are interested in attractors—atoms—numbers 1, 3 and 4, which are the carbon atoms. The AIM method places the positive charge near the hydrogen atoms, while the carbon atoms have very little excess positive charge (although there is slightly more on the central carbon).

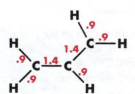

The predicted bond order for a given bond is listed at the intersection of the two atoms of interest in the bond orders table. The illustration at the left shows the predicted bond orders for this molecule (where 1.0 is a traditional single bond, 2.0 is a double bond, and so on). The C-H bonds all have predicted bond orders of about .9, while the C-C bonds have predicted bond orders of about 1.4. The latter are consistent with the known resonance structure for allyl cation. ■

```
*************************************************************
  Properties of atoms in molecules using the MP2 density.
*************************************************************
...
III. PROPERTIES OF ATTRACTORS
-------------------------------------------------
Attr.       Number of electrons          Charge
               total        spin
-------------------------------------------------
  1          5.944591     0.000000      0.055409
  2          0.828548     0.000000      0.171452
  3          5.984502     0.000000      0.015498
  4          5.984502     0.000000      0.015498
  5          0.805474     0.000000      0.194526
  6          0.823431     0.000000      0.176569
  7          0.805474     0.000000      0.194526
  8          0.823431     0.000000      0.176569
-------------------------------------------------
Total       21.999953    0.000000      1.000047
-------------------------------------------------

...
******* AOM-Derived covalent bond orders *******
-------------------------------------------------------------------------------
          C  1      H  2     C  3     C  4     H  5     H  6     H  7     H  8
-------------------------------------------------------------------------------
C  1     3.84223
H  2     0.92340   0.30060
C  3     1.43926   0.03790  4.02685
C  4     1.43926   0.03790  0.30949  4.02686
H  5     0.03419   0.00270  0.92595  0.00957  0.29015
H  6     0.03604   0.00403  0.92721  0.01494  0.01621  0.30005
H  7     0.03419   0.00270  0.00957  0.92594  0.00074  0.00064  0.29015
H  8     0.03604   0.00403  0.01494  0.92721  0.00064  0.00536  0.01621  0.30005
-------------------------------------------------------------------------------
```

Advanced Exercise 8.7: Si⁺ + Silane Potential Energy Surface

file: **8_07**

Silicon cluster reactions are an example of a newly emerging field of research which is very amenable to study with electronic structure methods. This exercise will examine the potential surface for silicon cation reacting with silane (SiH_4). Such reactions are central to the growth of large silicon clusters, which occurs by sequential additions of $-SiH_2$:

$$Si^+ + SiH_4 \rightarrow Si_2H_2^+ \rightarrow Si_3H_4^+ \rightarrow Si_4H_6^+ \rightarrow Si_5H_{10}^+ ...,$$

with H_2 also produced in each step.

We will examine the first addition reaction:

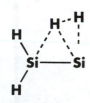

In his search of the $Si_2H_4^+$ potential energy surface, the original researcher, Krishnan Raghavachari, found the following minima (in addition to the reactants):

The rightmost structure is a weak complex of the products (having a binding energy of 1 kcal mol^{-1}), and for our purposes may be construed as the reaction end point.

Raghavachari also found the transition structure at the left.

Determine which of the minima are connected by this transition structure and predict the activation barriers for the reactions. Run your frequency and IRC calculations at the HF/6-31G(d) level, and compute final energies using the MP4 method with the same basis set.

Include these keywords in the route section of the IRC calculation:

IRC=(RCFC, StepSize=30, MaxPoints=15) SCF=QC.

These options to the **IRC** keyword increase the maximum number of points on each side of the path to 15 and the step size between points to 0.3 amu$^{-1/2}$ bohr (30 units of 0.1 amu$^{-1/2}$ bohr), where the defaults are 6 steps and 0.1 amu$^{-1/2}$ bohr, respectively. The **SCF=QC** keyword requests the quadratic convergence SCF procedure, a somewhat slower but significantly more reliable SCF procedure.

Once you have determined which minima the transition state connects, calculate the activation barrier for the corresponding reaction. Here is the energy data for the systems listed previously (these are the raw ZPE's; you'll need to scale them yourself):

System	E	ZPE
$SiH_4 + Si^+$	-579.96683	0.03347
$SiH_4...Si^+$ complex	-580.00136	0.03363
$H_3Si—SiH^+$	-580.01258	0.03378
$H_2Si—SiH_2^+$	-580.03101	0.03394
$H_2Si—Si^+...H_2$ complex	-579.97532	0.02725
Transition State	-579.96322	
$H_2 + H_2Si—Si^+$	-579.97312	0.02693

Make a plot of the relative energies of the various systems, indicating any known paths between them. You'll be able to provide the zero point energy for the transition state from your calculations.

Solution   Completing this exercise will require three parts:

✦ A frequency calculation to verify the transition structure, compute its zero point energy, and prepare for the IRC (the optimized structure is given in the input file for this exercise).

✦ An IRC calculation to determine which minima the transition structure connects.

✦ A UMP4/6-31G(d,p) energy calculation to determine the transition structure's total energy.

The frequency calculation of the given transition structure does produce one imaginary frequency, as required for a transition structure. The computed zero point energy is 0.03062 hartrees. When scaled and added to the MP4 total energy, it produces a relative energy of 0.63 kcal mol^{-1} compared to the starting reactants.

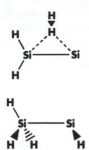

The IRC yields the following two structures at the two ends of the reaction path. The structure on the top is the weakly bound $H_2Si—Si^+...H_2$ complex. Some drawing programs will even render this data as two distinct molecules. The other structure is also easily identified as tending toward $SiH_3—SiH^+$. It essentially has the structure of silylsilene ion; the major difference is that the H–Si–Si–H dihedral angle is 170° rather than 180°. Thus, this transition structure connects the products[†] with silylsilene ion, and it is thus a transition structure for the H_2 elimination reaction.

Here is a plot of the part of the $Si_2H_4^+$ potential energy surface that we've just explored:

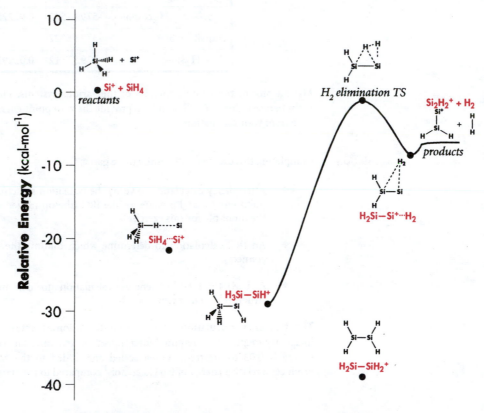

The other known minima are linked by other transition structures. ∎

---

† Or, more precisely, a complex very close to the products.

To The Teacher: Further Investigation of the $Si_2H_4^+$ PES

The reference for this exercise contains considerably more detail about this potential energy surface, so considerably more elaborate studies of it are feasible. For example, the complete reaction sequence connecting the products and the reactants through the given transition state could be studied:

$Si\ H_4 + Si^+ \rightarrow$
$SiH_4 \ldots Si^+$ (*the ion-molecule complex*) $\rightarrow$
$H_3Si—SiH^+$ (*insertion of Si^+ into the Si–H bond*) $\rightarrow$
$H_2Si—Si^+\ldots H_2$ (*1,2 hydrogen migration*) $\rightarrow$
$H_2 + Si_2H_2^+$ (*dissociation into products*)

One can also explore how the other minimum we noted is located on the potential energy surface. Here is a more complete diagram:

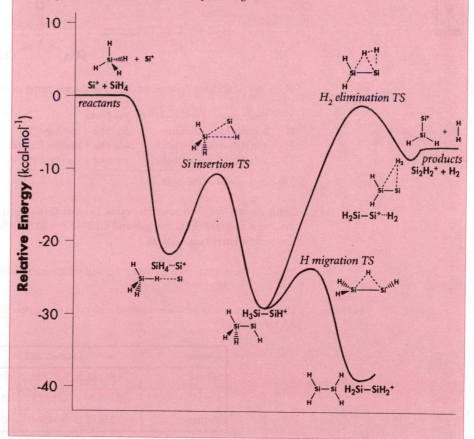

Here are the transition structures for the silicon insertion reaction (left) and the 1,2 hydrogen migration reaction:

 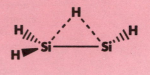

Advanced Exercise 8.8: Isodesmic Reactions

file: 8_08

In this exercise, we will consider additional isodesmic reactions of the form:

where the substituent X varies according to the following table:

X	Reactants	Products
H†	acetaldehyde + ethane	acetone + methane
F	acetyl fluoride + ethane	acetone + methyl fluoride
Cl	acetyl chloride + ethane	acetone + methyl chloride

† Already completed as Example 8.5.

Compute ΔH for each reaction, using the B3LYP/6-31G(d) model chemistry for structures and zero-point energies and the B3LYP/6-311+G(3df,2p) model chemistry for the final energy calculations.

Which of these reactions are exothermic and which are endothermic?

Solution   Here are our results for the individual molecules (we repeat the results from Example 8.5 for reference):

System	E	Scaled ZPE	E^0
Ethane	-79.86142	0.07286	-79.78856
Acetaldehyde	-153.89170	0.05474	-153.83695
Methane	-40.53678	0.04364	-40.49314

System	E	Scaled ZPE	E^0
Acetone	-193.23038	0.08214	-193.14824
Acetyl Fluoride	-253.19499	0.04846	-253.14653
Methyl Fluoride	-139.79898	0.03876	-139.76022
Acetyl Chloride	-613.53937	0.04667	-613.49270
Methyl Chloride	-500.15881	0.03718	-500.12163

These values result in the following predictions for ΔH:

X	Reactant/Product	ΔH Calc.	ΔH Exp.
H	acetaldehyde/methane	-9.95	-9.9±0.3
F	acetyl fluoride/methyl fluoride	16.71	17.9±1.3
Cl	acetyl chloride/methyl chloride	7.14	6.6±0.3

All of the calculated values are in very good agreement with experiment. The theoretical calculations correctly predict the direction of each reaction: only the first one is exothermic.

Wiberg and coworkers (the researchers who wrote the paper from which this example is drawn) used a somewhat different method for predicting ΔH. They performed the final energy calculation at the MP3/6-311++G(d,p) level. The following table compares our results to theirs (the HF and MP2 values are computed from the corresponding energies reported as part of the MP3 calculation):

X	B3LYP/ 6-311+G(3df,2p)	HF/ 6-311++G(d,p)	MP2/ 6-311++G(d,p)	MP3/ 6-311++G(d,p)	Experiment
H	-9.95	-9.3	-9.9	-9.4	-9.9±0.3
Fl	16.71	14.6	17.6	16.1	17.9±1.3
Cl	7.14	2.2	8.7	6.4	6.6±0.3

The Hartree-Fock values range from good to quite poor. For the first reaction, cancellation of errors allows Hartree-Fock theory to predict a good value for ΔH (it overestimates the energies for both ethane and acetone, and underestimates the one for acetaldehyde).

In all three reactions, MP2 theory overcompensates for electron correlation (as it often does). Of the methods used in the original study, only the MP3 level provides an adequate treatment of these reactions. Note, however, it is the special characteristics of isodesmic reactions that enables MP3 to do so well.

Semi-empirical methods are sometimes suggested for studying isodesmic reactions. We performed this same study using the AM1 method; the results are given in the following table:

X	AM1	HF	Experiment
H	-9.95	-9.3	-9.9±0.3
F	5.97	14.6	17.9±1.3
Cl	-0.06	2.2	6.6±0.3

AM1 benefits from the same cancellation of errors for the first reaction as Hartree-Fock theory. However, it performs even more poorly for the other two reactions. ■

To The Teacher: Additional Isodesmic Reactions

You could expand the discussion of the isodesmic reactions by considering additional similar reactions (e.g., X= NH_2, SiH_3, PH_2, CN, SH, CF_3). You could also run the computations at the MP4 level to discuss the relative merits of the MP2, MP3 and MP4 levels of theory and to compare the B3LYP results to them.

Advanced Exercise 8.9: Heats of Formation via Isodesmic Reactions

files: **8_09a** **(CH$_3$F)**
      8_09b **(benzene)**

Predict the heats of formation for methyl fluoride and benzene by modeling appropriate isodesmic reactions. Here are some experimental values for heats of formation (0 K) that you may find useful:

System	ΔH_f^{exp} (kcal-mol^{-1})
methane	-16.0
trifluoromethane	-164.0
ethane	-16.4
ethylene	14.5

Use the same model chemistries as in Exercise 8.5. Here are results from earlier calculations that may be helpful:

System	E	ZPE	E⁰
Methane	-40.53678	0.04364	-40.49314
Ethane	-79.86142	0.07286	-79.78856
Methyl Fluoride	-139.79898	0.03876	-139.76022

You may also want to draw on the benzene optimization we performed in Chapter 3.

Solution

These are the isodesmic reactions that we studied:

$$CHF_3 + 2CH_4 \rightarrow 3CH_3F$$
$$C_6H_6 + 6CH_4 \rightarrow 3C_2H_6 + 3C_2H_4$$

They are each among the simplest bond formation/separation reactions involving the system of interest. The following table summarizes our results for these reactions and the corresponding predicted values of ΔH_f at 0 K:

System	E	ZPE	E⁰	ΔH_f^{exp}
CHF₃	-338.37059	0.02333	-338.34726	-164.00
CH₃F	-139.79898	0.03876	-139.76022	?
methane	-40.53678	0.04364	-40.49314	-16.00
benzene	-232.32751	0.09203	-232.23548	?
ethane	-79.86142	0.07286	-79.78856	-16.40
ethylene	-78.62105	0.04679	-78.57426	14.5

System	ΔH^{calc}	ΔH_f^{calc}	Exp.
CH₃F	33.18	-54.27	-55.9±2.0, -59.0
benzene	66.41	23.89	24.0±0.2

Both values are in excellent agreement with the experimental heats of formation. Note that the experimental value for fluoromethane is quite uncertain. ∎

Advanced Exercise 8.10: An S$_N$2 Reaction

file: **8_10**

S$_N$2 reactions are characterized by an exchange of substituents between two species and have the general form:

$$N^- + RX \leftrightarrow RN + X^-$$

These reactions proceed via a collision between the reactants, with the nucleophilic species attacking the opposite side of the molecule with respect to the ionic substituent that it liberates. Such a process yields a transition structure in which the ion and neutral reactants are weakly bound.

The potential surface for such a reaction has the following general shape:

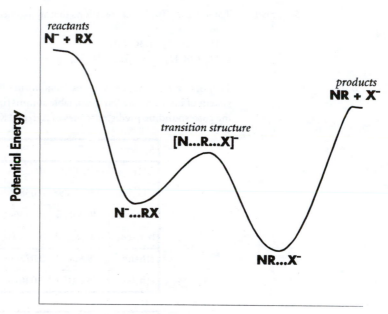

The reactants and products are at the two ends of the curve. The transition structure for the reaction connects two minima. These minima are two ion-molecule complexes, intermediate species through which the reaction proceeds.

Predict the structure of the transition state and the two intermediate ion-molecule complexes for the S$_N$2 reaction:

$$F^- + CH_3Cl \rightarrow Cl^- + CH_3F$$

What are the energies for each species? Plot the general shape of the potential energy curve for this reaction.

Run your study at the Hartree-Fock level, using the 6-31+G(d) basis set. Use a step size of 0.2 amu$^{-1/2}$ bohr for the IRC calculation (i.e., include **IRC=(RCFC, StepSize=20)** in the route section). You will also find the **CalcFC** option helpful in the geometry optimizations.

Here are the energy data for the products and reactants:

System	Total Energy	ZPE†
Cl$^-$	-459.53966	0.0
F$^-$	-99.41859	0.0
CH$_3$Cl	-499.09416	0.04065
CH$_3$F	-139.04423	0.04234

† Unscaled.

Solution

This study requires these calculations:

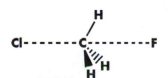

- ◆ An optimization of the transition structure.
- ◆ A frequency job for the transition structure.
- ◆ An IRC calculation starting from the transition structure.
- ◆ Two geometry optimizations to find the intermediate minima.
- ◆ Two frequency calculations to find their zero point energies.

The predicted transition structure is at the left. The frequency calculation confirms that it is a transition structure, as well as providing its zero-point energy.

Here are the two intermediate minima:

The IRC calculation confirms that the preceding transition structure does indeed connect these two minima. The C-Cl bond length increases as it proceeds in the forward direction along the reaction path, and this bond decreases in length in the reverse direction (naturally, the C-F bond length changes in the complementary manner).

Here are the zero-point corrected energies for the various stationary points:

System	E^0 (hartrees)	Δ (kcal-mol^{-1})
Reactants	-598.47652	50.9
Products	-598.54521	7.8
Transition State	-598.49386	40.0
Minimum 1 (TS $\leftrightarrow$ Products)	-598.49840	37.2
Minimum 2 (Reactants $\leftrightarrow$ TS)	-598.55761	0.0

The IRC calculation verifies that the transition structure does indeed connect these two minima. Here is an illustration of the potential energy surface for this reaction:

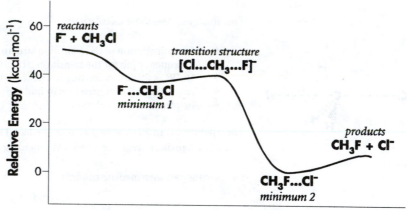

It follows the general shape for S_N2 reactions. ∎

References

Rotational Barrier of Allyl Cation	J. B. Foresman, M. W. Wong, K. B. Wiberg, and M. J. Frisch, "A Theoretical Investigation of the Rotational Barrier in Allyl and 1,1,3,3-Tetramethylallyl Ions," *J. Am. Chem. Soc.*, **115**, 2220 (1993).
Reaction Path Following	C. Gonzalez and H. B. Schlegel, *J. Phys. Chem.*, **90**, 2154 (1989).
	C. Gonzalez and H. B. Schlegel, *J. Phys. Chem.*, **94**, 5523 (1990).
	S. S. Shaik, H. B. Schlegel, and S. Wolfe, *Theoretical Aspects of Physical Organic Chemistry: The S_N2 Mechanism*. Wiley, New York, 1992.
Formaldehyde Dissociation	*Theoretical*: L. B. Harding, H. B. Schlegel, R. Krishnan, and J. A. Pople, *J. Phys. Chem.*, **84**, 3394 (1980).
	Experimental: P. Ho, D. J. Bamford, R. J. Buss, Y. T. Lee, and C. B. Moore, *J. Chem. Phys.*, **76**, 3630 (1982).
	W. M. Gelbart, M. L. Elert, and D. F. Heller, *J. Chem. Rev.*, **80**, 403 (1980).
C-H Bond Dissociation in Methane	R. J. Duchovic, W. L. Hase, H. B. Schlegel, M. J. Frisch, and K. Raghavachari, *Chem. Phys. Lett.*, **85**, 145 (1981).
Silicon Cluster Reactions	K. Raghavachari, *J. Chem. Phys.*, **88**, 1688 (1988).
S_N2 Reaction	Z. Shi and R. J. Boyd, *J. Am. Chem. Soc.*, **111**, 1575 (1989).
Hydration Reactions	J. E. Del Bene, H. D. Mettee, M. J. Frisch, B. T. Luke, and J. A. Pople, *J. Phys. Chem.*, **87**, 3279 (1983).
Isodesmic Reactions	K. B. Wiberg, C. M. Hadad, P. A. Rablen, and J. Cioslowski, *J. Am. Chem. Soc.*, **114**, 8644 (1992).
	K. B. Wiberg and J. W. Ochterski, *J. Comp. Chem.*, accepted (1996).
Fluoromethanes Heats of Formation	R. J. Berry, D. R. F. Burgess, Jr., M. R. Nyden, M. R. Zachariah and M. Schwartz, *J. Phys. Chem.*, **99**, 17145 (1995).
Thermochemical Data	J. B. Pedley, *Thermochemical Data and Structures of Organic Compounds*, (Thermodynamics Research Center, College Station, TX, 1994).
	S. G. Lias, J. E. Bartmess, J. F. Liebman, J. L. Holmes, R. D. Levin and W. G. Mallard, *Gas-Phase Ion and Neutral Thermochemistry, J. Phys. & Chem. Ref. Data*, **17**, Supplement 1 (1988), ACS and Amer. Inst. Phys., New York, 1988.

Chapter 9

Modeling Excited States

In This Chapter:

The Chemistry of Excited States

Running CI-Singles Calculations

The CASSCF Method (Advanced Exercises)

So far, we've examined molecular systems only in their ground states: the lowest energy configuration of the electrons within the various molecular orbitals. *Excited states* are stable, higher energy electronic configurations of molecular systems. For example, such states are produced when a sample is exposed to the light source in a UV/visible spectrophotometer. Excited states are relevant to many areas of chemistry, including photochemistry and electronic spectroscopy.

There is comparatively little theoretical data on molecules in their excited states. Modeling excited states and predicting their properties is a difficult problem; the theoretical method must avoid always ending up at the ground state. Currently, *Gaussian* offers the Configuration Interaction approach, modeling excited states as combinations of single substitutions out of the Hartree-Fock ground state; the method is thus named *CI-Singles*. CI-Singles is described by its developers as "an adequate zeroth-order treatment for many of the excited states of molecules." In this sense, CI-Singles is comparable to Hartree-Fock theory for ground state systems in that it is qualitatively accurate if not always highly quantitatively predictive.[†]

Like Hartree-Fock theory, CI-Singles is an inexpensive method that can be applied to large systems. When paired with a basis set, it also may be used to define excited state model chemistries whose results may be compared across the full range of practical systems.

Running Excited State Calculations

The following *Gaussian* keywords and options are useful for excited state calculations:

Keyword(Option)	Description
CIS	Requests a CI-Singles excited states calculation. **CIS** is a method keyword, and so can be preceded by **R** or **U** for restricted and unrestricted computations, respectively.
CIS=(Root=n)	Specifies which excited state is to be studied (used for geometry optimizations, population analysis, and other single-state procedures). The default is the first (lowest) excited state (n=1).

[†] Despite these comparisons to Hartree-Fock theory, the CI-Singles method does include some electron correlation.

Keyword(Option)	Description
CIS=(NStates=*n***)**	Specifies how many excited states are to be predicted. The default is 3. Note that if you are searching for some specific number of excited states, especially in conjunction with spectroscopic data, you will want to set **NStates** to a somewhat higher number to take into account the forbidden and degenerate states that are very likely to be interspersed within the states you are looking for.
CIS=50-50	Predicts both singlet and triplet excited states (by default, only singlets are computed; the **Triplets** option will restrict the calculation to triplet excited states). When this option is used, the value specified for **NStates** specifies how many states of each type are to be found.
CIS=Read	Reads the initial guesses for the CI-Singles states from the checkpoint file. This option is used to perform an additional job step for an excited state computed during the previous job step. It is accompanied by **Guess=Read** and **Geom=Check**.
Density=Current	Specifies that population analysis procedures use the excited state density matrix rather than the ground state SCF density.
Pop=Reg	Requests additional output from the population analysis procedures, including the molecular orbital coefficients.

Example 9.1: Ethylene Excited States

file: **e9_01**

We'll consider the four lowest excited states of ethylene as our first example. This system has been well-studied, both experimentally and theoretically. Merer and Mulliken offered excellent qualitative descriptions of the four lowest energy excited states of ethylene based upon the available experimental evidence; their results are summarized in the following table:

State	Multiplicity	Symmetry		Transition
		Modern Terminology	Mulliken's Terminology	
1	Triplet	B_{1u}	T	π-π^*
2	Triplet	B_{3u}	TR	π-3s
3	Singlet	B_{3u}	R	π-3s
4	Singlet	B_{1u}	V	π-π^*

We'll compute the first four excited states using the CI-Singles method and then compare their character to Mulliken's findings as well as with experimental determinations of the excitation energies.

Here is the route section for our job:

```
# RCIS=(NStates=2,50-50)/6-31+G(d) Test
```

Since we need to find both triplet and singlet excited states, we've included the **50-50** option to the **CIS** keyword. We've asked for two states of each type, the exact number we require for this well-studied system. When examining new systems, however, it's often a good idea to request slightly more states than you initially want to allow for degenerate states and other unexpected results.

Note that we have included diffuse functions in the basis set. Diffuse functions are essential to obtaining good results for excited state calculations.

We'll look at the output from this job in the next subsection.

CI-Singles Output

This banner opens the excited states output for ethylene produced by *Gaussian*:

```
**********************************************************
 Excited States from <AA,BB:AA,BB> singles matrix:
**********************************************************
```

Slightly later in the output, *Gaussian* gives the energies, excitation energies and oscillator strengths for each computed excited state:

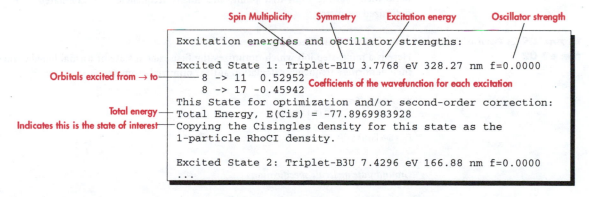

Here are the results from this job:

State	Symmetry	Excitation Energy (eV)	
		Calc.	Exp.
1	$^3B_{1u}$	3.78	4.36
2	$^3B_{3u}$	7.43	7.66
3	$^1B_{3u}$	7.83	6.98
4	$^1B_{1u}$	7.98	7.15

All of the predicted excitation energies are in good agreement with the experimental values. It should also be noted that the experimental excitation energy for the third state measured the adiabatic transition rather than the vertical transition, so this value must be assumed to be somewhat lower than the true vertical excitation energy. A larger basis set is needed to produce better agreement with experiment.

Excited State Optimizations and Frequencies

Geometry optimizations and frequency calculations for systems in an excited state are also possible using *Gaussian's* CI-Singles feature. We will do so in stages: first, the excited state of interest is located via an energy calculation, then an optimization is performed, starting from that point, and finally frequencies are calculated at the optimized geometry.

Example 9.2: Formaldehyde Excited State Optimization
file: e9_02

Here is a multi-step job which optimizes the first excited state of formaldehyde and then performs a frequency calculation at the optimized geometry:

```
%Chk=es_form
#T RCIS/6-31+G(D) Test

Formaldehyde Excited States

0 1
Ground state molecule specification

--Link1--
%Chk=es_form
%NoSave
#T RCIS(Root=1,Read)/6-31+G(D) Opt Freq
   Geom=Check Guess=Read Test
```

The first job step computes the energies of the three lowest excited states. The second job step uses its results to begin the optimization by including the **Read** option to the **CIS** keyword, **Geom=Check**, and **Guess=Read** (and of course the commands to name and save the checkpoint file). The **Freq** keyword computes the frequencies at the optimized structure.

Here is the stationary point found by the optimization, in its standard orientation:

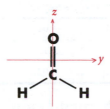

Center	Atomic	Coordinates (Angstroms)		
Number	Number	X	Y	Z
1	6	0.00	0.000000	-0.561638
2	8	0.00	0.000000	0.693881
3	1	0.00	0.944051	-1.090608
4	1	0.00	-0.944051	-1.090608

Unfortunately, the frequency job finds an imaginary frequency, indicating that this structure is not a minimum. Here are the displacements corresponding to this frequency:

```
              1
             B1
 Frequencies --  -371.3727
 ...
 Atom  AN   X     Y     Z
   1   6   0.17  0.00  0.00
   2   8  -0.04  0.00  0.00
   3   1  -0.70  0.00  0.00
   4   1  -0.70  0.00  0.00
```

We can see that the carbon is moving above the plane of the molecule, while the other atoms are moving below it, suggesting a pyramidalized structure. The original molecular structure constrained the structure to be planar, and it will need to be modified to produce the correct optimized geometry (excited state optimizations do not currently take advantage of the redundant internal coordinates features, so specifying a planar structure as the starting geometry will result in an optimized structure that is also planar). We will conclude this study as our second exercise.

Exercises

Exercise 9.1: Methylenecyclopropene Excited States

file: **9_01**

Methylenecyclopropene was first synthesized by Staley and Norden in the mid-1980's. They observed three peaks in the UV spectrum of this system, which they identified as follows:

Location (nm)	Symmetry	Energy (eV)	Relative Area
309	$^1B_2$	4.01	0.2
242	$^1B_1$	5.12	0.01
206	$^1A_1$	6.02	1.5

Their semi-empirical calculations also predicted a second $^1B_1$ transition below the $^1A_1$ which they did not observe; they explained this discrepancy by noting that the missing band "was probably obscured by the long-wavelength tail of the 206-nm band."

They also noted a strong solvent dependence in the lowest energy band, which corresponds to the lowest excited state of this molecule. This suggests that the dipole moment will change sign as the molecule moves from its ground state to the first excited state.

Perform a CI-Singles study of this system, and compare your excited state results with this experimental data. In addition, calculate the dipole moment for the ground and first excited state.

Solution   We performed our study using the ground state geometry computed with the MP2/6-31G(d) model chemistry (your results will differ slightly if a different geometry is used).

Here is the route section we used for our job:

```
# RCIS(NStates=5)/6-31+G(D) Density=All Test
```

We've specified five excited states with **NStates=5** (the reasons will be clear in a moment). The **Density=All** keyword tells *Gaussian* to perform the population analysis using all available densities: the SCF (ground state) density, the CI one-particle density, and the CI (CI-Singles) density. The population analyses using excited state densities will be performed for the first excited state (the default if the **Root** option is not included), which is the one in which we are interested.

Here are the predicted excited states:

State	Symmetry	Energy (eV) Calc.	Energy (eV) Exp.	Oscillator Strength
1	$^1B_2$	5.48	4.01	0.05
2	$^1B_1$	5.91	5.12	0.02
3	$^1A_2$	6.30		0.0
4	$^1B_1$	6.38		0.03
5	$^1A_1$	6.41	6.02	0.37

The first two predicted and observed excited states match up easily, and there is reasonable agreement between the two energies (especially for the second excited state). We also identify the fifth predicted excited state with the third observed peak, based on the identical symmetry and its relative oscillator strength with respect to the other predicted excited states; it is the strongest state seen here, just as the observed $^1A_1$ peak has the greatest relative area.

We are not surprised that the third and fourth predicted excited states are not observed. The third state has an oscillator strength of 0, which means that it is a forbidden state which cannot be observed by single photon experiments such as UV spectroscopy. The fourth state is very close in energy to the fifth state, and is expected to be much less strong (based on its oscillator strength), making it likely that the observed peak corresponding to the fifth predicted excited state will obscure the one arising from the fourth predicted state. (This is essentially the same conclusion as the original researchers reached.)

Here are the predicted dipole moments and atomic charges:

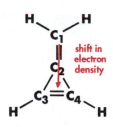

shift in electron density

Density	μ	Charges C_1	C_2	C_3	C_4
SCF	-2.39 z	-0.5	-0.2	-0.1	-0.1
CI 1-Particle	4.75 z	-0.004	-0.06	-0.4	-0.4
CI	2.56 z	-0.2	-0.2	-0.3	-0.3

Both methods for computing the excited state dipole moment exhibit the expected change in sign. However, the CI one-particle density greatly overestimates its magnitude, and shows correspondingly excessive shifts in the charges on the various carbon atoms. This method is the traditional one for computing excited state dipole moments. However, because it is based only on the square of the wavefunction, it is prone to errors such as this one. Accordingly, we strongly recommend using the true

CI density method, which uses analytic derivatives of the wavefunction to compute the dipole moments, resulting in much more accurate predictions, as is illustrated in this case. You can request the CI density by including either **Density=CI** or **Density=Current** in the route section of a CI-Singles calculation. n

---

To The Teacher: Charge Distribution Difference Density

This exercise would be a good place to compute a charge distribution difference density between the ground state and the first excited state, and plot it using an available graphics package.

Exercise 9.2: Formaldehyde Excited State Optimization

file: 9_02

Determine the optimized structure of the first excited state of formaldehyde, completing the study we began in Example 7.2. Compare the predicted frequencies with experimental spectroscopic results:

Peak (cm^{-1})	Corresponding Normal Mode
683	Out-of-plane bend
898	CH_2 rock
1173	C-O stretch
1290	CH_2 scissor
2847	Symmetric C-H stretch
2968	Asymmetric C-H stretch

Solution

Here is the Z-matrix we used for our optimization:

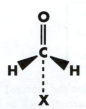

```
C
O 1 RCO
X 1 1.0 2 ACO
H 1 RCH 3 ACH 2  90.0
H 1 RCH 3 ACH 2 -90.0
   Variables:
RCO=1.25
RCH=1.08
ACO=145.0
ACH=60.0
```

The dummy atom is used to make it easy to specify the angles that the various other atoms make with the carbon atom. This Z-matrix no longer constrains the molecule to be planar, and the optimized structure does indeed show pyramidalization:

The frequency job for this structure finds no imaginary frequencies, confirming that it is a minimum.

Here are the predicted frequencies for the first excited state of formaldehyde, along with the corresponding experimental values (the scale factor is the same as for Hartree-Fock frequencies: 0.8929):

Mode Assignment	Calc.	Scaled	Exp.
Out-of-plane bend	495	442	683
CH$_2$ rock	978	873	898
CH$_2$ scissor	1426	1273	1290
C-O stretch	1647	1471	1173
Symm. C-H stretch	3200	2857	2847
Asymm. C-H stretch	3295	2942	2968

We've matched up the predicted to observed frequencies by examining the displacements for each normal mode and determining the type of motion to which it corresponds (just as we did for ground state frequencies). The scaled frequencies are generally in excellent agreement with the observed spectrum. ■

To The Teacher: CI vs. One-Particle Dipole Moments

Formaldehyde also provides another excellent opportunity to compare the dipole moments computed via one-particle and CI-Singles methods. In order to do so, you'll need to do two things:

✦ Change the option for the **Density** keyword from **Current** to **All** in the frequency calculation.

✦ Change the orientation of the molecule so that the dipole moment axis is the one used for the analysis of Stark effect experiments: an axis going through the carbon atom, making an angle of 1.7° with the C-O axis, and forming a 180° dihedral angle with the bisector of the H-C-H angle. Use the **NoSymm** keyword to retain this non-standard orientation.

Here is a Z-matrix which conforms to these specifications:

```
X
C 1 1.
O 2 RO 1 1.7
X 2 1. 3 AOOP 1 180.
H 2 RH 4 HALF 3 90.
H 2 RH 4 HALF 3 -90.
 Variables:
RH=1.084781
RO=1.258059
HALF=58.791505
AOOP=152.147348
```

Here are the results we obtained:

Method	μ
1-Particle	0.48
CI-Singles	1.37
Experiment	1.56

The CI-Singles prediction is in good agreement with experiment, while the value produced via the one-particle wavefunction grossly overestimates the amount of charge transfer from the oxygen to the carbon. These results, along with those for methlyenecyclopropene, serve to emphasize the importance of evaluating properties using the properly relaxed derivative expressions (i.e., by computing analytic derivatives of the wavefunction rather than performing a crude approximation to them).

Exercise 9.3: Acrolein Excited State Optimization

file: **9_03**

Determine the optimized structure of the first excited state of acrolein, and then compare it to the ground state structure. Compare the change in structure for acrolein to what occurs in formaldehyde. What is the effect of substituting the vinyl group for the hydrogen in formaldehyde?

In addition, compare the predicted frequencies for the first excited state with these experimental results:

Symmetry	Peak (cm^{-1})
A"	250
A"	333
A' (C-C-O bend)	488
A"	582
A"	644
A"	909
A'	1133
A' (C-O stretch)	1266
A' (C-C stretch)	1410

Solution

Here are the structures of the ground state (left) and first excited state of acrolein:

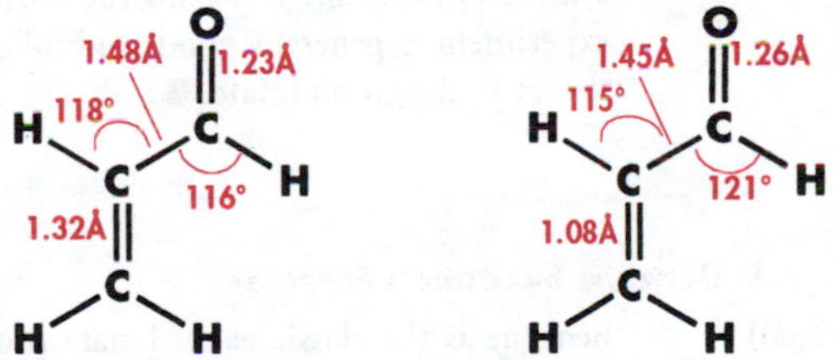

Unlike formaldehyde, acrolein retains its planar structure in the first excited state. Moving to the first excited state principally affects the C-C-H bond angle, decreasing it almost 5°, and the C-C-C bond angle, increasing it about the same amount. The C-O bond also stretches slightly.

The frequency job confirms that this structure is a minimum, finding no imaginary frequencies. Here are the predicted frequencies, compared to the experimental values given earlier:

Symmetry	Peak (cm^{-1}) Exp.	Calc. (scaled)
A"	250	142
A"	333	373
A' (C-C-O bend)	488	466
A"	582	604
A"	644	886
A"	909	981
A'	1133	1058
A' (C-O stretch)	1266	1479
A' (C-C stretch)	1410	1538

Note that the frequency calculation produces many more frequencies than those listed here. We've matched calculated frequenices to experimental frequencies using symmetry types and analyzing the normal mode displacements. The agreement with experiment is generally good, and follows what might be expected of Hartree-Fock theory in the ground state. ■

Advanced Exercise 9.4: Benzene Excitation Energies

files: **9_04a (6-31G(d))**
     9_04b (6-31+G(d))

Benzene is the classic excited state problem for organic chemists. It is a bit more complicated than some other systems we've examined (which is why we saved it for the final exercise). As we consider benzene's excited states, we'll want to keep in mind this caution included by the developers of CI-Singles in their original paper:

> We can further conclude that the success of the CI-Singles method often depends critically on the chosen basis set. Diffuse (Rydberg-like) excited states usually require the addition of one or two diffuse functions to a split-valence basis set.

Benzene will clearly illustrate this effect. Compare the first six excited states, as predicted using the 6-31G and 6-31+G basis sets. When setting up the route section for these jobs, include the **NStates=8** option. Although we are only looking for six excited states, benzene is known to have two low-level doubly degenerate states, and each doubly degenerate state will appear in the output as a pair of states with equal energy.

Include the keywords **IOP(9/40=3)** and **Pop=Full** in the route section of your jobs. The latter requests that all molecular orbitals (occupied and virtual) be included in the population analysis, while the former specifies that all wavefunction coefficients greater than 0.001 be included in the excited state output (by default, only those greater than 0.1 are listed).

The excited states of benzene exemplify the importance of the following points in any theoretical study of excited states:

✦ Theoretical predictions must be compared to appropriate high quality experimental results. Allowed transitions (having oscillator strength greater than 0) may be compared to standard one-photon spectroscopic data. However, forbidden transitions must be compared to multi-photon experiments, and both types must be considered before a complete characterization of a system's excited states can be made.

✦ The symmetry of each excited state must be used when matching up predicted and observed states. You cannot simply assume that the theoretical excited state ordering corresponds to the experimental. In most cases, *Gaussian* will identify the symmetry for each excited state. In those relatively rare instances when it cannot[†]—as will be true for benzene—you will need to determine it by examining the transition wavefunction coefficients and molecular orbitals.

Here is the beginning of the output for the first predicted excited state (using the 6-31G(d) basis set):

```
CIS wavefunction symmetry could not be determined.
Excited State 1: Singlet-?Sym  6.5110 eV  190.42 nm  f=0.0000
  7 -> 35      -0.00280
 -8 -> 27       0.00314
  8 -> 31      -0.00396
  ...
```

The first line indicates that the symmetry could not be determined for this state (the symmetry itself is given as ?Sym). We will need to determine it ourselves. Molecular symmetry in excited states is related to how the orbitals transform with respect to the ground state. From group theory, we know that the overall symmetry is a function of symmetry products for the orbitals, and that only singly-occupied orbitals are

---

[†] Which usually involve degenerate point groups.

significant in determining the symmetry of the excited state (since the fully-occupied sets of symmetry-related orbitals are totally symmetric).

We will find an excitation which goes from a totally symmetric representation into a different one as a shortcut for determining the symmetry of each excited state. For benzene's point group, this totally symmetric representation is A_{1g}. We'll use the wavefunction coefficients section of the excited state output, along with the listing of the molecular orbitals from the population analysis:[†]

```
      6         7         8         9        10
   (B1U)--O  (A1G)--O  (E1U)--O  (E1U)--O  (E2G)--O
   ...
     31        32        33        34        35
   (E2G)--V  (E2G)--V  (E1U)--V  (E1U)--V  (B2U)--V
```

What we want to do is to find an A_{1g} orbital within the transition list; the symmetry of the virtual orbital into which it is excited will give us the symmetry for that excited state. Orbital 7 has A_{1g} symmetry, and for the first excited state, the first entry is:

```
7 -> 35  ...
```

When we examine orbital 35, we find that its symmetry is B_{2u}, so we assign this symmetry to this excited state. Note that the coefficient for this transition is very small, illustrating why we needed the input keyword requesting a larger range of coefficients.

If we want to determine the specific type of orbital transformation for this transition, we will need to examine the molecular orbitals for the largest components of the transition, indicated by the largest wavefunction coefficients. In this case, this is the relevant entry:

```
20 -> 22  ...
```

These two orbitals are of symmetry types E_{1g} and E_{2u} respectively.[‡]

From the standard orientation, we see that the plane of the molecule is the XY plane. Both orbitals are composed of only p_z components, indicating that they are π orbitals. Thus, this excited state corresponds to the $\pi \rightarrow \pi^*$ transition.

[†] You can also use the orbital listing labeled `Orbital Symmetries` if you did not include **Pop=Full** in the route section.

[‡] The 21→23 excitation has an equally large coefficient; these are the other halves of the two pairs of doubly degenerate orbitals.

We perform a similar analysis procedure for each excited state for the two basis sets. Here are the final results of the two jobs, along with the corresponding experimental excitation energies:

Symmetry	6-31G(d)		6-31+G(d)		Exp.
	Ex. E	f	Ex. E	f	Ex. E
B_{2u} ($\pi \rightarrow \pi^*$)	6.51	0.0	6.32	0.0	4.9
B_{1u} ($\pi \rightarrow \pi^*$)	6.73	0.0	6.50	0.0	6.2
E_{1g} ($\pi \rightarrow 3s$)			7.25	0.0	6.33
A_{2u} ($\pi \rightarrow 3p$)			7.53	0.1	6.93
E_{2u} ($\pi \rightarrow 3p$)			7.84	0.0	6.95
E_{1u} ($\pi \rightarrow \pi^*$)	8.75	1.2	8.08	0.9	7.0

The calculation done without including diffuse functions in the basis set fails to find three of the lower excited states. It does still compute excitation energies for six excited states, but the other three states are higher in energy than the 8.75 eV E_{1u} state, and do not correspond to the missing states observed by experiment. The three missing states are Rydberg states, observable via multiphoton ionization experiments.

The excitation energies obtained with the 6-31+G(d) basis set are in good qualitative agreement with the experimental values. The quantitative agreement is reasonably good, with the exception of the first excited state. However, modeling this excited state is known to be a correlation-level problem, and so we should not anticipate a more accurate result from a zeroth-order method.

This example once again illustrates the fact that CI-Singles excited state calculations can find states which are detectable only by some mechanism other than optical spectroscopy. ■

Advanced Exercise 9.5: Using the CASSCF Method to Study Excited State Systems

files: **9_05a (orbitals)**
9_05b (CAS)

In this exercise, we will introduce the Complete Active Space Multiconfiguration SCF (CASSCF) method, using it to compute the excitation energy for the first excited state of acrolein (a singlet). The CIS job we ran in Exercise 9.3 predicted an excitation energy of 4.437 eV, which is rather far from the experimental value of 3.72 eV. We'll try to improve this prediction here.

A CASSCF calculation is a combination of an SCF computation with a full Configuration Interaction calculation[†] involving a subset of the orbitals. The orbitals involved in the CI are known as the *active space*. In this way, the CASSCF method optimizes the orbitals appropriately for the excited state. In contrast, the CI-Singles method uses SCF orbitals for the excited state. Since Hartree-Fock orbitals are biased toward the ground state, a CASSCF description of the excited state electronic configuration is often an improvement.

A CASSCF calculation is requested in *Gaussian* with the **CASSCF** keyword, which requires two integer arguments: the number of electrons and the number of orbitals in the active space. The active space is defined assuming that the electrons come from as many of the highest occupied molecular orbitals as are needed to obtain the specified number of electrons; any remaining required orbitals are taken from the lowest virtual orbitals.

For example, in a 4-electron, 6-orbital CAS—specified as **CASSCF(4,6)**—performed on a singlet system, the active space would consist of the two highest occupied molecular orbitals (where the four electrons reside) and the four lowest virtual orbitals. Similarly, for a 6-electron, 5-orbital CAS on a triplet system, the active space would consist of the four highest occupied MO's—two of which are doubly-occupied and two are singly-occupied—and the LUMO (the keyword is **CASSCF(6,5)**).

The **Guess=Alter** keyword is used to ensure that the orbitals of interest are included in the active space. This keyword allows orbitals to be swapped in order within the initial guess. A prior run with **Guess=Only** and/or **Pop=Full** can be used to quickly determine the orbital symmetries and decide which ones should be placed within the active space.

Perform a series of CASSCF calculations on acrolein to predict the excitation energy of its first excited state. In order to complete a CASSCF study of this excited state, you will need to complete the following steps:

♦ Run a preliminary **UHF/STO-3G Pop=NaturalOrbitals** job on *triplet* acrolein to generate and examine the starting orbitals and their symmetries. Select those that will make up the active space; you will want to create an active

---

[†] See Appendix A for a description of the CI method.

space that contains the π orbital from the C-O bond and the oxygen atom lone pair, since in the first excited state, an electron moves from the lone pair into the π space.

Use the geometry optimized at the **CASSCF(6,5)/6-31G(d) level** that we have provided in the file **9_05.pdb**.

✦ Predict the energies of the ground state and the excited state using the 6-31G(d) basis set. CASSCF wavefunctions can be difficult to converge, so we will build up to this level in stages:

❖ Run a **CASSCF(6,5,UNO)/STO-3G Guess=(Read,Alter)** calculation, again on triplet acrolein, modifying the orbital ordering from the checkpoint file in order to place the orbitals of interest into the active space. We begin with the triplet rather than the singlet as it is easier to converge because it is a pure diradical, and hence a more constrained problem than the π-π* singlet which will have significant ionic character. Thus, we will use (Note that the **CASSCF=UNO** option says to use the natural orbitals in the CAS.)

❖ Run a second job with the 6-31G(d) basis set, starting from the STO-3G converged wavefunction.

❖ Compute the energy of the excited state singlet with the 6-31G(d) basis set. Once again, begin the calculation with the converged wavefunction from the previous job step. Include **Geom=Check** in the route section for the job, and specify a spin multiplicity of 1 for this job step. You will also need to give the option **NRoot=2** to the **CASSCF** keyword to specify the excited state.

✦ Finally, run another **CASSCF(6,5)/6-31G(d)** job to predict the energy of the ground state, using the same strategy as for the excited state. Retrieve the initial guess from the checkpoint file from the excited state calculation.

The excitation energy will then be given by the difference of the energies predicted by the final two calculations.

CAS is not for the faint hearted! You should be aware that the CAS method is not a black box in the same way that, say, Hartree-Fock or CI-Singles are. Designing and completing these calculations successfully will require considerable care and patience. Note that starting a CASSCF computation from the default initial guess is almost never successful. Choosing an appropriate active space requires a good understanding of the problem under investigation as well as a fair amount of trial and error (which gets easier with experience). Do not be discouraged by difficulties that you may encounter. If you get stuck at any point, examine the input files we have provided to determine how to proceed.

Solution   We'll look at the input files for this exercise more closely than we often do. Here is the structure of the first set of jobs designed for examining the orbitals and planning the active space (note that we save the checkpoint file for later reuse):

```
%chk=acro_cas
#T UHF/STO-3G Test Pop=NaturalOrbitals

UHF on triplet acrolein at CAS(6,5) 6-31G(d) geometry

0 3
molecule specification

--Link1--
%chk=acro_cas
#T CAS(6,5,UNO) Guess=(Read,Only) Test Geom=Check
...
```

Here are the orbital symmetries from the converged wavefunction from the second, **Guess=Only** job (at the beginning of the population analysis):

```
Orbital Symmetries:
     Occupied  (A') (A') (A') (A') (A') (A") (A') (A') (A') (A')
               (A') (A') (A') (A") (A') (A")
     Virtual   (A") (A') (A') (A') (A') (A') (A') (A')
```

The active space will consist of the four highest occupied MO's and the lowest virtual MO. We want four A" and one A' orbital in the active space. This suggests that we want to move orbital 6 into the active space, replacing either orbital 13 or 15. As always, however, we must examine the relevant MO's themselves to ensure that they are what and where we expect them to be. In this case, we want to retain the A' orbital corresponding to the oxygen lone pair. Orbital 15 has large $2p_x$ and $2p_y$ on the oxygen atom and no large coefficients elsewhere, so this is the orbital we want to retain.[†]

Accordingly, we will swap orbitals 6 and 13. We define the active space to comprise these orbitals by using the **Guess=Alter** keyword in the route section for the first job step in our second calculation series:

```
%chk=acro_cas
#T CAS(6,5,UNO)/STO-3G Test Geom=Check Guess=(Read,Alter)

CAS 6,5 using triplet UNO orbitals

0 3

! Bring A" into the active space
6,13
```

[†] Note that these orbital numbers may vary in your output due to small numerical differences produced by differing computer architectures.

The final section of the file gives the input to **Guess=Alter**: swap orbitals 6 and 13, as we had previously decided.

The output of the calculation will be the new CASSCF description of the triplet state. We will use this as the starting point for further calculations: first, another CAS on the triplet with the target basis set, and then a CAS on the singlet excited state:

```
--Link1--
%Chk=acro_cas
#T CAS(6,5)/6-31G(d) Test Geom=Check Guess=Read

CAS 6,5 in extended basis set

0 3

--Link1--
%Chk=acro_cas
#T CAS(6,5,NRoot=2)/6-31G(d) Test Geom=Check Guess=Read

Singlet n-pi state (should have similar orbitals)

0 1
```

The orbital alteration will be carried along into each subsequent job.

The final job step predicts the energy of the ground state (also a singlet) via another CAS calculation:

```
--Link1--
%Chk=acro_cas
%NoSave
#T CAS(6,5)/6-31G(d) Test Geom=Check Guess=Read

Ground state starting from excited state orbitals

0 1
```

The predicted energy is given in the final CAS iteration (this is from the ground state calculation):

```
ITN= 32 MaxIt= 64 E=   -190.8250224914 DE=-8.55D-06 Acc= 1.00D-05
```

1 Hartree = 27.2116 eV

In our case, the predicted excitation energy is given by -190.67673 − -190.82502 Hartrees = 4.035 eV, which is reasonably close to the experimental value of 3.72 eV, and is an improvement on the CIS value. ■

Advanced Exercise 9.6: Using CASSCF to Study Butadiene Photochemistry

files: 9_06a (GS orbitals)
      9_06b (GS 4,4)
      9_06c (GS 4,6)
      9_06d (CI)

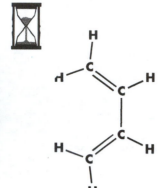

The photochemical behavior of butadienes has been closely studied. When these compounds are exposed to light, they move from the ground state to an excited state. This excited state eventually returns to one of the ground state conformations via a process that includes a radiationless decay (i.e., without emitting a photon) from the excited state potential energy surface back to the ground state potential energy surface.

Such radiationless decay has been explained in two different ways. The traditional view holds that the location where the molecule crosses from the excited state PES to the ground state PES is an *avoided crossing minimum*: a region that is a minimum on the excited state PES which is only slightly higher in energy than the ground state PES at the same points. However, Olivucci, Ragazos, Bernardi and Robb have argued that the decay occurs via a *conical intersection*: a region in which the ground state and excited state potential energy surfaces overlap (are degenerate).

The following illustration depicts the process proposed by these researchers:

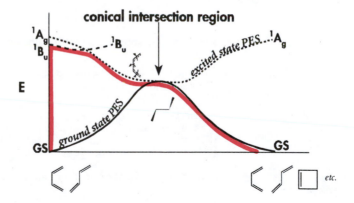

The red line follows the progress of the reaction path. First, a butadiene compound is excited into its first excited state (either the cis or trans form may be used—we will be considering the cis conformation). What we have illustrated as the lower excited state is a singlet ^1B_u state, resulting from a single excitation from the HOMO to the LUMO of the π system. The second excited state is a ^1A_g state, corresponding to a double excitation from HOMO to LUMO. The ordering of these two excited states is not completely known, but internal conversion from the ^1B_u state to the ^1A_g state is known to occur almost immediately (within femtoseconds).

Accordingly, the reaction path then proceeds via the ^1A_g excited state on the excited state PES until the conical intersection region is reached, passing through an excited state minimum. At the conical intersection, the molecule drops down to the ground state PES, and the molecule then takes on one of its ground state conformations (perhaps even the very one it began as).

In this exercise, we will examine a small part of this process. We will predict the relative energies of the three states at the ground state geometry, and we will locate the conical intersection. We've provided you with an optimized ground state (cis) structure and a starting structure for the conical intersection in the files 9_06_gs.pdb and 9_06_ci.pdb, respectively.

For the ground state study, complete the following steps:

✦ Compute and examine the orbitals at the RHF/3-21G level in order to select the active space. We will be performing a 4-electron CAS, using 4 and 6 active orbitals. The orbitals we want are those corresponding to the π system (where the excited electrons go); therefore, the orbitals we want will be pairs of symmetry A_2 and B_1. Reorder the orbitals so that six appropriate orbitals make up the active space.

✦ Perform a series of *state-averaged* 4,4 CAS calculations on the ground state, using the active space you have selected. Normally, a CAS calculation optimizes the orbitals and hence the wavefunction for the state of interest (as specified by the **NRoot** option). However, in a state-averaged CAS, orbitals are optimized to provide the best description of the specified group of states as a whole that is possible with a single set of orbitals.

For a state-averaged CAS calculation, you must specify the states to be averaged by selecting the highest state of interest with the **NRoot** option. All states between that one and the ground state will be averaged. You must also provide the weights for each state to be averaged in a separate input section, in format nF10.8.

We are interested in the three lowest states, and we want each state to be treated equally, so we will specify **NRoot=3** and all three weights as 0.3333333. We will run a series of state-averaged CAS(4,4) calculations (the option is **StateAverage**) on the ground state structure, using this sequence of basis sets: 3-21G, 4-31G, 6-31G(d) and 6-31+G(d,p). Begin the first computation using the wavefunction computed in the RHF calculation.

Include **#P** in the route section of the final job. The various states will be described in the output following the final CAS iteration and introduced by the line:

```
VECTOR  EIGENVALUES          CORRESPONDING EIGENVECTOR

    1   -154.8747374   0.95038483   -0.32993992E-01   ...
```

State number   Energy   Coefficients of each
(starts at 1)   electronic configuration

The coefficients indicate the composition of the electronic state in terms of a linear combination of the various electronic configurations defined earlier in the output. Here is an example from a 4,4 CAS showing the first two excited state configurations:

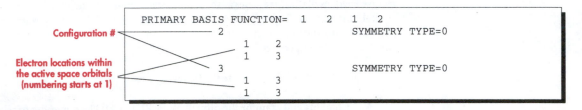

Configuration 2 is a single excitation, with one electron moving from the second to third orbital within the active space (where the ground state is configuration 1, denoted: 1 2 1 2 for this system). Configuration 3 is a double excitation: both electrons originally in the second active space orbital move to the third orbital within the active space. The coefficients for state 1 (given on the previous page) indicate that it is primarily composed of configuration 1, the ground state.

✦ Once your jobs have completed, characterize the two predicted excited states and compare their energies.

✦ You can continue to improve upon this CAS description of this system by running a second series of state-averaged 4x6 CAS calculations on the lowest three states, starting from the results of the final job of the 4x4 series, using the 3-21G, 4-31G, 6-31G(d) and 6-31+G(d,p) basis sets in succession. How do the results change with the larger active space?

For the study of the conical intersection, complete these steps:

✦ Using the starting structure that we have provided, begin the study with a **UHF/STO-3G Guess=Mix Pop=NaturalOrbitals NoSymm** job. Examine the orbitals. You should be able to use the default ordering to define the active space.

✦ Build up to a good CAS description of this structure by running two state-averaged 4,4 CAS calculations beginning with the wavefunction from the first step (since we will be looking for a conical intersection, we will average the lowest two states using equal weights of 0.5). Use the STO-3G basis set for the first job, along with the **UNO** and **NoFullDiag** options to the **CASSCF** keyword; use the 4-31G basis set for the second job. Include the **NoSymm** keyword on both jobs.

✦ Locate the conical intersection by running a **CAS Opt=Conical** jobs. Include **NoSymm** and **IOp(1/8=5)** in the route section.

✦ Run a final state-averaged calculation at the fully-optimized conical intersection using the 4-31G basis set and **#P** to predict the energies of the two states and view the configuration coefficients. (This step will not be necessary if you chose to use **#P** for the final conical intersection optimization job; you'll find the relevant output in the CAS output for the final optimization step, preceding the table giving the stationary point geometry.)

Solution

The table below summarizes the results of the study of the cis ground state:

Method	Excited State 1	Excited State 2	ΔE (Hartrees)
CAS(4,4)/6-31+G(d,p)	$2\ {}^1A_g$	$1\ {}^1B_u$	0.03702
CAS(4,6)/6-31+G(d,p)	$2\ {}^1A_g$	$1\ {}^1B_u$	0.00540

In both cases, the double excitation ^1A_g state is lower in energy than the singe excitation ^1B_u state. However, the energy difference continuously decreases as the CAS description is improved. Adding an MP2 correction would decrease it even further.

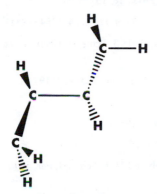

The search for a conical intersection is also successful. The predicted structure is at the left. The predicted energies of the two states—the ground state and the first excited state—differ by about 0.00014 Hartrees, confirming that they are degenerate at these points on the two potential energy surfaces. ■

References

CI-Singles Method; Ethylene & Formaldehyde Studies

J. B. Foresman, M. Head-Gordon, J. A. Pople, and M. J. Frisch, *J. Phys. Chem.*, **96**, 135 (1992).

CI-Singles Method; Benzene Excitation Energies

J. B. Foresman and H. B. Schlegel, "Application of the CI-Singles Method in Predicting the Energy, Properties and Reactivity of Molecules in Their Excited States" in *Molecular Spectroscopy: Recent Experimental and Computational Advances*, ed. R. Fausto, NATO-ASI Series C, Kluwer Academic, The Netherlands, 1993.

Formaldehyde Frequencies

C. M. Hadad, J. B. Foresman, and K. B. Wiberg, "The Excited States of Carbonyl Compounds. I. Formaldehyde and Acetaldehyde," *J. Phys. Chem.*, **97**, 4293 (1993).

Ethylene Excited States

A. J. Merer and R. S. Mulliken, *Chem. Rev.*, **69**, 639 (1969).

Methylenecyclopropene Spectra

S. W. Staley and T. D. Norden, *J. Am. Chem. Soc.*, **106**, 3699 (1984).

Formaldehyde Experimental Data

V. A. Job, V. Sethuraman, and K. K. Innes, *J. Mol. Spectrosc.*, **30**, 365 (1969).

D. E. Freeman and W. J. Klemperer, *J. Chem. Phys.*, **45**, 52 (1966).

V. T. Jones and B. J. Coon, *J. Mol. Spectrosc.*, **31**, 137 (1969).

J. L. Hardwick and S. M. Till, *J. Chem. Phys.*, **70**, 2340 (1979).

W. E. Henke, H. L. Selzle, T. R. Hays, E. W. Schlag, and S. H. Lin, *J. Chem. Phys.* **76**, 1327 (1982).

Formaldehyde Dipole Moment Orientation   A. D. Buckingham, D. A. Ramsey, and J. Tyrrell, *Can. J. Phys.*, **48**, 1242 (1970).

Acrolein Experimental Data   R. R. Birge, W. C. Pringle, and P. A. Leermakers, *J. Am. Chem. Soc.*, **93**, 6715 (1971).

CASSCF Study of Butadiene Photochemistry   M. Olivucci, I. N. Ragazos, F. Bernardi and M. A. Robb, *J. Am. Chem. Soc.*, **115**, 3710 (1993).

CASSCF Method   B. O. Roos, P. R. Taylor and P. E. M. Siegbahn, *Chem. Phys.*, **48**, 157 (1980).

P. E. M. Siegbahn, J. Amlöf, J. Heiberg and B. O. Roos, *J. Chem. Phys.*, **74**, 2384 (1981).

N. Yamamoto, T. Vreven, M. A. Robb, M. J. Frisch and H. B. Schlegel, *Chem. Phys. Lett.*, **250**, 373 (1996).

M. J. Bearpark, M. A. Robb and H. B. Schlegel, *Chem. Phys. Lett.*, **223**, 269 (1994).

D. Hegarty and M. A. Robb, *Mol. Phys.* **38**, 1795 (1979).

R. H. E. Eade and M. A. Robb, *Chem. Phys. Lett.* **83**, 362 (1981).

H. B. Schlegel and M. A. Robb, *Chem. Phys. Lett.* **93**, 43 (1982).

F. Bernardi, A. Bottini, J. J. W. McDougall, M. A. Robb and H. B. Schlegel, *Far. Symp. Chem. Soc.* **19**, 137 (1984).

Modeling Systems in Solution

In This Chapter:

Chemistry in Solution

Self-Consistent Reaction Field Methods

Running Calculations Including Solvent Effects

So far, all of the calculations we've done have been in the gas phase. While gas phase predictions are appropriate for many purposes, they are inadequate for describing the characteristics of many molecules in solution. Indeed, the properties of molecules and transition states can differ considerably between the gas phase and solution. For example, electrostatic effects are often much less important for species placed in a solvent with a high dielectric constant than they are in the gas phase.

Reaction Field Models of Solvation

One family of models for systems in non-aqueous solution are referred to as Self-Consistent Reaction Field (SCRF) methods. These methods all model the solvent as a continuum of uniform dielectric constant ε: the *reaction field*. The solute is placed into a cavity within the solvent. SCRF approachs differ in how they define the cavity and the reaction field. Several are illustrated below.

The simplest SCRF model is the Onsager reaction field model. In this method, the solute occupies a fixed spherical cavity of radius a_0 within the solvent field. A dipole in the molecule will induce a dipole in the medium, and the electric field applied by the solvent dipole will in turn interact with the molecular dipole, leading to net stabilization.

Onsager (Dipole & Sphere) Model
SCRF=Dipole

Tomasi's PCM Model
SCRF=PCM

Isodensity Model
SCRF=IPCM

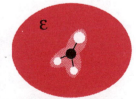
Self-consistent Isodensity Model
SCRF=SCIPCM

Tomasi's Polarized Continuum Model (PCM) defines the cavity as the union of a series of interlocking atomic spheres. The effect of polarization of the solvent continuum is represented numerically: it is computed by numerical integration rather than by an approximation to the analytical form used in the Onsager model. The two isodensity surface-based SCRF models also use a numerical representation of the solvent field.

The Isodensity PCM (IPCM) model defines the cavity as an isodensity surface of the molecule. This isodensity is determined by an iterative process in which an SCF cycle is performed and converged using the current isodensity cavity. The resultant wavefunction is then used to compute an updated isodensity surface, and the cycle is repeated until the cavity shape no longer changes upon completion of the SCF.

An isodensity surface is a very natural, intuitive shape for the cavity since it corresponds to the reactive shape of the molecule to as great a degree as is possible (rather than being a simpler, pre-defined shape such as a sphere or a set of overlapping spheres).

However, a cavity defined as an isosurface and the electron density are necessarily coupled. The Self-consistent Isodensity Polarized Continuum Model (SCI-PCM) was designed to take this effect fully into account. It includes the effect of solvation in the solution of the SCF problem. This procedure solves for the electron density which minimizes the energy, including the solvation energy—which itself depends on the cavity which depends on the electron density. In other words, the effects of solvation are folded into the iterative SCF computation rather than comprising an extra step afterwards.[†] SCI-PCM thus accounts for the full coupling between the cavity and the electron density and includes coupling terms that IPCM neglects.

Limitations of the Onsager Model

Note that systems having a dipole moment of 0 will not exhibit solvent effects for the Onsager SCRF model, and therefore Onsager model (**SCRF=Dipole**) calculations performed on them will give the same results as for the gas phase. This is an inherent limitation of the Onsager approach.

[†] Note that this approach results in a proper variational condition.

Running SCRF Calculations

The **SCRF** keyword in the route section of a *Gaussian* job requests a calculation in the presence of a solvent. SCRF calculations generally require an additional input line following the molecule specification section's terminating blank line, having the following form:

Model	Required Input	Example
SCRF=Dipole	$a_0(\text{Å})$ ε	2.92 2.0
SCRF=PCM	ε *pts/sphere*	2.0 100
SCRF=IPCM	ε	2.0
SCRF=SCIPCM	ε	2.0

Remember that ε is the dielectric constant of the solvent. The examples show the value for cyclohexane (2.0).

Molecular Volume Calculations

Gaussian also includes a facility for estimating molecular volumes for **SCRF=Dipole** calculations. An energy calculation run with the **Volume** keyword will produce an estimate value for a_0. For example, here is the output indicating the recommended value for a_0 for formaldehyde (RHF/6-31+G*):

```
Recommended a0 for SCRF calculation = 2.92 angstrom ( 5.51 bohr)
```

The value indicated is 0.5Å larger than the computed molecular volume in order to account for the van der Waals radii of the surrounding solute molecules.

Example 10.1: Dichloroethane Conformer Energy Difference by Solvent

files: **e10_01a (IPCM)**
      e10_01b (Dipole)

We will consider the energy difference between the trans and gauche conformations of dichloroethane in different environments:

trans   gauche

We ran an SCRF single point energy calculation for gauche dichloroethane conformers in cyclohexane ($\varepsilon=2.0$), using the Onsager model at the Hartree-Fock and MP2 levels of theory ($a_0=3.65$) and using the IPCM model at the B3LYP level. The 6-31+G(d) basis set was used for all jobs. We also ran gas phase calculations for both conformations at the same model chemistries, and an IPCM calculation for the trans conformation (**SCRF=Dipole** calculations are not necessary for the trans conformation since it has no dipole moment).

Locating Results in *Gaussian* Output

The predicted energies in solution are generally given in the same location within the *Gaussian* output as for gas phase calculations, with the following variations:

♦ Gas phase results are given as the first iteration of IPCM calculations (so separate gas phase jobs at B3LYP/6-31+G(d) are not needed).

♦ The predicted energy in solution is given in the SCF summary section preceding the `Convergence Achieved` message in an IPCM calculation (indicating the final iteration).

♦ For Onsager model calculations, the energy in solution is marked as `Total energy (include solvent energy)` in the output. This value is the same as that given in the regular SCF output (i.e., prefaced by `SCF Done`) for Hartree-Fock calculations. For MP2 calculations, *only* the value in the solvation summary section includes all of the solvent effects, and in particular, energy values immediately following this section should not be mistaken for the energy in solution.

We specified tight SCF convergence criteria for all jobs (**SCF=Tight**). Here are the results of our calculations, as well as the computed and observed energy differences:

| | $E^{\text{gas phase}}$ | | | $E^{\text{cyclohexane}}$ | | |
| | | | | Onsager | | IPCM |
Medium	HF	MP2	B3LYP	HF	MP2	B3LYP
trans	-997.03286	-997.55740	-999.02324	N/A	N/A	-999.02486
gauche	-997.02974	-997.55499	-999.02043	-997.03075	-997.55583	-999.02254

| | $\Delta E^{\text{gauche - trans}}$ (kcal-mol^{-1}) | | | |
| | Onsager | | IPCM | |
Medium	HF	MP2	B3LYP	Exp.
Gas Phase	1.96	1.51	1.76	1.20
Cyclohexane ($\varepsilon=2.0$)	1.32	0.99	1.46	0.91
Solvent Effect	-0.64	-0.52	-0.30	-0.29

The Onsager MP2 and IPCM B3LYP values are in pretty good agreement with the experimental data. When we consider the *solvent effect*—the *change* in the energy difference produced by the solvent—then the IPCM model is in the closest agreement with the experimental value of -0.29 kcal-mol^{-1} (gas phase $\rightarrow$ solution), followed by the Onsager model at the MP2 level. Electron correlation is known to be important in predicting gas phase properties for this system, so it is not surprising that correlation produces significantly better results in solution as well.

We will continue this study in the first exercise.

Example 10.2: Formaldehyde Frequencies in Acetonitrile

files: e10_02a (gas+Vol)
e10_02b (SCIPCM)
e10_02c (Dipole)

Next, we will consider the vibrational frequencies of formaldehyde in acetonitrile, using the Onsager SCRF model and the SCIPCM model. Acetonitrile is a highly polar solvent, with an ε value of 35.9. In order to predict the vibrational frequencies, we'll first need to optimize the structure for formaldehyde in this medium. Thus, we'll be running these jobs:

- ✦ A ground state optimization at the HF/6-31+G(d) level.
- ✦ A molecular volume calculation to estimate a_0 for the Onsager model.
- ✦ An SCRF geometry optimization, beginning at the optimized gas phase structure, for each model.
- ✦ An SCRF frequency calculation at the two SCRF optimized structures. Note that frequency calculations must be run as a separate job step for SCRF calculations (**Opt Freq** does not do what might be expected).

The volume calculation results in a cavity radius of 3.65. The acetonitrile solution produces only subtle changes in the molecule's structure. The only significant change is a decrease of 0.3-0.4° in the O-C-H bond angle.

Here are the predicted frequencies (scaled, in cm^{-1}) in the gas phase and in solution:

	Model	Frequency (Symmetry)					
		$v_1 (B_1)$	$v_2 (B_2)$	$v_3 (A_1)$	$v_4 (A_1)$	$v_5 (A_1)$	$v_6 (B_2)$
Gas Phase	Calculated	1190	1227	1489	1792	2829	2896
	Experimental	1167	1249	1500	1746	2782	2843
Acetonitrile	Onsager	1202	1222	1488	1766	2848	2924
	SCIPCM	1205	1223	1485	1757	2860	2934
	Experimental		1247	1503	1723	2797	2876

A useful way of analyzing this data is to compute the frequency shifts on going from the gas phase to acetonitrile solution:

Model	$\Delta\nu_1$	$\Delta\nu_2$	$\Delta\nu_3$	$\Delta\nu_4$	$\Delta\nu_5$	$\Delta\nu_6$
Onsager	+12	-5	-1	-26	+19	+28
SCI-PCM	+15	-4	-4	-35	+31	+38
Experiment		-2	+3	-23	+15	+33

As this table indicates, the SCRF facility in *Gaussian* produces very good agreement with experiment. The solvent produces fairly small but significant shifts in the locations of the major peaks, as predicted by both SCRF models.

Exercises

Exercise 10.1: Dichloroethane Conformer Energy Differences

files: **10_01a (IPCM)**
      10_01b (HF)
      10_01c (MP2)

Predict the energy difference between the gauche and trans conformers of dichloroethane in its liquid state ($\varepsilon=10.1$) and in acetonitrile ($\varepsilon=35.9$). Plot the predicted and experimental energy differences for the four media examined in Example 8.2 and this exercise. The experimental values for pure liquid and acetonitrile are 0.31 and 0.15 kcal mol^{-1}, respectively. You may use either the Onsager (HF or MP2) or IPCM (B3LYP) SCRF models (IPCM takes much longer than either Onsager model), with the 6-31+G(d) basis set. Use tight SCF convergence criteria (**SCF=Tight**) for all jobs.

Remember that the trans form of dichloroethane has no dipole moment, so it is not necessary to compute its energy in solution with the Onsager model.

Solution   Here are the predicted energy differences and solvent effects in the four solvent environments:

	$\Delta E^{\text{gauche - trans}}$ (kcal-mol^{-1})			
	Onsager		IPCM	Exp.
Medium	HF	MP2	B3LYP	
Gas Phase	1.96	1.51	1.76	1.20
Cyclohexane	1.32	0.99	1.45	0.91
Pure Liquid	0.50	0.29	0.90	0.31
Acetonitrile	0.30	0.13	0.73	0.15

| Medium | Solvent Effect | | | |
| | Onsager | | IPCM | Exp. |
	HF	MP2	B3LYP	
Cyclohexane	-0.64	-0.52	-0.30	-0.29
Pure Liquid	-1.46	-1.22	-0.86	-0.89
Acetonitrile	-1.66	-1.38	-1.03	-0.95

The graph on the right plots the predicted energy difference by SCRF method and solvent environment, and the graph on the left plots the predicted solvent effect for the various methods and solvents.

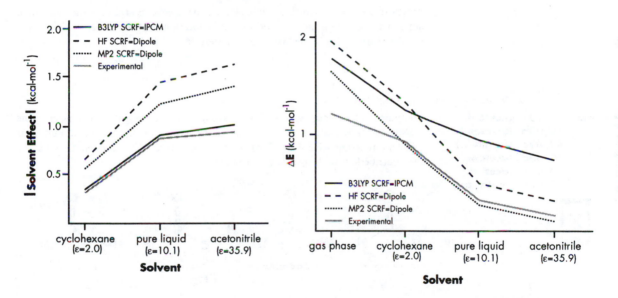

As the plot of ΔE indicates, the energy difference between the two forms decreases in more polar solvents, and becomes nearly zero in acetonitrile. The left plot illustrates the fact that the IPCM model (at the B3LYP/6-31+G(d) level of theory) does a much better job of reproducing the observed solvent effect than the two Onsager SCRF models. In contrast, the Onsager model at the MP2 level treats the solvated systems more accurately than it does the gas phase system, leading to a poorer value for the solvent effect. ■

Exercise 10.2: Formaldehyde Frequencies

file: **10_02**

Predict the vibrational frequencies for formaldehyde in solution with cyclohexane. Use the RHF/6-31+G(d) level of theory with Onsager SCRF method.

Solution

The geometry optimization reveals that the structure of formaldehyde in cyclohexane is essentially the same as it is in acetonitrile. Here are the predicted frequency shifts with respect to the gas phase for the two media:

Medium	Δv_1	Δv_2	Δv_3	Δv_4	Δv_5	Δv_6
Cyclohexane	+5	-1	0	-8	+7	+19
Acetonitrile	+12	-5	-1	-26	+19	+28

As we can see, cyclohexane has a much less dramatic effect on the peak locations than acetonitrile; although the same peaks change location for both solvents, the shift is less than half as large in the case of cyclohexane. ■

Exercise 10.3: Carbonyl Stretch in Solution

files: 10_03a (acetald.)
10_03b (acrolein)
10_03c (formam.)
10_03d (acetone)
10_03e (acet. cl.)
10_03f (meth. ac.)

Compute the frequency associated with carbonyl stretch in solution with acetonitrile for the carbonyl systems we looked at in the gas phase in Chapter 4. Run your calculations using RHF/6-31+G(d) with the Onsager SCRF model. Discuss the substituent effect on the predicted solvent effects.

formaldehyde   acetaldehyde   acrolein   formamide

acetone   acetyl chloride   methyl acetate

The following table lists recommended values of a_0 for the various systems. It also includes the published frequency (scaled) associated with carbonyl stretch in the gas phase for each compound that we gave in Chapter 4:

System	a_0	Frequency Calc.	Exp.
Formaldehyde	2.92	1773	1746
Acetaldehyde	3.27	1777	1746
Acetone	3.65	1750	1737
Acrolein	3.48	1787	1723
Methyl Acetate	3.71	1789	1761
Acetyl Chloride	3.54	1771	1822
Formamide	3.20	1832	1740

Solution   A geometry optimization and frequency calculation (both in solution) are needed for each system (we ran the formaldehyde calculations earlier in this chapter). Here are the resulting scaled frequencies associated with carbonyl stretch for each system, along with the corresponding experimental values:

System	Gas Phase Calc.	Exp.	Acetonitrile Calc.	Exp.	Frequency Shift Calc.	Exp.
Formaldehyde	1773	1746	1766	1723	-21	-23
Acetaldehyde	1777	1746	1768	1723	-16	-23
Acetone	1750	1737	1755	1713	-14	-24
Acrolein	1787	1723	1740	1698	-28	-25
Methyl Acetate	1789	1761	1752	1741	-14	-20
Acetyl Chloride	1771	1822	1816	1805	-10	-17
Formamide	1832	1740	1695	1702	-46	-38

Once again, frequency shifts provide a good way of examining the solvent effect. The highly polar solvent produces about the same shift for each compound with the exception of formamide, where it is quite a bit greater, the result of combining the polar solvent with formamide's rather large dipole moment. ∎

Advanced Exercise 10.4: Rotational Barrier in Solution for N-Methyl-2-Nitrovinylamine

files: **10_04a (E form)**
10_04b (Z form)
10_04c (TS)

Compute the rotational barrier about the C=C bond in solution for the E and Z forms of n-methyl-2-nitrovinylamine in a solution of ortho-dichlorobenzene (ε=9.9). Completing this study will require the following steps:

✦ Optimize the two equilibrium structures in solution, using the Onsager SCRF method and the RHF/6-31G(d) model chemistry. You'll of course need to determine the appropriate cavity radius first.

✦ Locate the transition structure connecting these two minima, optimizing its structure in solution.

✦ Perform frequency calculations on all three optimized structures, using the same SCRF method and model chemistry.

✦ Compute the energies of the three structures using the SCI-PCM SCRF model and the B3LYP/6-31+G(d) model chemistry.[†]

✦ Compute the two rotational barriers. The experimental value for the Z form is 21.10 kcal-mol^{-1}.

[†] The input files we provide begin with this step.

Solution   Here are the three optimized structures:

E Form

Z Form

Transition Structure

The following table summarizes the results of our calculations:

System	E	Thermal Energy Correction (Rel. to Z form)	ΔE^{rot} (kcal-mol^{-1}) Calc.	Exp.
E form	-377.79443	-0.22	27.51	
Z form	-377.79801	0.0	29.54	21.10
TS	-377.74886	-1.31		

The corresponding predicted gas phase rotational barrier is 41.8 kcal-mol^{-1}. As is observed, the rotational barrier decreases considerably in solution. ∎

Advanced Exercise 10.5: Comparing SCRF Methods on Furfuraldehyde

files: 10_05a (anti)
10_05b (syn)

Compute the energy difference between the anti (left) and syn forms of furfuraldehyde in a solution of dimethyl ether (ε=12.0), using either the Onsager (MP2/6-31+G(d)) or the SCIPCM (B3LYP/6-31+G(d)) SCRF models. The observed energy difference is -0.53 kcal-mol^{-1}.

Solution   The following table lists the energy differences that we computed as well as the original researchers' HF/6-31+G(d) Onsager and B3LYP/6-31+G(d) SCRF=IPCM results:

Model	$\Delta E^{syn-anti}$
HF/6-31+G(d) SCRF=Dipole	-0.13
MP2/6-31+G(d) SCRF=Dipole	-0.60
B3LYP/6-31+G(d) SCRF=IPCM	-0.39
B3LYP/6-31+G(d) SCRF=SCIPCM	-0.10

Both the MP2 Onsager calculation and the IPCM calculaton are in good agreement with experiment. The SCI-PCM and Hartree-Fock Onsager SCRF calculations perform significantly less well for this problem. ∎

References

SCRF Methods and Applications   J. B. Foresman, T. A. Keith, K. B. Wiberg, J. Snoonian and M. J. Frisch, "Solvent Effects. 5. The Influence of Cavity Shape, Truncation of Electrostatics, and Electron Correlation on Ab Initio Reaction Field Calculations," *J. Phys. Chem.*, submitted (1996). [Discusses the IPCM SCRF model.]

K. B. Wiberg, T. A. Keith, M. J. Frisch and M. Murcko, *J. Phys. Chem.*, **99**, 9072 (1995).

M. W. Wong, M. J. Frisch, and K. B. Wiberg, *J. Am. Chem. Soc.*, **113**, 4776 (1991)

M. W. Wong, K. B. Wiberg, and M. J. Frisch, *J. Chem. Phys.*, **95**, 8991 (1991)

M. W. Wong, K. B. Wiberg, and M. J. Frisch, *J. Am. Chem. Soc.*, **114**, 523 (1992)

M. W. Wong, K. B. Wiberg, and M. J. Frisch, *J. Am. Chem. Soc.*, **114**, 1645 (1992)

M. M. Karelson, T. Tamm, A. R. Katritzky, M. Szefran, and M. C. Zerner, *Int. J. Quantum Chem.*, **37**, 1 (1990)

M. M. Karelson, A. R. Katritzky, and M. C. Zerner, *Int. J. Quantum Chem.*, **20**, 521 (1986).

Onsager Reaction Field Model   L. Onsager, *J. Am. Chem. Soc.*, **58**, 1486 (1938).

J. G. Kirkwood, *J. Chem. Phys.* **2**, 351 (1934).

Dichloroethane & Onsager Model   K. B. Wiberg and M. A. Murcko, *J. Phys. Chem.*, **91**, 3616 (1987).

PCM Model   S. Miertus and J. Tomasi, "Approximate Evaluations of the Electrostatic Free Energy and Internal Energy Changes in Solution Processes," *Chem. Phys.* **65**, 239 (1982).

S. Miertus, E. Scrocco and J. Tomasi, "Electrostatic Interaction of a Solute with a Continuum. A Direct Utilization of ab initio Molecular Potentials for the Prevision of Solvent Effects," *Chem. Phys.* **55**, 117 (1981).

SCI-PCM Model   T. A. Keith and M. J. Frisch, "A Fully Self-Consistent Polarizable Continuum Model of Solvation with Analytic Energy Gradients," in preparation (1996).

N-Methyl-2-Nitrovinylamine Experimental Rotational Barrier   R. R. Pappalardo, E. S. Marcos, M. F. Ruiz-Lopez, D. Rinaldi and J-L. Rivail, *J. Am. Chem. Soc.*, **115**, 3722 (1993).

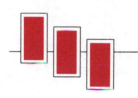

Appendices

The Theoretical Background

Ab initio molecular orbital theory is concerned with predicting the properties of atomic and molecular systems. It is based upon the fundamental laws of quantum mechanics and uses a variety of mathematical transformation and approximation techniques to solve the fundamental equations. This appendix provides an introductory overview of the theory underlying ab initio electronic structure methods. The final section provides a similar overview of the theory underlying Density Functional Theory methods.

The Schrödinger Equation

Quantum mechanics explains how entities like electrons have both particle-like and wave-like characteristics. The Schrödinger equation describes the wavefunction of a particle:

$$\left\{ \frac{-h^2}{8\pi^2 m} \nabla^2 + \mathbf{V} \right\} \Psi(\vec{r}, t) = \frac{ih}{2\pi} \frac{\partial \Psi(\vec{r}, t)}{\partial t} \qquad [1]$$

In this equation, Ψ is the wavefunction, m is the mass of the particle, h is Planck's constant, and $\mathbf{V}$ is the potential field in which the particle is moving.[†] The product of Ψ with its complex conjugate ($\Psi^*\Psi$, often written as $|\Psi|^2$) is interpreted as the probability distribution of the particle.

The Schrödinger equation for a collection of particles like a molecule is very similar. In this case, Ψ would be a function of the coordinates of all the particles in the system as well as t.

The energy and many other properties of the particle can be obtained by solving the Schrödinger equation for Ψ, subject to the appropriate boundary conditions. Many different wavefunctions are solutions to it, corresponding to different stationary states of the system.

[†] The differential operator on the left side of the equation is known as "del-squared." The operator del is equivalent to partial differentiation with respect to x, y, and z components:

$$\nabla = \frac{\partial}{\partial x}\hat{\mathbf{i}} + \frac{\partial}{\partial y}\hat{\mathbf{j}} + \frac{\partial}{\partial z}\hat{\mathbf{k}}$$

If **V** is not a function of time, the Schrödinger equation can be simplified using the mathematical technique known as separation of variables. If we write the wavefunction as the product of a spatial function and a time function:

$$\Psi(\vec{r}, t) = \psi(\vec{r})\,\tau(t) \tag{2}$$

and then substitute these new functions into Equation 1, we will obtain two equations, one of which depends on the position of the particle independent of time and the other of which is a function of time alone. For the problems in which we are interested, this separation is valid, and we focus entirely on the familiar time-independent Schrödinger equation:

$$\mathbf{H}\psi(\vec{r}) = E\psi(\vec{r}) \tag{3}$$

where E is the energy of the particle, and **H** is the *Hamiltonian operator*, equal to:

$$\mathbf{H} = \frac{-h^2}{8\pi^2 m}\nabla^2 + \mathbf{V} \tag{4}$$

The various solutions to Equation 3 correspond to different stationary states of the particle (molecule). The one with the lowest energy is called the *ground state*. Equation 3 is a non-relativistic description of the system which is not valid when the velocities of particles approach the speed of light. Thus, Equation 3 does not give an accurate description of the core electrons in large nuclei.

Note also that Equation 3 is an *eigenvalue equation*: an equation in which an operator acting on a function produces a multiple of the function itself as its result, having the general form:

$$\mathbf{Op}\,f = c\,f \tag{5}$$

where **Op** is an operator, f is a function, and c is a constant. The set of functions for which the equation holds are its *eigenfunctions*, each of which has an associated value for c, known as its *eigenvalue*. In the case of the Schrödinger equation, the eigenvalues are the energies corresponding to the different stationary states of the molecular system.

The Molecular Hamiltonian

For a molecular system, Ψ is a function of the positions of the electrons and the nuclei within the molecule, which we will designate as $\mathbf{r}$ and $\mathbf{R}$, respectively. These symbols are a shorthand for the set of component vectors describing the position of each particle. We'll use subscripted versions of them to denote the vector corresponding to a particular electron or nucleus: $\mathbf{r}_i$ and $\mathbf{R}_I$. Note that electrons are treated individually, while each nucleus is treated as an aggregate; the component nucleons are not treated individually.

The Hamiltonian is made up of kinetic and potential energy terms:

$$\mathbf{H} = \mathbf{T} + \mathbf{V} \tag{6}$$

The kinetic energy is a summation of ∇^2 over all the particles in the molecule:

$$\mathbf{T} = -\frac{h^2}{8\pi^2} \sum_k \frac{1}{m_k}\left(\frac{\partial^2}{\partial x_k^2} + \frac{\partial^2}{\partial y_k^2} + \frac{\partial^2}{\partial z_k^2}\right) \tag{7}$$

The potential energy component is the Coulomb repulsion between each pair of charged entities (treating each atomic nucleus as a single charged mass):

$$\mathbf{V} = \frac{1}{4\pi\varepsilon_0} \sum_j \sum_{k<j} \frac{e_j e_k}{\Delta r_{jk}} \tag{8}$$

where Δr_{jk} is the distance between the two particles, and e_j and e_k are the charges on particles j and k. For an electron, the charge is $-e$, while for a nucleus, the charge is Ze, where Z is the atomic number for that atom. Thus,

$$\mathbf{V} = \frac{1}{4\pi\varepsilon_0}\left(- \overset{electrons}{\sum_i} \overset{nuclei}{\sum_I} \left(\frac{Z_I e^2}{\Delta r_{iI}}\right) + \overset{electrons}{\sum_i} \sum_{j<i} \left(\frac{e^2}{\Delta r_{ij}}\right) + \overset{nuclei}{\sum_I} \sum_{J<I} \left(\frac{Z_I Z_J e^2}{\Delta R_{IJ}}\right)\right) \tag{9}$$

The first term corresponds to electron-nuclear attraction, the second to electron-electron repulsion, and the third to nuclear-nuclear repulsion.

Atomic Units

The fundamental equations of quantum chemistry are usually expressed in units designed to simplify their form by eliminating fundamental constants. The atomic unit of length is the *Bohr radius*:

$$a_0 = \frac{h^2}{4\pi^2 m_e e^2} = 0.52917725\text{Å} \qquad [10]$$

Coordinates can be transformed to bohrs by dividing them by a_0. Energies are measured in *hartrees*, defined as the Coulomb repulsion between two electrons separated by 1 bohr:

$$1\,hartree = \frac{e^2}{a_0} \qquad [11]$$

Masses are also specified in terms of electron mass units (i.e. define $m_e=1$).

We will use these units in all future equations.

The Born-Oppenheimer Approximation

The Born-Oppenheimer approximation is the first of several approximations used to simplify the solution of the Schrödinger equation. It simplifies the general molecular problem by separating nuclear and electronic motions. This approximation is reasonable since the mass of a typical nucleus is thousands of times greater than that of an electron. The nuclei move very slowly with respect to the electrons, and the electrons react essentially instantaneously to changes in nuclear position. Thus, the electron distribution within a molecular system depends on the positions of the nuclei, and not on their velocities. Put another way, the nuclei look fixed to the electrons, and electronic motion can be described as occurring in a field of fixed nuclei.

The full Hamiltonian for the molecular system can then be written as:

$$\mathbf{H} = \mathbf{T}^{elec}(\vec{\mathbf{r}}) + \mathbf{T}^{nucl}(\vec{\mathbf{R}}) + \mathbf{V}^{nucl\text{-}elec}(\vec{\mathbf{R}}, \vec{\mathbf{r}}) + \mathbf{V}^{elec}(\vec{\mathbf{r}}) + \mathbf{V}^{nucl}(\vec{\mathbf{R}}) \qquad [12]$$

The Born-Oppenheimer approximation allows the two parts of the problem to be solved independently, so we can construct an electronic Hamiltonian which neglects the kinetic energy term for the nuclei:

$$\mathbf{H}^{elec} = -\frac{1}{2} \overset{electrons}{\underset{i}{\sum}} \left(\frac{\partial^2}{\partial x_i^2} + \frac{\partial^2}{\partial y_i^2} + \frac{\partial^2}{\partial z_i^2} \right) - \overset{electrons}{\underset{i}{\sum}} \overset{nuclei}{\underset{I}{\sum}} \left(\frac{Z_I}{|\vec{\mathbf{R}}_I - \vec{\mathbf{r}}_i|} \right)$$

$$+ \overset{electrons}{\underset{i}{\sum}} \underset{j<i}{\sum} \left(\frac{1}{|\vec{\mathbf{r}}_i - \vec{\mathbf{r}}_j|} \right) + \overset{nuclei}{\underset{I}{\sum}} \underset{J<I}{\sum} \left(\frac{Z_I Z_J}{|\vec{\mathbf{R}}_I - \vec{\mathbf{R}}_J|} \right)$$

[13]

Note that the fundamental physical constants drop out with the use of atomic units.

This Hamiltonian is then used in the Schrödinger equation describing the motion of electrons in the field of fixed nuclei:

$$\mathbf{H}^{elec} \psi^{elec} (\vec{\mathbf{r}}, \vec{\mathbf{R}}) = \mathrm{E}^{eff} (\vec{\mathbf{R}}) \psi^{elec} (\vec{\mathbf{r}}, \vec{\mathbf{R}})$$

[14]

Solving this equation for the electronic wavefunction will produce the effective nuclear potential function E^{eff}.[†] It depends on the nuclear coordinates and describes the potential energy surface for the system.

Accordingly, E^{eff} is also used as the effective potential for the nuclear Hamiltonian:

$$\mathbf{H}^{nucl} = \mathbf{T}^{nucl} (\vec{\mathbf{R}}) + \mathrm{E}^{eff} (\vec{\mathbf{R}})$$

[15]

This Hamiltonian is used in the Schrödinger equation for nuclear motion, describing the vibrational, rotational, and translational states of the nuclei. Solving the nuclear Schrödinger equation (at least approximately) is necessary for predicting the vibrational spectra of molecules.

From this point on, we will focus entirely on the electronic problem. We will omit the superscripts on all operators and functions.

Restrictions on the Wavefunction

We've noted that ψ^2 is interpreted as the probability density for the particle(s) it describes. Therefore, we require that ψ be *normalized*; if we integrate over all space,

---

[†] For a given set of nuclear coordinates, this corresponds to the total energy predicted by a single point energy calculation, although such calculations, of course, do not solve this equation exactly. The approximation methods used to solve it will be discussed in subsequent sections of this appendix.

the probability should be the number of particles (the particles *are* somewhere). Accordingly, we multiply ψ by a constant such that:

$$\int_{-\infty}^{+\infty} |c\psi|^2 \, dv = n_{particles} \quad^{\dagger}$$

[16]

We can do this because the Schrödinger equation is an eigenvalue equation, and in general, if f is a solution to an eigenvalue equation, then cf is also, for any value of c. For the Schrödinger equation, it is easy to show that $H(c\psi) = cH(\psi)$ and that $E(c\psi) = c(E\psi)$; thus, if ψ is a solution to the Schrödinger equation, then $c\psi$ is as well.

Secondly, ψ must also be *antisymmetric*, meaning that it must change sign when two identical particles are interchanged. For a simple function, antisymmetry means that the following relation holds:

$$f(i,j) = -f(j,i)$$

[17]

For an electronic wavefunction, antisymmetry is a physical requirement following from the fact that electrons are fermions.[‡] It is essentially a requirement that ψ agree with the results of experimental physics. More specifically, this requirement means that any valid wavefunction must satisfy the following condition:

$$\psi(\vec{r}_1, ..., \vec{r}_i, ..., \vec{r}_j, ..., \vec{r}_n) = -\psi(\vec{r}_1, ..., \vec{r}_j, ..., \vec{r}_i, ..., \vec{r}_n)$$

[18]

Hartree-Fock Theory

The underlying physical laws necessary for the mathematical theory of a large part of physics and the whole of chemistry are thus completely known, and the difficulty is only that the exact application of these laws leads to equations much too complicated to be soluble.

— P. A. M. Dirac, 1929

[†] If ψ is complex, the integral becomes: $c^*c\int\int\int_{-\infty}^{+\infty} \psi^*\psi \, dx \, dy \, dz = n$

[‡] Fermions are particles that have the properties of antisymmetry and a half-integral spin quantum number, among others.

An exact solution to the Schrödinger equation is not possible for any but the most trivial molecular systems. However, a number of simplifying assumptions and procedures do make an approximate solution possible for a large range of molecules.

Molecular Orbitals

The first approximation we'll consider comes from the interpretation of $|\psi|^2$ as a probability density for the electrons within the system. Molecular orbital theory decomposes ψ into a combination of molecular orbitals: ϕ_1, ϕ_2, ... To fulfill some of the conditions on ψ we discussed previously, we choose a normalized, orthogonal set of molecular orbitals:

$$\iiint \phi_i^* \phi_i \, dx \, dy \, dz = 1$$

$$\iiint \phi_i^* \phi_j \, dx \, dy \, dz = 0; \qquad i \neq j$$

[19]

The simplest possible way of making ψ as a combination of these molecular orbitals is by forming their *Hartree product*:

$$\psi(\vec{\mathbf{r}}) = \phi_1(\vec{\mathbf{r}}_1) \ \phi_2(\vec{\mathbf{r}}_2) \cdots \phi_n(\vec{\mathbf{r}}_n)$$

[20]

However, such a function is not antisymmetric, since interchanging two of the $\vec{\mathbf{r}}_i$'s —equivalent to swapping the orbitals of two electrons—does not result in a sign change. Hence, this Hartree product is an inadequate wavefunction.

Electron Spin

The simplest antisymmetric function that is a combination of molecular orbitals is a determinant. Before forming it, however, we need to account for a factor we've neglected so far: electron spin. Electrons can have spin up ($+\frac{1}{2}$) or down ($-\frac{1}{2}$). Equation 20 assumes that each molecular orbital holds only one electron. However, most calculations are closed shell calculations, using doubly occupied orbitals, holding two electrons of opposite spin. For the moment, we will limit our discussion to this case.

We define two spin functions, α and β, as follows:

$$\alpha(\uparrow) = 1 \qquad\qquad \alpha(\downarrow) = 0$$

$$\beta(\uparrow) = 0 \qquad\qquad \beta(\downarrow) = 1$$

[21]

The α function is 1 for a spin up electron, and the β function is 1 when the electron is spin down. The notation $\alpha(i)$ and $\beta(i)$ will designate the values of α and β for electron i; thus, $\alpha(1)$ is the value of α for electron 1.

Multiplying a molecular orbital function by α or β will include electron spin as part of the overall electronic wavefunction ψ. The product of the molecular orbital and a spin function is defined as a *spin orbital*, a function of both the electron's location and its spin.[†] Note that these spin orbitals are also orthonormal when the component molecular orbitals are.

We can now build a closed shell wavefunction by defining $n/2$ molecular orbitals for a system with n electrons, and then assigning electrons to these orbitals in pairs of opposite spin:

$$\psi(\vec{\mathbf{r}}) = \frac{1}{\sqrt{n!}} \begin{vmatrix} \phi_1(\vec{\mathbf{r}}_1)\alpha(1) & \phi_1(\vec{\mathbf{r}}_1)\beta(1) & \phi_2(\vec{\mathbf{r}}_1)\alpha(1) & \phi_2(\vec{\mathbf{r}}_1)\beta(1) & \cdots & \phi_{\frac{n}{2}}(\vec{\mathbf{r}}_1)\alpha(1) & \phi_{\frac{n}{2}}(\vec{\mathbf{r}}_1)\beta(1) \\ \phi_1(\vec{\mathbf{r}}_2)\alpha(2) & \phi_1(\vec{\mathbf{r}}_2)\beta(2) & \phi_2(\vec{\mathbf{r}}_2)\alpha(2) & \phi_2(\vec{\mathbf{r}}_2)\beta(2) & \cdots & \phi_{\frac{n}{2}}(\vec{\mathbf{r}}_2)\alpha(2) & \phi_{\frac{n}{2}}(\vec{\mathbf{r}}_2)\beta(2) \\ \vdots & & & & & & \\ \phi_1(\vec{\mathbf{r}}_i)\alpha(i) & \phi_1(\vec{\mathbf{r}}_i)\beta(i) & \phi_2(\vec{\mathbf{r}}_i)\alpha(i) & \phi_2(\vec{\mathbf{r}}_i)\beta(i) & \cdots & \phi_{\frac{n}{2}}(\vec{\mathbf{r}}_i)\alpha(i) & \phi_{\frac{n}{2}}(\vec{\mathbf{r}}_i)\beta(i) \\ \phi_1(\vec{\mathbf{r}}_j)\alpha(j) & \phi_1(\vec{\mathbf{r}}_j)\beta(j) & \phi_2(\vec{\mathbf{r}}_j)\alpha(j) & \phi_2(\vec{\mathbf{r}}_j)\beta(j) & \cdots & \phi_{\frac{n}{2}}(\vec{\mathbf{r}}_j)\alpha(j) & \phi_{\frac{n}{2}}(\vec{\mathbf{r}}_j)\beta(j) \\ \vdots & & & & & & \vdots \\ \phi_1(\vec{\mathbf{r}}_n)\alpha(n) & \phi_1(\vec{\mathbf{r}}_n)\beta(n) & \phi_2(\vec{\mathbf{r}}_n)\alpha(n) & \phi_2(\vec{\mathbf{r}}_n)\beta(n) & \cdots & \phi_{\frac{n}{2}}(\vec{\mathbf{r}}_n)\alpha(n) & \phi_{\frac{n}{2}}(\vec{\mathbf{r}}_n)\beta(n) \end{vmatrix}$$ [22]

Each row is formed by representing all possible assignments of electron i to all orbital-spin combinations. The initial factor is necessary for normalization. Swapping two electrons corresponds to interchanging two rows of the determinant, which will have the effect of changing its sign.

This formulation is not just a mathematical trick to form an antisymmetric wavefunction. Quantum mechanics specifies that an electron's location is not deterministic but rather consists of a probability density; in this sense, it can be anywhere. This determinant mixes all of the possible orbitals of all of the electrons in the molecular system to form the wavefunction.

[†]Some texts use a separate notation for spin orbitals. We will not do so here.

Basis Sets

The next approximation involves expressing the molecular orbitals as linear combinations of a pre-defined set of one-electron functions known as basis functions. These basis functions are usually centered on the atomic nuclei and so bear some resemblance to atomic orbitals. However, the actual mathematical treatment is more general than this, and any set of appropriately defined functions may be used.

An individual molecular orbital is defined as:

$$\phi_i = \sum_{\mu=1}^{N} c_{\mu i} \chi_\mu \qquad [23]$$

where the coefficients $c_{\mu i}$ are known as the *molecular orbital expansion coefficients*. The basis functions $\chi_1 \ldots \chi_N$ are also chosen to be normalized. We follow the usual notational convention of using roman subscripts on molecular orbital functions and Greek subscripts on basis functions. Thus, χ_μ refers to an arbitrary basis function in the same way that ϕ_i refers to an arbitrary molecular orbital.

Gaussian and other ab initio electronic structure programs use gaussian-type atomic functions as basis functions. Gaussian functions have the general form:

$$g(\alpha, \vec{r}) = c x^n y^m z^l e^{-\alpha r^2} \qquad [24]$$

where $\vec{r}$ is of course composed of x, y and z. α is a constant determining the size (radial extent) of the function. In a gaussian function, $e^{-\alpha r^2}$ is multiplied by powers (possibly 0) of x, y, and z, and a constant for normalization, so that:

$$\int_{all\ space} g^2 = 1 \qquad [25]$$

Thus, c depends on α, *l, m* and *n*.

Here are three representative gaussian functions (s, p_y and d_{xy} types, respectively):

$$g_s(\alpha, \vec{r}) = \left(\frac{2\alpha}{\pi}\right)^{3/4} e^{-\alpha r^2}$$

$$g_y(\alpha, \vec{r}) = \left(\frac{128\alpha^5}{\pi^3}\right)^{1/4} y e^{-\alpha r^2} \qquad [26]$$

$$g_{xy}(\alpha, \vec{r}) = \left(\frac{2048\alpha^7}{\pi^3}\right)^{1/4} xy e^{-\alpha r^2}$$

Linear combinations of *primitive gaussians* like these are used to form the actual basis functions; the latter are called *contracted gaussians* and have the form:

$$\chi_\mu = \sum_p d_{\mu p} g_p \qquad [27]$$

where the $d_{\mu p}$'s are fixed constants within a given basis set. Note that contracted functions are also normalized in common practice.

All of these constructions result in the following expansion for molecular orbitals:

$$\phi_i = \sum_\mu c_{\mu i} \chi_\mu = \sum_\mu c_{\mu i} \left(\sum_p d_{\mu p} g_p\right) \qquad [28]$$

The Variational Principle

The problem has now become how to solve for the set of molecular orbital expansion coefficients, $c_{\mu i}$. Hartree-Fock theory takes advantage of the variational principle, which says that for the ground state of any antisymmetric normalized function of the electronic coordinates, which we will denote Ξ, then the expectation value for the energy corresponding to Ξ will always be greater than the energy for the exact wavefunction:

$$E(\Xi) > E(\Psi); \qquad \Xi \neq \Psi \qquad [29]$$

In other words, the energy of the exact wavefunction serves as a lower bound to the energies calculated by any other normalized antisymmetric function. Thus, the problem becomes one of finding the set of coefficients that minimize the energy of the resultant wavefunction.

The Roothaan-Hall Equations

The variational principle leads to the following equations describing the molecular orbital expansion coefficients, $c_{\nu i}$, derived by Roothaan and by Hall[†]:

$$\sum_{\nu = 1}^{N} (F_{\mu\nu} - \varepsilon_i S_{\mu\nu})\, c_{\nu i} = \mathbf{0} \qquad \mu = 1, 2, ..., N$$

[30]

Equation 30 can be rewritten in matrix form:

$$FC = SC\varepsilon$$

[31]

where each element is a matrix. ε is a diagonal matrix of orbital energies, each of its elements ε_i is the one-electron orbital energy of molecular orbital χ_i.

F is called the *Fock matrix*, and it represents the average effects of the field of all the electrons on each orbital. For a closed shell system, its elements are:

$$F_{\mu\nu} = H_{\mu\nu}^{core} + \sum_{\lambda = 1}^{N} \sum_{\sigma = 1}^{N} P_{\lambda\sigma} \left[(\mu\nu|\lambda\sigma) - \tfrac{1}{2}(\mu\lambda|\nu\sigma) \right]$$

[32]

where $H_{\mu\nu}^{core}$ is another matrix representing the energy of a single electron in the field of the bare nuclei, and P is the *density matrix*, defined as:

$$P_{\lambda\sigma} = 2 \sum_{i = 1}^{occupied} c_{\lambda i}^{*} c_{\sigma i}$$

[33]

The coefficients are summed over the occupied orbitals only, and the factor of two comes from the fact that each orbital holds two electrons.

Finally, the matrix S from Equation 31 is the *overlap matrix*, indicating the overlap between orbitals.

Both the Fock matrix—through the density matrix—and the orbitals depend on the molecular orbital expansion coefficients. Thus, Equation 31 is not linear and must be solved iteratively. The procedure which does so is called the *Self-Consistent Field*

[†] We alter the subscripts slightly here from what has preceded in order to follow common usage.

(SCF) method. At convergence, the energy is at a minimum, and the orbitals generate a field which produces the same orbitals, accounting for the method's name. The solution produces a set of orbitals, both *occupied* ($\phi_{i,j...}$) and *virtual* (unoccupied, conventionally denoted $\phi_{a,b...}$). The total number of orbitals is equal to the number of basis functions used.

The term $(\mu\nu|\lambda\sigma)$ in Equation 32 signifies the *two-electron repulsion integrals*. Under the Hartree-Fock treatment, each electron sees all of the other electrons as an average distribution; there is no instantaneous electron-electron interaction included. Higher level methods attempt to remedy this neglect of electron correlation in various ways, as we shall see.

The general strategy used by the SCF method (after initial setup steps) is as follows:

✦ Evaluate the integrals. In a conventional algorithm, they are stored on disk and read in for each iteration. In a direct algorithm, integrals are computed a few at a time as the Fock matrix is formed.

✦ Form an initial guess for the molecular orbital coefficients, and construct the density matrix.

✦ Form the Fock matrix.

✦ Solve for the density matrix.

✦ Test for convergence. If it fails, begin the next iteration. If it succeeds, go on to perform other parts of the calculation (such as population analysis).

Open Shell Methods

So far, we have considered only the restricted Hartree-Fock method. For open shell systems, an unrestricted method, capable of treating unpaired electrons, is needed.[†] For this case, the alpha and beta electrons are in different orbitals, resulting in two sets of molecular orbital expansion coefficients:

$$\phi_i^{\alpha} = \sum_{\mu} c_{\mu i}^{\alpha} \chi_{\mu}$$

$$\phi_i^{\beta} = \sum_{\mu} c_{\mu i}^{\beta} \chi_{\mu}$$

[34]

[†] Refer also to the discussion of open shell calculations in Chapter 1 (page 10).

The two sets of coefficients result in two sets of Fock matrices (and their associated density matrices), and ultimately to a solution producing two sets of orbitals. These separate orbitals produce proper dissociation to separate atoms, correct delocalized orbitals for resonant systems, and other attributes characteristic of open shell systems. However, the eigenfunctions are not pure spin states, but contain some amount of *spin contamination* from higher states (for example, doublets are contaminated to some degree by functions corresponding to quartets and higher states).

Electron Correlation Methods

As we've noted several times, Hartree-Fock theory provides an inadequate treatment of the correlation between the motions of the electrons within a molecular system, especially that arising between electrons of opposite spin.

When Hartree-Fock theory fulfills the requirement that $|\Psi^2|$ be invarient with respect to the exchange of any two electrons by antisymmetrizing the wavefunction, it automatically includes the major correlation effects arising from pairs of electrons with the same spin. This correlation is termed *exchange correlation*. The motion of electrons of opposite spin remains uncorrelated under Hartree-Fock theory, however.

Any method which goes beyond SCF in attempting to treat this phenomenon properly is known as an *electron correlation* method (despite the fact that Hartree-Fock theory does include some correlation effects) or a *post-SCF* method. We will look briefly at two different approaches to the electron correlation problem in this section.

Configuration Interaction

Configuration Interaction (CI) methods begin by noting that the exact wavefunction Ψ cannot be expressed as a single determinant, as Hartree-Fock theory assumes. CI proceeds by constructing other determinants by replacing one or more occupied orbitals within the Hartree-Fock determinant with a virtual orbital.

In a *single substitution*, a virtual orbital, say ϕ_a, replaces an occupied orbital ϕ_i within the determinant. This is equivalent to exciting an electron to a higher energy orbital.

Similarly, in a *double substitution*, two occupied orbitals are replaced by virtual orbitals: $\phi_a \leftarrow \phi_i$ and $\phi_b \leftarrow \phi_j$; for example, $\Psi_{ia} = | \phi_1, \dots \phi_i, \phi_{a+1}, \dots \phi_{i-1}, \phi_a, \dots \phi_n|$. *Triple substitutions* would exchange three orbitals, and so on.

Full CI

The full CI method forms the wavefunction ψ as a linear combination of the Hartree-Fock determinant and all possible substituted determinants:

$$\psi = b_0\psi_0 + \sum_{s>0} b_s\psi_s \qquad [35]$$

where the 0-indexed term is the Hartree-Fock level, and *s* runs over all possible substitutions. The b's are the set of coefficients to be solved for, again by minimizing the energy of the resultant wavefunction.

At a physical level, Equation 35 represents a mixing of all of the possible electronic states of the molecule, all of which have some probability of being attained according to the laws of quantum mechanics. Full CI is the most complete non-relativistic treatment of the molecular system possible, within the limitations imposed by the chosen basis set. It represents the possible quantum states of the system while modelling the electron density in accordance with the definition (and constraints) of the basis set in use. For this reason, it appears in the rightmost column of the following methods chart:

		Electron Correlation →					
Basis Set Type	HF	MP2	MP3	MP4	QCISD(T)	...	Full CI
Minimal						...	
Split-valence						...	
Polarized						...	
Diffuse						...	
High ang. momentum						...	
...	...	...	...	...	...		...
∞	*HF Limit*					...	**Schrödinger Equation**

As the basis set becomes infinitely flexible, full CI approaches the exact solution of the time-independent, non-relativistic Schrödinger equation.

Limited Configuration Interaction

The full CI method has many of the desirable features of a theoretical model.[†] It is well-defined, size-consistent, and variational. However, it is also very expensive and impractical for all but the very smallest systems.

Practical configuration interaction methods augment the Hartree-Fock by adding only a limited set of substitutions, truncating the CI expansion at some level of substitution. For example, the CIS method adds single excitations to the Hartree-Fock determinant, CID adds double excitations, CISD adds singles and doubles, CISDT adds singles, doubles, and triples, and so on.

A disadvantage of all these limited CI variants is that they are not size-consistent. The Quadratic Configuration Interaction (QCI) method was developed to correct this deficiency. The QCISD method adds terms to CISD to restore size consistency.[‡] QCISD also accounts for some correlation effects to infinite order. QCISD(T) adds triple substitutions to QCISD, providing even greater accuracy. Similarly, QCISD(TQ) adds both triples and quadruples from the full CI expansion to QCISD.

Møller-Plesset Perturbation Theory

Another approach to electron correlation is Møller-Plesset perturbation theory. Qualitatively, Møller-Plesset perturbation theory adds higher excitations to Hartree-Fock theory as a non-iterative correction,[§] drawing upon techniques from the area of mathematical physics known as many body perturbation theory.

Perturbation theory is based upon dividing the Hamiltonian into two parts:

$$\mathbf{H} = \mathbf{H}_0 + \lambda \mathbf{V} \qquad [36]$$

such that $\mathbf{H}_0$ is soluble exactly. $\lambda \mathbf{V}$ is a *perturbation* applied to $\mathbf{H}_0$, a correction which is assumed to be small in comparison to it. (Note that the perturbation operator $\mathbf{V}$ is not related to the potential energy.)

The assumption that $\mathbf{V}$ is a small perturbation to $\mathbf{H}_0$ suggests that the perturbed wavefunction and energy can be expressed as a power series in $\mathbf{V}$. The usual way to do so is in terms of the parameter λ:

[†] Refer to the section "Model Chemistries" in Chapter 1 for a discussion of the desirable features of a theoretical model and for the definition of the terms in this paragraph.

[‡] The QCISD method is also very closely related to coupled cluster theory, with singles and doubles (CCSD).

[§] In contrast to QCISD.

$$\psi = \psi^{(0)} + \lambda\psi^{(1)} + \lambda^2\psi^{(2)} + \lambda^3\psi^{(3)} + \dots$$

$$E = E^{(0)} + \lambda E^{(1)} + \lambda^2 E^{(2)} + \lambda^3 E^{(3)} + \dots \tag{37}$$

The perturbed wavefunction and energy are substituted back into the Schrödinger equation:

$$(\mathbf{H}_0 + \lambda\mathbf{V})\,(\psi^{(0)} + \lambda\psi^{(1)} + \dots) = (E^{(0)} + \lambda E^{(1)} + \dots)\,(\psi^{(0)} + \lambda\psi^{(1)} + \dots) \tag{38}$$

After expanding the products, we can equate the coefficients on each side of the equation for each power of λ, leading to a series of relations representing successively higher orders of perturbation. Here are the first three such equations (after some rearranging), corresponding to powers of 0, 1, and 2 of λ:

$$(\mathbf{H}_0 - E^{(0)})\,\psi^{(0)} = \mathbf{0}$$

$$(\mathbf{H}_0 - E^{(0)})\,\psi^{(1)} = (E^{(1)} - \mathbf{V})\,\psi^{(0)} \tag{39}$$

$$(\mathbf{H}_0 - E^{(0)})\,\psi^{(2)} = (E^{(1)} - \mathbf{V})\,\psi^{(1)} + E^{(2)}\psi^{(0)}$$

So far, we've presented only general perturbation theory results. We'll now turn to the particular case of Møller-Plesset perturbation theory. Here, $\mathbf{H}_0$ is defined as the sum of the one-electron Fock operators:[†]

$$\mathbf{H}_0 = \sum_i \mathbf{F}^i \tag{40}$$

The Hartree-Fock determinant and all of the substituted determinants are eigenfunctions of $\mathbf{H}_0$; these are the solutions to the part of the divided Hamiltonian for which we have a solution. Thus:

$$\mathbf{H}_0\psi_s = E_s\psi_s \tag{41}$$

for all substituted determinant wavefunctions.

[†] $\mathbf{F}^i$ is the Fock operator acting on the ith electron.

We'll consider each of the relations in Equation 39 in turn. In the first case, by forming the inner product of each side with $\langle\psi^{(0)}$, we obtain the following expression for $E^{(0)}$:

$$\langle\psi^{(0)}|H_0 - E^{(0)}|\psi^{(0)}\rangle = 0 \quad \Rightarrow$$

$$\langle\psi^{(0)}|H_0|\psi^{(0)}\rangle = E^{(0)}\langle\psi^{(0)}|\psi^{(0)}\rangle = E^{(0)} \tag{42}$$

Since the ψ's are orthonormal, the inner product of any with itself is one, and the inner product of any distinct two of them is 0.

Since H_0 is the sum of Fock operators, then $E^{(0)}$ is the sum of the orbital energies:

$$E^{(0)} = \langle\psi^{(0)}|H_0|\psi^{(0)}\rangle = \sum_i \varepsilon_i \tag{43}$$

The expression for $E^{(1)}$ also follows easily from simple linear algebra. We begin by again forming the inner product of both sides of the second relation from Equation 39 with $\langle\psi^{(0)}$:

$$\langle\psi^{(0)}|(H_0 - E^{(0)})|\psi^{(1)}\rangle = \langle\psi^{(0)}|(E^{(1)} - V)|\psi^{(0)}\rangle \quad \Rightarrow$$

$$\langle\psi^{(0)}|H_0|\psi^{(1)}\rangle - E^{(0)}\langle\psi^{(0)}|\psi^{(1)}\rangle = E^{(1)}\langle\psi^{(0)}|\psi^{(0)}\rangle - \langle\psi^{(0)}|V|\psi^{(0)}\rangle \tag{44}$$

Now, since $H_0\psi^{(0)}=E^{(0)}\psi^{(0)}$ and H_0 is an Hermitian operator ($H_0\psi^{(0)}=\psi^{(0)}H_0$), the left hand side of the final Equation 44 goes to 0, leaving this expression for $E^{(1)}$:

$$E^{(1)} = \langle\psi^{(0)}|V|\psi^{(0)}\rangle \tag{45}$$

Adding $E^{(0)}$ and $E^{(1)}$ yields the Hartree-Fock energy (since H_0+V is the full Hamiltonian):

$$E^{(0)} + E^{(1)} = \langle\psi^{(0)}|H_0|\psi^{(0)}\rangle + \langle\psi^{(0)}|V|\psi^{(0)}\rangle$$

$$= \langle\psi^{(0)}|(H_0 + V)|\psi^{(0)}\rangle = \langle\psi^{(0)}|H|\psi^{(0)}\rangle = E^{HF} \tag{46}$$

We'll begin examining the third relation in Equation 39 in the same way:

$$\langle \psi^{(0)} | (H_0 - E^{(0)}) | \psi^{(2)} \rangle = \langle \psi^{(0)} | (E^{(1)} - V) | \psi^{(1)} \rangle + E^{(2)} \langle \psi^{(0)} | \psi^{(0)} \rangle \Rightarrow$$

$$E^{(2)} = \langle \psi^{(0)} | (V - E^{(1)}) | \psi^{(1)} \rangle = \langle \psi^{(0)} | V | \psi^{(1)} \rangle \qquad [47]$$

We need to find $\psi^{(1)}$ before we can determine $E^{(2)}$. We will form it as a linear combination of substituted wavefunctions and solve for the coefficients:

$$\psi^{(1)} = \sum_s a_s \psi_s \quad \ni \quad H_0 \psi_s = E_s \psi_s \qquad [48]$$

We will return to the second relation in Equation 39, and this time use it to find the coefficients for $\psi^{(1)}$:

$$(H_0 - E^{(0)}) \sum_s a_s \psi_s = (E^{(1)} - V) \psi^{(0)} \qquad [49]$$

We will form the inner product of both sides of Equation 49 with an arbitrary substituted wavefunction ψ_t, and then solve for a_t :

$$\langle \psi_t | (H_0 - E^{(0)}) | \sum_s a_s \psi_s \rangle = \langle \psi_t | (E^{(1)} - V) | \psi^{(0)} \rangle \Rightarrow$$

$$\sum_s a_s \langle \psi_t | (H_0 - E^{(0)}) | \psi_s \rangle = E^{(1)} \langle \psi_t | \psi^{(0)} \rangle - \langle \psi_t | V | \psi^{(0)} \rangle \Rightarrow \qquad [50]$$

$$\sum_s a_s \left(\langle \psi_t | H_0 | \psi_s \rangle - \langle \psi_t | E^{(0)} | \psi_s \rangle \right) = E^{(1)} \langle \psi_t | \psi^{(0)} \rangle - \langle \psi_t | V | \psi^{(0)} \rangle$$

The left side of the final Equation 50 is nonzero only when $s=t$, yielding:

$$a_t (E_t - E^{(0)}) = -\langle \psi_t | V | \psi^{(0)} \rangle \Rightarrow$$

$$a_t = \frac{\langle \psi_t | V | \psi^{(0)} \rangle}{E^{(0)} - E_t} \qquad [51]$$

The result in Equation 51 indicates that substitutions close in energy to the ground state make larger contributions to the perturbation. Similarly, the more strongly mixed a state is with the ground state, the larger its contribution to the perturbation. Both of these observations are in line with (quantum mechanical) intuition.

These coefficients result in the following expression for $\psi^{(1)}$:

$$\psi^{(1)} = \sum_t \left(\frac{\langle \psi_t | V | \psi^{(0)} \rangle}{E^{(0)} - E_t} \right) \psi_t \qquad [52]$$

We can now return to the expression for $E^{(2)}$:

$$E^{(2)} = \langle \psi^{(0)} | V | \psi^{(1)} \rangle = \langle \psi^{(0)} | V | \sum_t a_t \psi_t \rangle = \sum_t a_t \langle \psi^{(0)} | V | \psi_t \rangle$$

$$= \sum_t \frac{\langle \psi^{(0)} | V | \psi_t \rangle \langle \psi_t | V | \psi^{(0)} \rangle}{E^{(0)} - E_t} = - \sum_t \frac{\left| \langle \psi^{(0)} | V | \psi_t \rangle \right|^2}{E_t - E^{(0)}} \qquad [53]$$

The two factors in the numerator of the first expression in the second line are one another's complex conjugates, and so reduce to the square of its modulus in the final expression.

Note that both the numerator and denominator in the final expression are always positive expressions; in the case of the denominator, we know this because $E^{(0)}$ is the lowest energy eigenvalue of the unperturbed system. (The denominator reduces to a difference in orbital energies.)

In addition, the numerator will be nonzero only for double substitutions. Single substitutions are known to make this expression zero by Brillouin's theorem. Triple and higher substitutions also result in zero value since the Hamiltonian contains only one and two-electron terms (physically, this means that all interactions between electrons occur pairwise).

Thus, the value of $E^{(2)}$, the first perturbation to the Hartree-Fock energy, will always be negative. Lowering the energy is what the exact correction should do, although the Møller-Plesset perturbation theory correction is capable of overcorrecting it, since it is not variational (and higher order corrections may be positive).

By a similar although more elaborate process, the third and fourth order energy corrections can be derived. For further details, consult the references.

Density Functional Theory

Density functional theory-based methods ultimately derive from quantum mechanics research from the 1920's, especially the Thomas-Fermi-Dirac model, and from Slater's fundamental work in quantum chemistry in the 1950's. The DFT approach is based upon a strategy of modeling electron correlation via general functionals[†] of the electron density.

Such methods owe their modern origins to the Hohenberg-Kohn theorem, published in 1964, which demonstrated the existence of a unique functional which determines the ground state energy and density exactly. The theorem does not provide the form of this functional, however.

Following on the work of Kohn and Sham, the approximate functionals employed by current DFT methods partition the electronic energy into several terms:

$$E = E^T + E^V + E^J + E^{XC} \qquad [54]$$

where E^T is the kinetic energy term (arising from the motion of the electrons), E^V includes terms describing the potential energy of the nuclear-electron attraction and of the repulsion between pairs of nuclei, E^J is the electron-electron repulsion term (it is also described as the Coulomb self-interaction of the electron density), and E^{XC} is the exchange-correlation term and includes the remaining part of the electron-electron interactions.

All terms except the nuclear-nuclear repulsion are functions of ρ, the electron density. E^J is given by the following expression:

$$E^J = \frac{1}{2} \iint \rho\,(\vec{r}_1)\,(\Delta r_{12})^{-1} \rho\,(\vec{r}_2)\,d\vec{r}_1 d\vec{r}_2 \qquad [55]$$

$E^T + E^V + E^J$ corresponds to the classical energy of the charge distribution ρ. The E^{XC} term in Equation 54 accounts for the remaining terms in the energy:

♦ The exchange energy arising from the antisymmetry of the quantum mechanical wavefunction.

♦ Dynamic correlation in the motions of the individual electrons.

[†] A *functional* is a function whose definition is itself a function: in other words, a function of a function.

Hohenberg and Kohn demonstrated that E^{XC} is determined entirely by the (is a functional of) the electron density. In practice, E^{XC} is usually approximated as an integral involving only the spin densities and possibly their gradients:

$$E^{XC}(\rho) = \int f(\rho_\alpha(\vec{r}), \rho_\beta(\vec{r}), \nabla\rho_\alpha(\vec{r}), \nabla\rho_\beta(\vec{r})) \, d^3\vec{r} \qquad [56]$$

We use ρ_α to refer to the α spin density, ρ_β to refer to the β spin density, and ρ to refer to the total electon density ($\rho_\alpha + \rho_\beta$).

E^{XC} is usually divided into separate parts, referred to as the *exchange* and *correlation* parts, but actually corresponding to same-spin and mixed-spin interactions, respectively:

$$E^{XC}(\rho) = E^X(\rho) + E^C(\rho) \qquad [57]$$

All three terms are again functionals of the electron density, and functionals defining the two components on the right side of Equation 57 are termed *exchange functionals* and *correlation functionals*, respectively. Both components can be of two distinct types: *local* functionals depend on only the electron density ρ, while *gradient-corrected* functionals depend on both ρ and its gradient, $\nabla\rho$.[†]

We'll now take a brief look at some sample functionals. The local exchange functional is virtually always defined as follows:

$$E^X_{LDA} = -\frac{3}{2}\left(\frac{3}{4\pi}\right)^{1/3}\int \rho^{4/3} d^3\vec{r} \qquad [58]$$

where ρ is of course a function of $\vec{r}$. This form was developed to reproduce the exchange energy of a uniform electron gas. By itself, however, it has weaknesses in describing molecular systems.

Becke formulated the following gradient-corrected exchange functional based on the LDA exchange functional in 1988, which is now in wide use:

$$E^X_{Becke88} = E^X_{LDA} - \gamma\int \frac{\rho^{4/3}x^2}{(1 + 6\gamma\sinh^{-1}x)} d^3\vec{r} \qquad [59]$$

[†] Note that this use of the term "local" does not coincide with the use of the term in mathematics; both local and gradient-corrected functionals are local in the mathematical sense.

where $x = \rho^{-4/3} |\nabla \rho|$. γ is a parameter chosen to fit the known exchange energies of the inert gas atoms, and Becke defines its value as 0.0042 Hartrees. As Equation 59 makes clear, Becke's functional is defined as a correction to the local LDA exchange functional, and it succeeds in remedying many of the LDA functional's deficiencies.

Similarly, there are local and gradient-corrected correlation functionals. For example, here is Perdew and Wang's formulation[†] of the local part of their 1991 correlation functional:

$$E^C = \int \rho \varepsilon_C \left(r_s \left(\rho \left(\vec{r} \right) \right), \zeta \right) d^3 \vec{r}$$

$$r_s = \left[\frac{3}{4\pi\rho} \right]^{1/3}$$

$$\zeta = \frac{\rho_\alpha - \rho_\beta}{\rho_\alpha + \rho_\beta} \qquad [60]$$

$$\varepsilon_C (r_s, \zeta) = \varepsilon_C (\rho, 0) + a_C (r_s) \frac{f(\zeta)}{f''(0)} (1 - \zeta^4) + [\varepsilon_C (\rho, 1) - \varepsilon_C (\rho, 0)] f(\zeta) \zeta^4$$

$$f(\zeta) = \frac{[(1+\zeta)^{4/3} + (1-\zeta)^{4/3} - 2]}{(2^{4/3} - 2)}$$

r_s is termed the density parameter. ζ is the relative spin polarization. $\zeta = 0$ corresponds to equal α and β densities, $\zeta = 1$ correponds to all α density, and $\zeta = -1$ corresponds to all β density. Note that $f(0) = 0$ and $f(\pm 1) = 1$.

The general expression for ε_C involves both r_s and ζ. Its final term performs an interpolation for mixed spin cases.

The following function G is used to compute the values of $\varepsilon_C(r_s, 0)$, $\varepsilon_C(r_s, 1)$ and $-a_C(r_s)$:

$$G(r_s, A, \alpha_1, \beta_1, \beta_2, \beta_3, \beta_4, P) = -2A(1 + \alpha_1 r_s) \ln \left(1 + \frac{1}{2A(\beta_1 r_s^{1/2} + \beta_2 r_s + \beta_3 r_s^{3/2} + \beta_4 r_s^{P+1})} \right) \qquad [61]$$

In Equation 61, all of the arguments to G except r_s are parameters chosen by Perdew and Wang to reproduce accurate calculations on uniform electron gases. The parameter sets differ for G when it is used to evaluate each of $\varepsilon_C(r_s, 0)$, $\varepsilon_C(r_s, 1)$ and $-a_C(r_s)$.

In an analogous way to the exchange functional we examined earlier, a local correlation functional may also be improved by adding a gradient correction.

[†] Which is very closely related to Vosko, Wilk and Nusair's local correlation functional (VWN).

Pure DFT methods are defined by pairing an exchange functional with a correlation functional. For example, the well-known BLYP functional pairs Becke's gradient-corrected exchange functional with the gradient-corrected correlation functional of Lee, Yang and Parr.

Hybrid Functionals

In actual practice, self-consistent Kohn-Sham DFT calculations are performed in an iterative manner that is analogous to an SCF computation. This similarity to the methodology of Hartree-Fock theory was pointed out by Kohn and Sham.

Hartree-Fock theory also includes an exchange term as part of its formulation. Recently, Becke has formulated functionals which include a mixture of Hartree-Fock and DFT exchange along with DFT correlation, conceptually defining E^{XC} as:

$$E_{hybrid}^{XC} = c_{HF}E_{HF}^{X} + c_{DFT}E_{DFT}^{XC} \qquad [62]$$

where the c's are constants. For example, a Becke-style three-parameter functional may be defined via the following expression:

$$E_{B3LYP}^{XC} = E_{LDA}^{X} + c_0\,(E_{HF}^{X} - E_{LDA}^{X}) + c_X\Delta E_{B88}^{X} + E_{VWN3}^{C} + c_C\,(E_{LYP}^{C} - E_{VWN3}^{C}) \qquad [63]$$

Here, the parameter c_0 allows any admixture of Hartree-Fock and LDA local exchange to be used. In addition, Becke's gradient correction to LDA exchange is also included, scaled by the parameter c_X. Similarly, the VWN3 local correlation functional is used, and it may be optionally corrected by the LYP correlation correction via the parameter c_C. In the B3LYP functional, the parameters values are those specified by Becke, which he determined by fitting to the atomization energies, ionization potentials, proton affinities and first-row atomic energies in the G1 molecule set: c_0=0.20, c_X=0.72 and c_C=0.81. Note that Becke used the the Perdew-Wang 1991 correlation functional in his original work rather than VWN3 and LYP. The fact that the same coefficients work well with different functionals reflects the underlying physical justification for using such a mixture of Hartree-Fock and DFT exchange first pointed out by Becke.

Different functionals can be constructed in the same way by varying the component functionals—for example, by substituting the Perdew-Wang 1991 gradient-corrected correlation functional for LYP—and by adjusting the values of the three parameters.

Integration Grids and DFT Calculations

In general, DFT calculations proceed in the same way as Hartree-Fock calculations, with the addition of the evaluation of the extra term, E^{XC}. This term cannot be evaluated analytically for DFT methods, so it is computed via numerical integration.

These calculations employ a grid of points in space in order to perform the numerical integration. Grids are specified as a number of radial shells around each atom, each of which contains a set number of integration points. For example, in the (75,302) grid, 75 radial shells each contain 302 points, resulting in a total of 22,650 integration points.

Uniform and *pruned* versions of many grids have been defined. Uniform grids contain the same number of angular points at each radial distance, while pruned grids are reduced from their full form so that fewer points are used on the shells near the core and far from the nucleus, where less density is needed for a given level of computational accuracy. Put another way, pruned grids are designed to be densest in the region of the atom where properties are changing most rapidly.

For example, the pruned (75,302) grid, denoted "(75,302)p" contains about 7,500 integration points per atom. In general, pruning reduces the size of a uniform grid by about 66%.

As of this writing, (75,302)p[†] is the default grid in *Gaussian* for all but single point calculations using standard SCF convergence (including **SCF=Tight** calculations). The SG1 grid, a pruned (50,194) grid containing about 3,600 points per atom is used for lower-accuracy single point calculations.

(75,302)p produces more accurate results than SG1, and it is accordingly strongly recommended for final energy calculations (where **SCF=Tight** should also be used in general), and for all geometry optimizations and frequency calculations. (75,302)p also has better rotational invarience properties than SG1, and it is much more suitable for molecular systems involving transition metals and calculations using pseudopotentials. The following example illustrates the differences in accuracy that can result from employing different grids.

Example A.1: Comparing Integration Grids

files: **ea_01a** (Si_5H_{12})
ea_01b (Al_4P_4)
ea_01c (**NoSymm**)

We ran a BLYP/6-31G(d) single point energy calculation, using tight SCF convergence, on Si_5H_{12} and Al_4P_4 (119 and 152 basis functions, respectively), using the SG1 and (75,302)p pruned grids, and the unpruned (50,194) and (99,434) grids.

[†] Also referred to by the option **FineGrid**.

Here are the predicted relative energies with respect to the results from the large (99,434) grid for each calculation:

Grid (Option)	$\Delta E^{(99,434)}$ (kcal-mol^{-1})	
	Si_5H_{12}	Al_4P_4
(50,194)p **Int=SG1**	0.292	-0.373
uniform (50,194) **Int(Grid=50194)**	0.277	-0.287
(75,302)p **Int=FineGrid**	-0.029	0.060

SG1 seems to have more trouble with second-row atoms than first-row atoms. The energy differences between the SG1 and the large (99,434) grids are small but significant. In contrast, the default (75,302)p grid reproduces the energy predictions of the larger grid very well. The energy differences between SG1 and the default grid are 0.321 and -0.313 for the Si_5H_{12} and Al_4P_4, respectively.

SG1 also suffers from substantial rotation invarience: changing the orientation of the molecule can substantially alter the predicted energy. All DFT methods using finite grids will exhibit some degree of rotational invarience, but SG1 is more sensitive than most grids—the effect is generally more pronounced with smaller grids—as the following results on Al_4P_4 indicate. This table gives the change in predicted energy when molecular symmetry is ignored in the calculation with respect to the default procedure (taking advantage of symmetry) for SG1 and the default grid:

Grid (Option)	ΔE^{NoSymm} (kcal-mol^{-1})
(50,194)p **Int=SG1**	0.354
(75,302)p **Int=FineGrid**	0.079

The default (75,302)p grid results in only minor changes in energy between the two molecular orientations. However, the SG1 grid's predicted energy is very different for the two orientations of the molecule.

The Complete Basis Set Extrapolation

As we noted in Chapter 7, the CBS family of methods all include a component which extrapolates from calculations using a finite basis set to the estimated complete basis set limit. In this section, we very briefly introduce this procedure.

The extrapolation to the complete basis set energy limit is based upon the Møller-Plesset expansion $E = E^{(0)} + E^{(1)} + E^{(2)} + E^{(3)} + E^{(4)} + ...$ as described earlier in this appendix. Recall that $E^{(0)} + E^{(1)}$ is the Hartree-Fock energy. We will denote $E^{(3)}$ and all higher terms as $E^{3 \to \infty}$, resulting in this expression for E:

$$E = E^{HF} + E^{(2)} + E^{3 \to \infty} \qquad [64]$$

Remember that the CBS models begin with a large enough SCF calculation to obtain the desired level of accuracy (see Chapter 7); therefore, no explicit extrapolation of the SCF energy is included. CBS extrapolation involves computing the second-order and infinite-order corrections to the energy.

Schwartz has shown that for a helium-like ion[†], the contribution to the second-order Møller-Plesset energy from the l angular momentum component can be approximated by the following expression:

$$\lim_{l \to \infty} \Delta E_l^{(2)} \approx -\frac{45}{256}\left(l + \frac{1}{2}\right)^{-4} \qquad [65]$$

This expression describes how the energy converges as we add successive s functions, p functions, d functions, f functions, and so on, to spherical atoms.

Petersson and coworkers have extended this two-electron formulation of asymptotic convergence to many-electron atoms. They note that the second-order Møller-Plesset correlation energy for a many-electron system may be written as a sum of pair energies, each describing the energetic effect of the electron correlation between that pair of electrons:

[†] In the limit of infinite nuclear charge.

$$E^{(2)} = \sum_{i,j}^{occ} e_{ij}^{(2)} = \sum_{i,j}^{occ} \sum_{a,b}^{virt} C_{ij}^{ab} V_{ij}^{ab}$$

$$V_{ij}^{ab} = \langle ij | (\Delta r_{12})^{-1} | ab \rangle \qquad [66]$$

$$C_{ij}^{ab} = \frac{V_{ij}^{ab}}{\varepsilon_i + \varepsilon_j - \varepsilon_a - \varepsilon_b}$$

where the V_{ij}^{ab} are Hamiltonian matrix elements coupling occupied orbitals i and j with virtual orbitals a and b. C_{ij}^{ab} are the coefficients of the first-order wavefunction.

For $\alpha\beta$ electron pairs, the coefficient matrix C may be diagonalized, yielding the *pair natural orbital* (PNO) expansion of the pair energies:

$$^{\alpha\beta}e_{ij}^{(2)} = \sum_{a}^{PNO} C_{ij}^{aa} V_{ij}^{aa} \qquad [67]$$

In natural orbital form, the asymptotic convergence of $^{\alpha\beta}e_{ij}^{(2)}$ has been shown to have the following form, resulting in the CBS limit, $e_{ij}^{(2)}(\mathbf{CBS})$:

$$^{\alpha\beta}e_{ij}^{(2)}(\mathbf{CBS}) = \lim_{N \to \infty} {}^{\alpha\beta}e_{ij}^{(2)}(N) - \left(\frac{25}{512}\right) {}^{\alpha\beta}f_{ij}(N + \delta_{ij})^{-1}$$

$$^{\alpha\beta}e_{ij}^{(2)}(N) = \sum_{a=2}^{N} C_{ij}^{aa} V_{ij}^{aa} \qquad [68]$$

f is the *overlap factor*, and it provides the exact attenuation of the interorbital pairs relative to intraorbital pairs for a model involving two infinitely-separated helium-like ions.

The parameter δ_{ij} serves to retain size consistency in the CBS extrapolation for finite values of N. Full CI pair energies, $^{\alpha\beta}e_{ij}^{(\infty)}(N)$, may be obtained from the diagonalization of the pair CI Hamiltonian:

$$\langle \phi_{ij}^{ab} | \mathbf{H} | \phi_{ij}^{cd} \rangle \qquad [69]$$

where ϕ_{ij}^{ab} is a configuration in which occupied orbitals i and j are replaced by virtual orbitals a and b. It has been shown that the resulting infinite-order pair energies converge to the CBS limit according to the following expression:

$$^{\alpha\beta}e_{ij}^{(\infty)}(CBS) = \lim_{N \to \infty} {}^{\alpha\beta}e_{ij}^{(\infty)}(N) - \left[\sum_{a=1}^{N} C_{ij}^{a_i, a_j} \right]^2 (\tfrac{25}{512}) \, {}^{\alpha\beta}f_{ij} \, (N + \delta_{ij})^{-1} \quad [70]$$

The sum over CI coefficients is an *interference factor* resulting from the fact that the full CI pair energies converge faster than the second-order pair energies.

CBS model chemistries make the correction resulting from these extrapolations to the second-order (MP2) correlation energy:

$$\Delta E^{(2)} = \sum_{ij} [\, e_{ij}^{(2)}(CBS) - e_{ij}^{(2)}(N) \,] \quad [71]$$

An infinite-order correction is similarly made to MP4 or QCISD(T) energies (approximate full CI energies):

$$\Delta E^{(\infty)} = \sum_{ij} \left\{ \left[\sum_{\mu_{ij}}^{N_{virt}+1} C_{\mu_{ij}} \right]^2 [e_{ij}^{(2)}(CBS) - e_{ij}^{(2)}(N)\,] \right\} \quad [72]$$

Because the interelectronic cusp is difficult to describe well with one-electron basis functions, pair correlation energies converge much more slowly (as N^{-1})[†] than SCF energies (which converge as l^{-6}). This fact makes the use of CBS extrapolations of the correlation energy very beneficial in terms of both accuracy and computational cost.

[†] $\alpha\alpha$ and $\beta\beta$ (triplet) pair energies converge as $N^{-5/3}$.

CBS extrapolation is illustrated in the following figure which depicts the extrapolation for the helium atom:

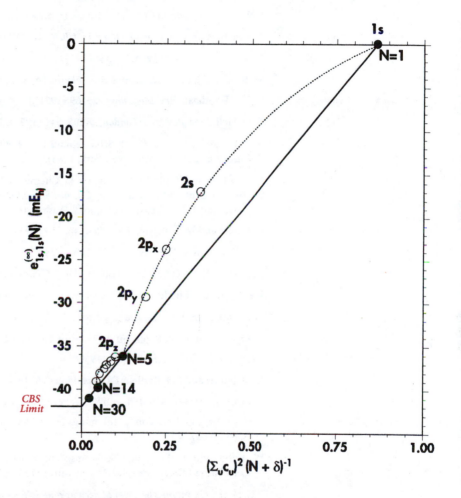

The filled and hollow circles indicate the contributions of each successive natural orbital. The filled circles correspond to complete shells. Only these points are useful for extrapolating to the complete basis set limit.

Consult the works listed in the references for a full discussion of CBS extrapolation.

References

Quantum Mechanics

L. I. Schiff, *Quantum Mechanics* (McGraw-Hill, New York, 1968).

I. N. Levine, *Quantum Chemistry*, 4th ed. (Prentice-Hall, Englewood Cliffs, NJ, 1991).

A. Hinchliffe, *Computational Quantum Chemistry* (Wiley, New York, 1988).

E. Schrödinger, *Ann. Physik*, **79**, 361 (1926).

M. Born and J. R. Oppenheimer, *Ann. Physik*, **84**, 457 (1927).

Electronic Structure Theory

C. C. J. Roothaan, *Rev. Mod. Phys.*, **23**, 69 (1951).

G. G. Hall, *Proc. Roy. Soc. (London)*, **A205**, 541 (1951).

W. J. Hehre, L. Radom, P. v.R. Schleyer, and J. A. Pople, *Ab Initio Molecular Orbital Theory*, Chapter 2 (Wiley, New York, 1986).

J. B. Foresman, "Ab Initio Techniques in Chemistry: Interpretation and Visualization," Chapter 14 in *What Every Chemist Should Know About Computing*, ed. M. L Swift and T. J. Zielinski (ACS Books, Washington, D.C., 1996).

MP Perturbation Theory

C. Møller and M. S. Plesset, *Phys. Rev.*, **46**, 618 (1934).

L. Brillouin, *Actualities Soc. Ind.*, **71**, 159 (1934).

J. A. Pople, R. Seeger, and R. Krishnan, *Int. J. Quantum Chem., Symp.*, **11**, 149 (1977).

J. A. Pople, J. S. Binkley, and R. Seeger, *Int. J. Quantum Chem., Symp.*, **10**, 1 (1976).

R. Krishnan, M. J. Frisch, and J. A. Pople, *J. Chem. Phys.*, **72**, 4244 (1980).

R. Krishnan and J. A. Pople, *Int. J. Quantum Chem.*, **14**, 91 (1978).

Coupled Cluster and QCI

J. Cizek, *Adv. Chem. Phys.*, **14**, 35 (1969).

G. D. Purvis and R. J. Bartlett, *J. Chem. Phys.*, **76**, 1910 (1982).

J. A. Pople, M. Head-Gordon, and K. Raghavachari, *J. Chem. Phys.*, **87**, 5968 (1987).

Density Functional Theory

P. Hohenberg and W. Kohn, "Inhomogeneous Electron Gas," *Physical Review,* **136**, B864 (1964).

W. Kohn and L. J. Sham, "Self-Consistent Equations Including Exchange and Correlation Effects," *Physical Review,* **140**, A1133 (1965).

J. C. Slater, *Quantum Theory of Molecular and Solids. Vol. 4: The Self-Consistent Field for Molecular and Solids* (McGraw-Hill, New York, 1974).

S. H. Vosko, L. Wilk and M. Nusair, "Accurate spin-dependent electron liquid correlation energies for local spin density calculations: a critical analysis," *Canadian J. Phys.*, **58**, 1200 (1980).

B. Miehlich, A. Savin, H. Stoll and H. Preuss, *Chem. Phys. Lett.,* **157**, 200 (1989).

C. Lee, W. Yang and R. G. Parr, "Development of the Colle-Salvetti correlation-energy formula into a functional of the electron density," *Physical Review B*, **37**, 785 (1988).

A. D. Becke, *Phys. Rev. A*, **38**, 3098 (1988).

A. D. Becke, *J. Chem. Phys.*, **98**, 1372 (1993).

A. D. Becke, "Density-functional thermochemistry. III. The role of exact exchange," *J. Chem. Phys.*, **98**, 5648 (1993).

J. P. Perdew and Y. Wang, "Accurate and Simple Analytic Representation of the Electron Gas Correlation Energy," *Phys. Rev. B*, **45**, 13244 (1992).

R. G. Parr and W. Yang, *Density-functional theory of atoms and molecules* (Oxford Univ. Press: Oxford, 1989).

D. R. Salahub and M. C. Zerner, eds., *The Challenge of d and f Electrons* (ACS, Washington, D.C., 1989).

G. W. Trucks and M. J. Frisch, "Rotational Invariance Properties of Pruned Grids for Numerical Integration," in preparation (1996).

CBS Extrapolation   C. Schwartz, *Phys. Rev.*, **126**, 1015 (1962).

C. Schwartz, in *Methods in Computational Physics*, vol.2, ed. B. Alder, S. Fernback and M. Rotenberg (Academic Press, New York, 1963).

M. R. Nyden and G. A. Petersson, *J. Chem. Phys.*, **75**, 1843 (1981).

G. A. Petersson and M. R. Nyden, *J. Chem. Phys.*, **75**, 3423 (1981).

G. A. Petersson, A. K. Yee and A. Bennett, *J. Chem. Phys.*, **83**, 5105 (1985).

G. A. Petersson and M. A. Al-Laham, *J. Chem. Phys.*, **94**, 6081 (1991).

J. W. Ochterski, G. A. Petersson and J. A. Montgomery, Jr., *J. Chem. Phys.*, **104**, 2598 (1996).

J. W. Ochterski, *Complete Basis Set Model Chemistries*, Ph. D. Thesis, (Wesleyan Univ., Middletown, CT, 1993), §2.8.

Overview of Gaussian Input

We've already looked briefly at *Gaussian* input in the *Quick Start*. Here we present a more formal definition and discuss the various molecule specification options.

Gaussian input is designed to be free-format and extremely flexible. For example, it is not case-sensitive, and keywords and options may be shortened to a unique abbreviation.

Input File Sections

Gaussian input (which is the same for all versions of the program, including the Window version) has the basic structure described in the following table. Note that the input sections marked with an asterisk are required in every input file:

Input Section	Contents
Link 0 Commands	*Defines the locations of scratch files and job resource limits.*
*Route Section	*Specifies the job type and model chemistry.*
*blank line	*Separates the route section from the title section.*
*Title Section	*Describes the job for the output and archive entry.*
*blank line	
*Molecule Specification	*Gives the structure of the molecule to be studied.*
*blank line	
Variables Section	*Specifies values for the variables used in the molecule specification.*
blank line	

Note that the separate input sections are separated from one another by blank lines. These blank lines are inserted automatically into input files created with the **Job Entry** window in the Windows version and need not be entered by the user. If you choose to create a *Gaussian* input file using an external Windows editor, however, you must follow the same rules for input as under other versions of *Gaussian*.

Note that some job types require additional sections not listed.

Input lines have a maximum length of 80 characters.

The Route Section

The first line of the route section always begins with a pound sign (#) in the first column. This section specifies the theoretical procedure, basis set, and desired type of calculation. It may also include other keywords. The ordering of keywords is not important. Some keywords require options; the following input line illustrates the possible formats for keywords with options:

```
#T RHF/6-31G(d)  SCF=Tight      Units=(Bohr,Radian)        Opt Test
```
Keyword with: **a single option**   **≥ 2 options**   **no options**

The amount of spacing between items is not significant in *Gaussian* input. In the route section, commas or slashes may be substituted for spaces if desired (except within parenthesized options, where slashes don't work). For example, the previous route section used a slash to separate the procedure and basis set, spaces to separate other keywords, and commas to separate the options to the **Units** keyword.

The route section may extend over more than one line if necessary. Only the first line need begin with a pound sign, although any others may. The route section is terminated by a blank line.

The Title Section

The title section consists of one or more lines of descriptive information about the job. It is included in the output and in the archive entry but is not otherwise used by *Gaussian*. This section is terminated by a blank line.

Specifying Molecular Structures

Gaussian accepts molecule specifications in several different formats:

- ✦ Cartesian coordinates
- ✦ Z-matrix format (internal coordinates)
- ✦ Mixed internal and Cartesian coordinates

All molecule specifications require that the *charge* and *spin multiplicity* be specified (as two integers) on the first line of this section. The charge is a positive or negative integer specifying the total charge on the molecule. Thus, 1 or +1 would be used for a singly-charged cation, -1 designates a singly-charged anion, and 0 represents a neutral molecule.

Spin Multiplicity

The *spin multiplicity* is given by the equation $2S + 1$, where S is the total spin for the molecule. Paired electrons contribute nothing to this quantity. They have a net spin of zero since an alpha electron has a spin of $+\frac{1}{2}$ and a beta electron has a spin of $-\frac{1}{2}$. Each unpaired electron contributes $+\frac{1}{2}$ to S. Thus, a singlet—a system with no unpaired electrons—has a spin multiplicity of 1, a doublet (one unpaired electron) has a spin multiplicity of 2, a triplet (two unpaired electrons of like spin) has a spin multiplicity of 3, and so on.

Units

The units in a Z-matrix are angstroms for lengths and degrees for angles by default; the default units for Cartesian coordinates are angstroms. These are also the default units for lengths and angles used in *Gaussian* output. You can change them to bohrs and/or radians by including the **Units** keyword in the route section with one or both of its options: **Bohr** and **Radian**.

Cartesian Coordinate Input

Cartesian coordinate input consists of a series of lines of the form:

```
Atomic-symbol   X-coordinate   Y-coordinate   Z-coordinate
```

For example, here is the molecular structure for formaldehyde, given in Cartesian coordinates:

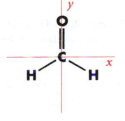

```
0 1
C   0.0    0.0  0.0
O   0.0    1.22 0.0
H   0.94 -0.54 0.0
H -0.94 -0.54 0.0
```

Z-Matrix Input

The other syntax for supplying molecular structures to *Gaussian 94* is the *Z-matrix*. A Z-matrix specifies the locations of and bonds between atoms using bond lengths, bond angles, and dihedral (torsion) angles.

Each atom in the molecule is described on a separate input line within the Z-matrix. As we consider the procedure for creating a Z-matrix, we'll use hydrogen peroxide as an example. These are the steps to do so:

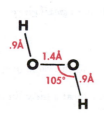

1. Choose a starting atom in the molecule, and conceptually place it at the origin in three dimensional space.

The first line of the Z-matrix consists solely of the label for this atom. An atom label is made up of its atomic symbol optionally followed by an integer (no spaces), used to distinguish it from the other atoms of the same type (e.g. H1 for the first hydrogen, H2 for the second one, and so on).

We'll use the left oxygen atom in the illustration as our first atom:

O1

2. Choose another atom bonded to the first atom. Place it along the Z-axis, and specify the length of the bond connecting the two atoms.

This second input line will include the atom label of the second atom, the label of the atom it is bonded to (the first atom), and the bond length, in that order. Items may be separated by spaces, tabs or commas.

We'll use the hydrogen atom bonded to the first oxygen for our second atom:

```
O1
H1 O1 .9
```

3. Choose a third atom bonded to either of the previous two atoms and specify the angle formed by the two bonds.

This angle locates the molecule's position in the XZ-plane. This input line will include the new atom's label, the atom it is bonded to and the bond length, the label of the other atom forming the bond angle, and the angle's value.

We have only one choice for the third atom in our Z-matrix, the second oxygen atom:

```
O1
H1 O1 0.9
O2 O1 1.4 H1 105.0
```

The new line illustrates an important point about numeric values within Z-matrices. Since they correspond to floating point quantities, they must include a decimal point, as in the value above. This is true even for a value of 0.

4. Describe the positions of all subsequent atoms by specifying:

✦ Its atom label.
✦ An atom it is bonded to and the bond length.
✦ A third atom bonded to it (or to the second atom), and the value of the resulting bond angle.
✦ A fourth atom bonded to either end of the previous chain, and the value of the dihedral (torsion) angle formed by the four atoms.

Dihedral angles describe the angle the fourth atom makes with respect to the plane defined by the first three atoms; their values range from 0 to 360 degrees, or from -180 to 180 degrees. Dihedral angles are easy to visualize using Newman projections. The illustration shows the Newman projection for hydrogen peroxide, looking down the O-O bond. Positive dihedral angles correspond to clockwise rotation in the Newman projection.

Obviously, we'll use the remaining hydrogen atom for the fourth line of our Z-matrix for hydrogen peroxide. Here is the completed molecule specification:

0 1	*Charge and multiplicity.*
O1	*Oxygen atom #1.*
H1 O1 .9	*Hydrogen #1, connected to oxygen #1 by a bond of 0.9 Å.*
O2 O1 1.4 H1 105.	*Oxygen #2: O2–O1 = 1.4 Å; – H1–O1–O2 = 105°.*
H2 O2 .9 O1 105. H1 120.	*Hydrogen #2: H2–O2 bond =0.9 Å; – H2–O2–O1 = 105°; dihedral angle H2–O2–O1–H1=120°.*

Sources for bond lengths, bond angles, and dihedral angles include the published literature, standard references like the CRC series, and previous calculations. Z-matrices may also be created by the **NewZMat** utility from data generated by a wide variety of drawing packages. Refer to the *Quick Start* for a sample conversion operation for your version of *Gaussian*.

Mixed Internal and Cartesian Coordinates

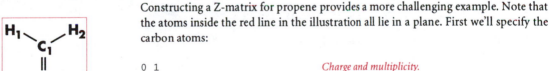

It is also possible to specify the molecular structure in a format which combines Cartesian coordinates and Z-matrix style input; this format is referred to as mixed internal and Cartesian coordinates. It is useful for systems where some parts of the molecule are more easily specified in Cartesian coordinates and others are more easily described as a Z-matrix. Consult Exercise C.2 (page 293) and Appendix B of the *Gaussian 94 User's Reference* for more information on this topic.

More Complex Z-Matrices

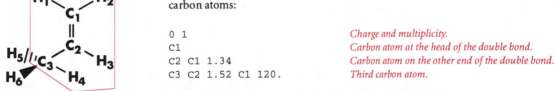

Constructing a Z-matrix for propene provides a more challenging example. Note that the atoms inside the red line in the illustration all lie in a plane. First we'll specify the carbon atoms:

0 1	*Charge and multiplicity.*
C1	*Carbon atom at the head of the double bond.*
C2 C1 1.34	*Carbon atom on the other end of the double bond.*
C3 C2 1.52 C1 120.	*Third carbon atom.*

Next, we'll specify the hydrogens on C1 and C2. The bond angles formed with the double-bonded carbons and each of these hydrogens is 120°. We'll pick simple dihedral angles for each of them:

```
H1 C1 1.09 C2 120. C3 0.
```
*The dihedral with respect to the C-C single bond is 0°. Note that the decimal point **must** be included.[†]*

```
H2 C1 1.09 C2 120. C3 180.
```
The dihedral with respect to the same bond is 180°, since it is on the opposite side of the double bond from carbon C3.

```
H3 C2 1.09 C1 120. H1 180.
```
This is an equivalent dihedral to the previous one, substituting H1 for the third carbon.

The planar hydrogen on C3 is specified in a similar manner:

```
H4 C3 1.09 C2 109.5 C1 180.
```
Just like the dihedral we formed for H2.

The geometry of the carbon we've labelled C3 is tetrahedral; the bond angle of each of the hydrogens with respect to the C3-C2 bond is about 109.5°.

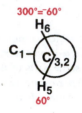

The dihedrals for the remaining two hydrogens are best visualized with a Newman projection. They are located above and below the plane of the C-C-C bond. H5 is the hydrogen below the plane, and its dihedral is 60°. The dihedral for H6 could be expressed as either 300° or -60°; we'll use the latter to express the symmetry of the molecule. Here are the Z-matrix lines for these atoms:

```
H5 C3 1.09 C2 109.5 C1  60.
H6 C3 1.09 C2 109.5 C1 -60.
```

Using Variables in a Z-matrix

Here is a complete input file for an optimization of this molecule:

```
#T RHF/6-31G(d) Opt Test

Propene Optimization

0 1
C1
C2 C1 CCD
C3 C2 CCS C1 A1
H1 C1 CH   C2 A1 C3 0.
H2 C1 CH   C2 A1 C3 180.
H3 C2 CH   C1 A1 H1 180.
H4 C3 CH   C2 A2 C1 180.
H5 C3 CH   C2 A2 C1  D
H6 C3 CH   C2 A2 C1 -D
```
Z-matrix with variables.

[†] Note that there are no blank lines within the Z-matrix, despite its appearance here. The extra spacing in this example is simply an artifact of the commentary.

```
        Variables:
CCD=1.34
CCS=1.52
CH=1.09
A1=120.0
A2=109.5
D=60.0
```
C-C double bond length.
C-C single bond length.
C-H bond length.
C-C-C and some C-C-H bond angles.
C-C-H bond angles for hydrogens on C3.
Magnitude of the dihedral angle for non-planar hydrogens.

This file introduces the concept of *variables* within the molecule specification. Here, variables are simply named constants; variable names are substituted for literal values within the Z-matrix, and their values are defined in a separate section following it. The two sections are separated by a blank line, or a line with a blank in the first column and the label Variables: placed elsewhere on it (this is one exception *Gaussian* makes in its requirement for completely blank lines).[†]

Notice that we used D and –D respectively for the dihedral angles for the non-planar hydrogens, as opposed to two separate variables. This is done to ensure symmetry within the molecule.

Exercise B.1: Z-Matrices for 1,2-Dichloro-1,2-Difluoroethane Isomers

Try your hand at constructing Z-matrices for these three isomers of 1,2-Dichloro-1,2-Difluoroethane:

RR   SS   meso

Solution   We'll construct the Z-matrix for the RR form first. We'll use the Cl-C-C-Cl plane as our major reference. Here are the lines for the carbons and chlorines:

```
C1
C2   C1 1.53
Cl1  C1 1.76 C2 109.5
Cl2  C2 1.76 C1 109.5 Cl1 180.
```
Bonded to C1 at a distance of 1.53A.
Bonded to C1 at 1.76Å; ∠Cl-C-C=109.5°.
Bonded to C2 (1.76A); ∠C-C-Cl =109.5°; and Cl-C-C-Cl dihedral angle is 180° (the 2 chlorines are on opposite sides of the carbon chain).

[†] Variables represent labels for the internal degrees of freedom being specified for the structure. As we note, the values of the variables are defined in a separate section below the Z-matrix. It is also possible to specify a third section for *constants*, which immediately follows the variables section; its separator line is either blank or it contains the label Constants: preceded by one or more spaces. In traditonal **Opt=Z-Matrix** geometry optimizations, the values of variables are optimized while the values of constants remain fixed throughout.

Newman projections are helpful in determining the proper dihedral angles for the fluorines and hydrogens. Here are diagrams for the RR isomer, looking down the C-C bond in both directions:

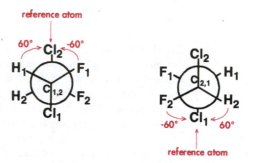

The left diagram places the C_1 carbon in front, and indicates the angles for the fluorine and hydrogen attached to it, using the two carbons and the chlorine attached to the other carbon (Cl_2) to form the dihedral angle:

```
F1  C1  1.37  C2  109.5  Cl2  -60.
H1  C1  1.09  C2  109.5  Cl2   60.
```

A similar process, using the Newman projection diagram on the right, which places C_2 in front of C_1, and uses Cl_1 as the third atom for the dihedral angles, results in the last two lines of the Z-matrix:

```
F2  C2  1.37  C1  109.5  Cl1  -60.
H2  C2  1.09  C1  109.5  Cl1   60.
```

Here is the complete Z-matrix for the RR form:

```
0  1
C1
C2   C1  1.53
Cl1  C1  1.76  C2  109.5
Cl2  C2  1.76  C1  109.5  Cl1 180.
F1   C1  1.37  C2  109.5  Cl2  -60.
H1   C1  1.09  C2  109.5  Cl2   60.
F2   C2  1.37  C1  109.5  Cl1  -60.
H2   C2  1.09  C1  109.5  Cl1   60.
```

In the SS form, the positions of the fluorine and the hydrogen on each carbon are interchanged. This results in a corresponding exchange of their dihedral angles, while all other values in the Z-matrix remain the same. Here is the complete Z-matrix for the SS form:

```
0  1
C1
C2   C1 1.53
Cl1  C1 1.76 C2 109.5
Cl2  C2 1.76 C1 109.5 Cl1 180.
F1   C1 1.37 C2 109.5 Cl2  60.
H1   C1 1.09 C2 109.5 Cl2 -60.
F2   C2 1.37 C1 109.5 Cl1  60.
H2   C2 1.09 C1 109.5 Cl1 -60.
```

The meso form swaps the hydrogen and fluorine on only one of the carbons, leaving the other two unchanged with respect to the RR form. This will result in the dihedral angles for the hydrogens and fluorines having different signs on the two carbons:

```
0  1
C1
C2   C1 1.53
Cl1  C1 1.76 C2 109.5
Cl2  C2 1.76 C1 109.5 Cl1 180.
F1   C1 1.37 C2 109.5 Cl2 -60.
H1   C1 1.09 C2 109.5 Cl2  60.
F2   C2 1.37 C1 109.5 Cl1  60.
H2   C2 1.09 C1 109.5 Cl1 -60.
```

Exercise B.2: Mixed Cartesian and Internal Coordinates

Here is a molecule specification for $Cr(CO)_6$, expressed in Cartesian coordinates:

```
0    1
Cr   0.00   0.00   0.00
C    1.93   0.00   0.00
C   -1.93   0.00   0.00
C    0.00   1.93   0.00
C    0.00  -1.93   0.00
C    0.00   0.00   1.93
C    0.00   0.00  -1.93
O    3.07   0.00   0.00
O   -3.07   0.00   0.00
O    0.00   3.07   0.00
O    0.00  -3.07   0.00
O    0.00   0.00  -3.07
O    0.00   0.00   3.07
```

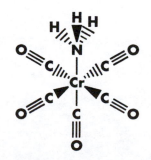

Replace one of the carbonyls with an ammonia group, and construct a new molecule specification.

Solution   We replace the final carbon atom with a nitrogen, specifying the Cr-N bond length as 2.27, and then express the three hydrogen atoms via a Z-matrix. Note that Cartesian coordinates are included within a Z-matrix by specifying the bonded-to-atom as **0**:

```
0    1
Cr 0 0.00   0.00   0.00
C 0   1.93  0.00   0.00
C 0  -1.93  0.00   0.00
C 0   0.00  1.93   0.00
C 0   0.00 -1.93   0.00
C 0   0.00  0.00   1.93
O 0   3.07  0.00   0.00
O 0  -3.07  0.00   0.00
O 0   0.00  3.07   0.00
O 0   0.00 -3.07   0.00
O 0   0.00  0.00  -3.07
N 0   0.00  0.00   2.27
H 12 R 1 A  2  0.
H 12 R 1 A 13  D
H 12 R 1 A 13 -D

R 1.02
A 115.0
D 120.0
```

See Appendix B of the *Gaussian 94 User's Reference* for more information about and examples of constructing Z-matrices. ■

Multi-Step Jobs

Multiple *Gaussian* calculations may be combined within a single input file. The input for each successive job is separated from that of the preceding job step by a line of the form:

```
--Link1--
```

Here is an example input file containing two job steps:

```
#T RHF/6-31G(d) Test          Route section for the first job step

Formaldehyde Energy           Title section for the first jobstep

0 1                           Molecule specification section
...
H2 O 1. H1 120.               End of Z-matrix
                              Blank line ending the molecule specification section
--Link1--                     Starts a new job step
```

```
#T RHF/6-31G(d) Test          Route section for the second job step

Peroxide Energy               Title section for the second job step
...                           Input continues...
```

When placing multiple jobs within a single input file, it is imperative that the final section of each job end with a blank line, a requirement that is not always strictly enforced for single-step jobs. If you want to run a single job from a multistep input file, you must copy the relevant lines to a new file, and then execute *Gaussian 94* using the new file.

Here is an example of an input file containing two job steps in which the second calculation depends upon and uses the results of the first job step:

```
%Chk=freq                     First job step
#T HF/6-31G(d) Freq

Frequencies at STP

Molecule specification

--Link1--                     Separator line
%Chk=freq                     Second job step
%NoSave
#T HF/6-31G(d) Geom=Check Guess=Read Freq=(ReadFC,ReadIsotopes)

Frequencies at 300 K

charge and multiplicity

300.0  2.0
Isotope specifications
```

This input file computes vibrational frequencies and performs thermochemical analysis at two different temperatures and pressures: first at 298.15 K and 1 atmosphere, and then again at 300 K and 2 atmospheres. Note that a blank line *must* precede the **‑‑Link1‑‑** line.

The **%Chk** command in each job step specifies the name for the checkpoint file—one of *Gaussian*'s scratch files—and it tells the program to save the file after the job finishes (normally, all scratch files are deleted automatically). The **%NoSave** command in the second job step tells the program to delete the checkpoint file after that step concludes even though **%Chk** has been included.

The most common purpose for specifying and saving the checkpoint file is so that molecular structures and other calculation results can be retrieved from it for use in a subsequent calculation. For example, in the second job step, the molecular structure, SCF initial guess, and frequency results are retrieved from the checkpoint file and used to predict thermochemical properties at a different temperature and pressure.

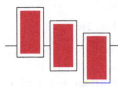

Index